THE ROMAN SYSTEM

OF

PROVINCIAL ADMINISTRATION

THE ROMAN SYSTEM

OF

PROVINCIAL ADMINISTRATION

TO THE

ACCESSION OF CONSTANTINE THE GREAT

BY THE LATE

W. T. ARNOLD, M.A.

FORMERLY SCHOLAR OF UNIVERSITY COLLEGE, OXFORD

'*Urbem fecisti quod prius orbis erat.*'—RUTILIUS
' . . . *the legions thunder past.*'—M. ARNOLD

THIRD EDITION

REVISED BY

E. S. BOUCHIER, M.A.

ARNOLD PRIZEMAN IN THE UNIVERSITY OF OXFORD
AUTHOR OF 'LIFE AND LETTERS IN ROMAN AFRICA,' 'SPAIN UNDER THE ROMAN EMPIRE'

ARES PUBLISHERS INC.
CHICAGO   MCMLXXIV

Unchanged Reprint of the Edition:
Oxford, 1914.
ARES   PUBLISHERS   INC.
150 E. Huron Street
Chicago, Illinois 60611
Printed in the United States of America
International Standard Book Number:
0-89005-027-9
Library of Congress Catalog Card Number:
74-77873

PREFACE

TO THE THIRD EDITION

This essay was originally composed by Mr. Arnold for the prize founded in the University of Oxford in honour of his grandfather, Thomas Arnold, headmaster of Rugby. Being awarded the prize he published the essay in book form in 1879. In spite of the exacting character of his work as a journalist, Mr. Arnold always remained keenly interested in subjects connected with Roman history, especially in the provincial administration and the parallels which may be drawn between it and the British rule in India. A number of essays bearing on such questions have been collected and published under the title of 'Studies of Roman Imperialism,' and many articles and reviews were contributed to the *English Historical Review* between 1886 and 1895.

For years Mr. Arnold entertained the hope of producing an enlarged and revised edition of the present work, carefully reading and noting any fresh publications or epigraphic evidence which promised to assist him. Failing health prevented the accomplishment of this design, and after his death in 1904 his notes were entrusted to the late Dr. E. S. Shuckburgh, of Emmanuel College, Cambridge. An enlarged edition accordingly appeared in 1906, embodying many of the additional facts which Mr. Arnold had himself collected, together with a few alterations in the text and a number of fresh references.

This edition being in turn exhausted, I have been asked to make some slight alterations in the plan, and have endeavoured to keep in view the needs of University students of Ancient History. Knowledge of the Roman world has developed so greatly in the thirty-five years since the essay was written, that a thorough treatment of a subject of this kind would run to many volumes, and would have to take account of the results of archæological explorations in an immense number of centres. Many teachers of ancient history have, however, expressed the opinion that this survey, in a moderate compass, of the main principles of administration, free from too much detail, and only touching lightly on the many controversial matters connected with the subject, meets a want not provided for by any other English work.

In the bibliography I have somewhat increased the proportion of English and French books, and made an attempt to classify them according to subject. In the foot-notes some of the less important references have been omitted, and many of the remainder corrected, or expanded by quotation. As the author attempted no geographical treatment of the subject, and the facts relating to the same province are scattered through several chapters, I have added an appendix giving a few leading points about each of the provinces, arranged as far as possible according to the order of acquisition. Another short appendix contains a chronological table of the chief events connected with the provincial system. The appendix on ancient Switzerland is due to Mr. Arnold himself, but in view of the great development of the knowledge about Roman Britain in recent years, and of the publication of Professor Haverfield's ‘ Romanisation of Roman Britain,’ and his appendix to the translation of Mommsen's ‘ Provinces,’ I have omitted the long note on this subject in Chapter IV.

E. S. BOUCHIER.

3, WINCHESTER ROAD,
OXFORD.
May, 1914.

BIBLIOGRAPHY

LAW AND CONSTITUTION.

Marquardt, J., Römische Staatsverwaltung, 3 vols. (French translation—Organisation de l'empire romain.)
Bruns, Fontes juris Romani, seventh edition, 1909.
Guiraud, Assemblées provinciales dans l'empire romain.
Hardy, E. G., Three Spanish Charters.
Reid, J. S., The Municipalities of the Roman Empire, 1913.
Kuhn, E., Die städtische und bürgerliche Verfassung des römischen Reichs.
Klein, Die Verwaltungsbeamten des römischen Reichs bis auf Diocletian, 1878.
Botsford, G. W., The Roman Assemblies, 1909.
Hirschfeld, O., Die Kaiserl. Verwaltungsbeamten bis auf Diocletian, 1905.
Willems, P., Le Sénat de la République romaine, 1878.
Le droit public romain, 1888.

LIFE AND MANNERS.

Friedländer, Roman Life and Manners under the Early Empire, 4 vols., English Translation, 1908-1912.
Mahaffy, J. P., The Greek World under Roman Sway, 1890.
Dill, S., Roman Society from Nero to Aurelius, 1905.
Fowler, W. W., Social Life at Rome in the Age of Cicero, 1909.
Ramsay, W. M., The Church in the Roman Empire, 1893.
Greenidge, A. H. J., Roman Public Life, 1901.

INSCRIPTIONS.

Rushforth, G. McN., Latin Historical Inscriptions, illustrating the History of the Early Empire, 1893.
Wilmanns, Exempla Inscriptionum Latinarum, 1873.
Fairley, W., Monumentum Ancyranum, Text and Translation.
Flach, La Table de bronze d'Aljustrel, 1879.
Dessau, Inscriptiones Latinae Selectae.
Zumpt, A. W., Commentationes Epigraphicae, 1850.
Zumpt, C. T., Decretum Tergestinum, 1867.
Orelli-Henzen, Inscr. Lat. Select. amplissima collectio, 1828-56.
Corpus Inscriptionum Latinarum (15 vols., several with supplements embodying most of the recently found inscriptions at first published in the *Ephemeris Epigraphica* and other periodicals. The arrangement is geographical, and the volumes relating to the provinces are II. Spain, III. Greek-speaking and Central European provinces, V. Cisalpine Gaul, VII. Britain, VIII. Africa, X. part 2, Sicily and Sardinia, XII. Narbonensis, XIII. Gaul and Germany).

vii

SPECIAL PROVINCES AND DISTRICTS.

Haverfield, F. J., The Romanisation of Roman Britain.
Desjardins, E., Géographie de la Gaule Romaine.
Jung, Die romanischen Landschaften des römischen Reichs.
Hübner, E., Römische Herrschaft in West Europa.
Boissier, G., L'Afrique Romaine (and trans. A. Ward, 1899).
Graham, A., Roman Africa, 1902.
Hardy, E. G., Studies in Roman History, seeond series, pp. 1-129,
'Armies and frontier relations of the German provinces.'
   Edit. of Pliny's Letters to Trajan (Bithynia).
Finlay, Hist. of Greece, ed. Tozer, vol. i.
Jung, Fasten der Provinz Dacien, 1894.
Milne, History of Egypt under Roman Rule.

GENERAL HISTORIES.

Republic.

Mommsen, History of Rome, English translation, 5 vols.
Ihne, Roman History, English translation, 5 vols.
Heitland, The Roman Republic, 3 vols., 1910.
Greenidge, History of Rome, 133-104 B.C., 1905.
Greenidge and Clay, Sources of Roman History, 133-70 B.C., 1904.
Watson, Select Letters of Cicero, 1891.

Early Empire.

Merivale, The Romans under the Empire (80 B.C.-A.D. 180) 8 vols.
Gardthausen, V., Augustus und seine Zeit, 1904.
Gsell, S., Essai sur le règne de l'empereur Domitien, 1894.
De la Berge, Essai sur le règne de Trajan, 1877.
Bury, Students' History of the Roman Empire.
Gregorovius, The Emperor Hadrian (English translation, 1898).
Mommsen, The Provinces of the Roman Empire (English translation, 2 vols.).

Later Empire to Diocletian.

Bussell, F. W., Essays on the Constitutional History of the Roman
   Empire from A.D. 81.
Duruy, History of Rome, 6 vols., 1886 (to Theodosius).
Peters, ed. of Scriptores Historiae Augustae, 2 vols.
Schiller, Geschichte der römischen Kaiserzeit (Augustus to Theo-
   dosius).
Ceuleneer, A. de, Essai sur la vie et le règne de Septime Sevère.
Preuss, T., Kaiser Diocletian und seine Zeit (Leipzig, 1869).
Seeck, O., Geschichte des Untergangs der Antiken Welt., 1893.
Jullian C., De la réforme provinciale attribuée à Dioclétien (Rév.
   Hist. 1882).
Gibbon, ed, Bury Vol. I. (Appendix I. reviews the ancient
   authorities for this period).

CONTENTS

CHAPTER I

CHAPTER II

CHAPTER III

CHAPTER IV

CHAPTER I.

Limits of Period and Subject.

TAKING the terms in their widest extent, the Roman Provincial Administration may be said to have lasted for some 700 years, from the final settlement of Sicily after the Second Punic War to the apparent destruction of the system by the barbarians. And as the fall of the Western Empire is a convenient external mark of the success of those barbarians and of the passing away of the old order of things, the date of that event, A.D. 476, might be taken as the limit in time between which and 210 B.C., that administration existed. But within this larger whole there are smaller wholes, each of which forms in itself a unity. And indeed if we press the terms Roman Provincial Administration closely, the limit might be put earlier, with the accession of Constantine. For then that administration ceased to be distinctively Roman. It has been said that with Constantine modern history begins; and there are many reasons which make the date of his accession a better division—where all such divisions are necessarily arbitrary—between the old world and the new than the date which marks the fall of the Empire of the West. The tendencies which came to their full growth in the reign of Constantine had many of them existed for centuries, all of them at least since Diocletian. But Constantine seems to gather up and concentrate in his reign the forces which were a legacy from the past and were to form the future. Constantine adopted a new religion and created a new capital. The one act marks the final adoption of

I

the religion which is that of the Western world, and the other brought into existence the Byzantine Empire, Europe's 'bulwark against the Ottoman.' The monarchy which he constituted, with its hierarchy of counts and its brilliant court, was the model which later princes copied ; and by his abandonment of Rome the Pope was made possible. But Constantine's reign, if it looks towards the future, can be only understood in the light of the past from which it grew. The division of the Empire into the four great prefectures was the thought of Diocletian. The principle at its base had long before been anticipated by the subdivision of the governments of Gaul and Syria[1] ; and the fatal change in the municipal towns, which shows itself so clearly in this reign, was the result of the slow canker of centuries. The division instituted between civil and military functions was mainly the work of Diocletian, but had been anticipated under the early Empire in the governments of Africa and Egypt. The counts (*comites*) of Constantine grew out of the retinue which accompanied the Emperor on a provincial progress ; and occur at least as early as the reign of M. Aurelius.[2] The centrifugal tendencies which had subsisted in the Empire along with its great and at one time prevailing tendencies to unity, had been already marked by Diocletian's practical aban-donment of Rome ; and indeed the division between East and West had always and necessarily existed, and could be made use of by Mark Antony as well as by Vespasian. Similarly Christianity was no new growth of the reign of Constantine, but only then won the fruit of centuries of enduring effort.

If then Constantine's reign, as consummating the past

[1] For the dread felt by the emperors of all the resources of Gaul or Syria being in one man's hands, see a discussion by Zumpt, *Comm. Epig.* ii. 133 ; Tac. *Ann.* xiii. 53, xiv. 57.

[2] See two inscriptions in Rénier, *Mélanges d'Epigraphie*, p. 80 and p. 76, where among a man's titles occur—'comiti divi Veri per Orientem,' and 'comiti ejusdem in Oriente.'

and as heralding the future, is a good limit to this great subject, we are still left with a period of 500 years, for which it is very necessary to find subdivisions. Fortunately this is not difficult. The immense and far-reaching changes which the Empire introduced into the administration of the provinces mark off in the clearest way, and yet without any absolute breach of continuity, the Republican period from the period of the early Empire. It may be questioned whether we should make this latter begin with Thapsus or with Actium, with Caesar or with Augustus. But the short span of eighteen months for which Caesar had supreme power in Rome was too little for him to do anything but sketch out the lines of a system which Augustus developed and realised, and we shall do better to fix the beginning of the Empire on the day of the fight in the bay of Actium. It is more open to dispute where the next break should come. The Julian Emperors in a sense, as being of the same blood and claiming the same divine origin, form a whole by themselves; and the terrible year of civil war which followed the last of them may be regarded as a cataclysm which marks the end of one period and the beginning of another. But for our purpose it is not so. The Flavian emperors who followed do not introduce new principles of administration, though their origin in the will of the army marks so far a new departure. Nor will the fact that Suetonius makes his collection end with Domitian induce us to regard the ' Twelve Caesars ' as vitally distinguished from the rest.

A happier era is inaugurated when the choice of the Senate becomes the origin of imperial authority in the person of Nerva; but otherwise the emperors from Trajan to Marcus Aurelius (A.D. 98-180), the Antonines as they are sometimes loosely called, may be regarded as continuing the best traditions of the Flavian emperors. With Marcus Aurelius comes a real break. He is the first emperor of the frontiers. From his time onwards the Empire has to maintain a long struggle with the barbarians; and the emperors that succeed one another in such breathless haste are the mere nominees of the soldiers. More important for our purpose are the changes in the administration which now became prominent, though some of them had been operating silently for a long time. Taxation for instance is now felt as an intolerable burden, and is continually rising. The municipia were more and more perverted from their original constitution; and the municipal offices became instruments of oppression. The progress of the provinces towards equality with Italy, which had been going on for centuries, completed itself with the edict of Caracalla. The progress towards administrative uniformity is shown by the perpetual provincial edict of M. Aurelius. Above all, the reforms of Diocletian were the most important changes that had taken place in the administration since Augustus. I propose therefore to make the second division of the subject at the death of M. Aurelius, not absolutely binding myself to a definite date, but taking that to be approximately the period at which the changes which distinguish the Early from the Later Empire most clearly manifested themselves. But I cannot hope to include all I have to say in three sections on the Republic, the Early Empire, and the Later Empire. The financial arrangements, for instance, are too important not to be discussed by themselves. Above all it is essential to form some idea of the constitution of the towns within a Roman province. The towns were the basis of the Roman administration; through them the taxes were collected, and in them justice was administered. But, more than this, a large share of local liberty was left to them. Even Rome would have found herself unequal to the burden of governing her heterogeneous empire if she had not left a good deal to the municipal administrations. Discoveries of the highest interest and importance have thrown a flood of light on the internal constitution of a provincial town. The active prosperous life of these innumerable towns is the fairest feature of Roman rule; and the question how much was left to the magistrates, and how much had to be referred to the governor at different periods, is perhaps the most interesting inquiry connected with our subject, as it is the most difficult.

So much for the way in which I propose to divide the subject. But there are one or two general remarks still to make. It is exceedingly difficult in discussing the provinces of Rome not to talk of them as a whole, and as a fixed whole. But in truth the Roman world is a world continually growing, developing, changing, always tending to a uniformity but never fully reaching it. The difference between East and West is never obliterated, and at last victoriously asserts itself. The Romans showed greater power of assimilation than has been shown by any other conquerors; but even they could not assimilate a civilisation like that of Greece, which was in some respects superior to their own. So the Greek East was not organised, after the strict type of the Roman province, into colonies and municipia until a late date. If we want to see typical examples of the Roman rule we must look to the West, not to the East; to the 'savage and barbarous tribes,' as Cicero[1] calls them (though they were by no means mere savages), of Africa, Gaul, or Spain, rather than to the polished Greeks of Achaia and Asia Minor. It is to the West also that we must look for instances of another important distinction, that between forward and backward provinces. By forward provinces I mean those which took kindly to Roman rule and flourished under it, for instance Spain and Gaul; by backward provinces those which either from having a different and equally advanced civilisa-

---

[1] *Ad Qu. Fr.* I. i. 9: 'Afris aut Hispanis aut Gallis . . . immanibus ac barbaris nationibus.' With these he contrasts the Greeks of Asia Minor—'quod est ex hominum omni genere humanissimum.' See § 1 of the same letter.

tion of their own, as Greece proper, or from a dead weight of barbarism, as Rhaetia or Britain, were unable to move in the ordinary Roman lines. On the whole, those provinces gained most where there was least to lose. Rome was extraordinarily successful in civilising barbarians, not perhaps so successful in dealing with races already of a high type. It is also to be borne in mind that there is a great difference between different parts of the same country; between Northern and Southern Gaul[1] and between Northern and Southern Spain.[2] So it is easy to understand the reason of these countries having been split up into several provinces, and the difference made between the different parts of Spain when the provinces were divided between the Senate and the Emperor. Or take the modern country of Switzerland, the western part of which was in Gaul and immensely rich and prosperous, full of important towns and possessing an extensive commerce, the eastern part in Rhaetia and comparatively uncivilised. Perhaps the modern division of languages in Switzerland is due to the way in which Roman civilisation had sunk into the western parts, so that the Alemanni could not wholly displace it, while in the eastern parts the tongue of the conquerors easily prevailed.[3]

These remarks illustrate the danger of general statements on the provinces as a whole. I shall therefore endeavour always to state to what particular province or provinces my statements specially refer. At the same time it would be absurd to ignore the large and increasing element of unity. The administration was everywhere of much the same type; a good governor in Cilicia was very similar to a good governor in Spain; and a Verres in Asia was much the same as a Verres in Sicily. The towns beginning with

---

[1] Mommsen, *Provinces* I. 79 and 81, notices the admixture of Iberians in the South and Germans in the North.

[2] Jung, *Die romanischen Landschaften*, pp. 19, 25, 33.

[3] Mommsen, *Schweiz in der Römischen Zeit*, p. 17.

the greatest possible varieties of constitution tended more and more to the one municipal type—a type which is generally accommodated to that of the Italian colonies and municipia, the account of which therefore has often to be given side by side with that of the municipia in the provinces; and by the time of the Later Empire the rights of individuals were the same over the Roman world. It is not therefore necessary to avoid generalisations altogether in speaking of the provinces; but it is necessary to be cautious in their employment.

CHAPTER II.

What a province was. How acquired. Use of client-princes. How secured and organised. Moral aspect of the Roman rule.

The word 'Provincia.' WHATEVER may be the derivation of the word 'Provincia,'[1] it is at any rate indisputable that it was not always used in the special sense which became attached to it under the later Republic. '*Provincia*,' says Mommsen, 'as is well known, denoted in the older language not what we now call *province*, a definite space assigned as a district to a standing chief magistrate, but simply the functions prescribed for the particular magistrate by law, decree of the senate, or agreement.' The word is of course frequently used in the early books of Livy long before there was any question of provinces in the later sense; and even under the Empire instances of a similar use occur. When the first transmarine provinces were formed their government was assigned to the existing magistrates, as the business which they had to discharge during their year of office.[2] Very soon and very naturally the word came to be applied

---

[1] The commonly received derivation is from *vincere*, to which Mommsen adheres, *Staatsr.* i. 50, note 2. Other suggestions are *providentia* (clearly wrong), and *vincire*, as though the meaning were 'obligation' (Fasc. 35 of Bibliothèque de l'Ecole des hautes études, p. 115). In Kuhn's *Zeitschrift*, viii. 289, Buden refers to Gothic *provius*. In *Class. Rev.*, vol. ii., p. 227, Mr. Cookson supposes an adj. *pròvincus*, of which the stem is *prov*, with which is connected O.H.G. *fro*, 'lord,' as in G. *frohnherrschaft*, the meaning therefore being 'lordship.' In its earlier use it is applicable to judicial (*Verr.* v. § 38) and financial (*Lex Acil.* § 67) functions.

[2] Mommsen, ii. 209.

to the district itself in which that government was exercised. The word 'Conventus' has had a similar history. Originally applied to the assembly of Roman citizens at a provincial town to meet the governor and act with him in trying law-suits on definite occasions, it came to be applied to the district from which the people assembled, and to the place in which the assembly was held.[1]

It does not come within the range of this work to narrate the history of Rome's foreign conquests. They may be said to have had their origin in the First and Second Punic Wars. Those wars had shown her the necessity of the possession of the 'suburban Sicily,' as Cicero calls it, if only for her own safety; and the same imperative reasons applied to Sardinia. The second war had brought Roman armies into Spain, and, once planted there, severe and unpopular though the service there was, they remained for many years. Philip of Macedonia's half-hearted assistance of Hannibal (together with his aggressive foreign policy) secured him the active enmity of Rome; and it had all along been obvious that in the struggle between Rome and Carthage Greece would necessarily be the prize of the conqueror. One may believe this without at all condemning the philhellenism of the better class of Romans as hypocritical and disingenuous. Having once decisively asserted herself in the world across the sea,[2] it was inevitable that in that chaos of factions and intrigues Rome should be called upon to play a more and more decisive part. There is evidence enough to warrant Mommsen[3] in his view that Rome's foreign conquests were not at first intentional and deliberate, but that her immediate aim was to make herself secure and all-powerful in Italy. But wars sprang up which she could not avoid, or which she had not

[Margin note: Origin and intention of Rome's foreign conquests.]

---

[1] Called in Greek διοίκησις (Cic. *Fam.* xiii. 53, 67).

[2] '*Provinciae quae mari dividuntur*' is Tacitus' name for the Greek East; *Ann.* ii. 43. So Vell. ii. 44, *Transmarinis provinciis.*

ii. 520-1. Cf. Freeman, *Essays*, 2nd Series, p. 253.

expected[1]; her clients and allies made demands upon her which it was impossible to refuse, and the Senate saw itself committed to the conquest and administration of half the known world, before having definitely made up its mind whether such conquests were advisable or the reverse. But when once there was a large army it was perhaps necessary to go on conquering,[2] and in any case it was not long before the sweets of conquest made themselves felt. The remission of the tribute paid by Roman citizens in the year 167 B.C. marks an epoch. That remission was the direct consequence of foreign conquest. The sums poured by Paullus into the treasury were so immense and unprecedented as to make it unnecessary to demand the money of Romans for the purposes of the state. When C. Gracchus added the taxation of Asia to the treasury, and fed the people by doles of foreign corn, the new system of things stands plainly revealed. The Romans are to rule and enjoy, their subjects to serve and pay. Along with these positive material advantages went an increase of the mere military spirit, of the love of conquest for its own sake, and of pride in the increasing extent of the subject territory, till we find under the Empire even so moderate and sensible a man as Agricola seriously meditating the barren conquest of Ireland, so that the Roman arms might be carried everywhere, and no country might be tempted from its allegiance by the spectacle of another's freedom.[3]

We must also have regard, in one case at all events, to the necessity which Rome lay under of securing herself against barbarian invasion. This was one of the reasons which led her on to the conquest of all Gaul. Cæsar [4] himself hints at the danger of the Germans being allowed to

---

[1] Cic. *pro Fonteio*, 19: 'cum tot bella aut a nobis necessario suscipiantur, aut subito atque improvisa nascantur.'

[2] Ne res disciplinae inimicissima, otium, corrumperet militem. Vell. Pat. ii. 78 (of Octavian's expedition to Illyria).

[3] Tac. *Agr.* 24.   [4] Caes. *B. G.* i. 33.

settle in that country, and there prepare themselves for a march southwards; and the facts seem to show that without Roman aid the Gauls could have made no effectual resistance to their invaders. The more rhetorical Cicero[1] in two well-known passages reminds his hearers of Rome's previous dangers from the 'savage natures and vast multitudes' of the Gauls, and congratulates them that the barrier of the Alps is no longer needed for the protection of Italy. The same reasons made it necessary for Rome in a later period to possess herself of the Danubian provinces. But conquest, whether deliberate or unintentional, was not the only means by which the Roman dominion spread. Pergamum, Bithynia, Cyrene,[2] were bequeathed to Rome by will; and Rome, though she hesitated, did not ultimately refuse the splendid gifts. That it was not really independent and powerful monarchs who so acted is, however, obvious; and a more particular account of these 'client-princes,' as Mommsen has called them, will make Rome's final success in administering and assimilating her provinces easier to understand.

This system lasted at least to the time of Trajan; but the period when it was most extensively used, and was least beneficial, was from the commencement of Roman conquest in the East up to the definite settlement of Macedonia. Till then the Roman Senate hardly seems to have made up its mind whether definitely to take over the countries it had conquered or not. So we find the petty kings of Asia Minor, 'Client-princes.'

---

[1] Cic. de prov. Cons. 13, in Pis. 33. Cf. Sall. Jug. 114. 'Cum Gallis pro salute non pro gloria certare.'

[2] The alleged bequest of Pergamum has had a somewhat different colour given it by the recovered fragment of the will, see Fränkel, Insch. von Pergamon, n. 249 (printed in Greenidge and Clay's Appendix to their Sources of Roman Hist.). ἐπεὶ βασιλεὺς Ἄτταλος μεθιστάμενος ἐξ ἀνθρώπων ἀπολέλοιπεν τὴν πατρίδα ἡμῶν ἐλεύθερον, δεῖ δὲ ἐπικυρωθῆναι τὴν διαθήκην ὑπὸ Ῥωμαίων. Sall. Ep. Mithr. also hints at fraud on the part of Rome. For Cyrene (bequeathed 96 B.C.) cf. Liv. Ep. 70, App. B. C. i. 111.

the Seleucidae of Syria, and the Ptolemies of Egypt left in possession of their dominions subject to the hegemony of Rome, which was rather practically understood than positively defined. So, as Mommsen[1] has pointed out, they had neither freedom nor order. They were not free, because Roman senatorial commissions were continually regulating their affairs ; and their constant quarrels with one another could neither come to a definite issue, nor be controlled by a sovereign authority. No wonder then that both the Romans and the princes themselves became tired of so unsatisfactory an arrangement. The latter did not care to leave to their children the empty shadow of power[2] with which there was neither honour nor profit ; and the Romans by their definite annexation of Macedonia showed that they had at last made up their minds to a more decided policy. But this is not the last of a system which we find in full force under Caligula and Claudius; and we may be sure that it would not have lasted so long if it had not possessed, in the eyes of the Romans, some positive advantages. Tacitus[3] speaks of it as 'the ancient and long-recognised practice of the Roman people, which seeks to secure among the instruments of dominion even kings themselves.' It was especially the system of Augustus, who describes his application of it in these words: 'When, after the murder of its king Artaxias, I could have made Greater Armenia a province, I preferred, according to the example of our ancestors, to entrust that kingdom to Tigranes, son of king Artavasdes, grandson of king Tigranes, through the agency of Tib. Nero, who was then my stepson. And the same nation, when it afterwards revolted, on its subjugation by my son Gaius, I entrusted for government to king Ariobarzanes, son of Artabanus king of the Medes, and after his

---

[1] Mommsen, iii. 236, and the whole chapter.
[2] 'Umbra regis' is the expression of Tacitus, *Ann.* xv. 6, for one of these princes.
[3] Tac. *Agr.* 14.

death to his son Artavasdes ; and when he too was slain, I sent Tigranes, who was sprung from the royal stock of Armenia, into that kingdom.'[1] But Cilicia is a better instance of the system than Armenia. Augustus made it his policy to encourage the petty kings in this quarter : thus we find a dynasty of Olbe, and a dynasty of Mount Amanus.[2] In this way we find the province cut short more and more till it meant only the plain country of Cilicia. This distinction between *Cilicia Campestris* and *Cilicia Aspera* is the key to the extensive use of the system in that country. No difficulty was found in thoroughly administering and Romanising the level country from an early date. Tarsus[3] was a very considerable city long before St. Paul mentions it. Very different was the condition of the fierce hillmen whom the Romans so often hunted down in their fastnesses, and with so little permanent effect. The description which Cicero[4] gives us of a siege of one of these hill-forts in Mount Amanus reads like a description of a raid upon the hillmen of Nepal or Afghanistan. The difference between the men of the plains and of the hills is strikingly illustrated by a passage where Tacitus[5] seems purposely to contrast the Clitae on their ' rocky mountains ' with the peaceful ' farmers,' ' townsfolk,' ' merchants,' ' shipowners,' whom they harried in the plain beneath. Rome could not have brought these districts and such as these directly under her rule without a large military force, and great expense with very little profit. And yet it was impossible for her to leave them altogether uncontrolled. So she interfered with their affairs so far as to appoint princes who would rule in her

---

[1] Mon. Ancyr. § 27. Cf. Suet. *Aug.* 48. The idea was that of interposing buffer states between Roman territories and the Parthians. See Ramsay, *Church in the Roman Empire*, p. 385.

[2] Marquardt, i. 227 ; Strab. xiv. 5, § 6.

[3] See, for instance, *Bell. Alex.* 66 ; Strab. xiv. 10, 12-15 ; *Acts* 21, 39.

[4] *Ad Att.* v. 20.

[5] Tac. *Ann.* vi. 41 ; xii. 55. Another form is Cietae, *Arch. Epigr. Mitt.* xvii. 1.

interest, and whose task it was to tame and civilise their subjects till they were fit to come directly under Roman rule. Factions within the tribe itself, or quarrels between different members of the ruling house, would give her frequent occasion for such interference; indeed we find that on more than one occasion kings are requested from her by nations beyond the frontier.[1] As it was to be expected that such princes should frequently have to control their subjects' disaffection, it was a common practice to support the Roman nominee by a small detachment of Roman troops. When the Tigranes whom Nero had appointed to the government of Armenia arrived in his province, 'he was supported with a force of a thousand legionaries, three allied cohorts, and two squadrons of cavalry, that he might the more easily secure his new kingdom.'[2] Two other passages of Tacitus[3] prove that these troops were permanently stationed in the country and garrisoned strong places in it. A few cohorts and a Roman knight protected the prince of the Bosporus; and such troops though insignificant in numbers would act as a nucleus for the native army[4] and form a model which princes like Deiotarus,[5] ambitious of having troops trained after the Roman fashion, would imitate. Even if there were not troops stationed

---

[1] Parthia, though not a client state, illustrates this attitude to native powers. See Tac. *Ann*. xii. 10, 11, xiii. 9, Mommsen *Provinces*, ch. ix.; and summary of Roman relations with Parthia under the first emperors by Church and Brodribb, p. 396. But the same thing occurs in the case of the Suevi, *Ann*. xii. 29, 30; Cherusci, *Ann*. xi. 16; see also Tac. *Germ*. 42; Bructeri, Plin. *Ep*. ii. 7. Arrian, writing to the emperor an account of his voyage round the coasts of the Black Sea, says (*Periplus*, § 15) 'Next to the Apsitae come the Abasci; their king is Rhesmagas; he holds his kingdom of you.' § 27 he says the same of the king of the Zilchi.

[2] Tac. *Ann*. xiv. 26.   [3] Ib. xii. 15, 45.

[4] Tac. *Ann*. iv. 44, iii. 7, 38; xii. 16; *Hist*. v. 1.

[5] *Bell. Alex*. 34; Cic. *Phil*. xi. 13, § 33; cf. Dio C. 42, 3 and 5 for the guards left by Gabinius in Egypt, where they became thoroughly denationalised.

actually within the kingdom, the governor of the neighbouring province would send them in case of need. For
instance, when the Clitae revolted against the process of
Romanisation which their king was applying to them, the
revolt was put down by troops sent by the governor of
Syria. The particular grievance against which the Clitae
revolted is an illustration of how these ' subject princes ' [1] of
Rome broke in their unruly subjects to the most unpleasant
necessities of the Roman rule. ' They were compelled in
Roman fashion to render an account of their revenue, and
submit to tribute,' says Tacitus.[2] We find the same thing
in Cappadocia, where king Ariobarzanes is instructed by
Cicero's predecessor, Appius, to levy a tribute upon his
subjects.[3] This was advised by Appius, apparently that
Ariobarzanes might be enabled to pay his debts; and if
other such princes were as heavily indebted to aristocratic
Roman usurers as was this unfortunate monarch, the
tribute must have been instituted everywhere. It should
be added that some, at all events, of these kingdoms paid a
tribute directly to Rome.

It is obvious of what service such a system as this
could be to Rome. If these princes were, as Tacitus[4]
says, protected by the greatness of Rome against external
Empires, it is also true that they acted as a barrier between
Rome and such Empires,[5] to defer or altogether prevent
the otherwise inevitable collisions. Without saddling herself with absolute responsibility or binding herself to interfere when it was inconvenient, Rome had her work done
for her in the way in which she would have it. These
princes were thoroughly subservient and responsible to
their masters[6]; were often themselves brought up at

---

[1] ' Inservientium regum '; Tac. *Hist.* ii. 81.

[2] Tac. *Ann.* vi. 41.   [3] Cic. *ad Att.* vi. 1. § 3.

[4] Tac. *Ann.* iv. 5.

[5] *Bell. Alex.* 78, provincias populi Romania barbaris atque inimicis regibus interposito amicissimo rege munivit.

[6] Tac. *Ann.* xi. 8.

Rome[1]; and quite understood what work Rome expected of them. A passage from Strabo[2] shows the nature of that work in a few words. He is describing the settlement of Africa after the destruction of Carthage. ' The Romans paid particular attention to Masanasses on account of his great abilities and friendship for them. For he it was who formed the Numidians to civil life, and directed their attention to husbandry.' If an inscription of Britain is correctly read, it seems to mention *Cogidubni Regis* (also known from Tac. *Agr.* 14) as *legati Augusti in Britannia;* Hübner supposes this to have been an honorary title only, though Henzen disputes this interpretation.[3] Add to this that in the coins struck by such provinces the Emperor's head appears on one side, and that of the prince on the other[4]; and the part played by such princes as representing Rome to their subjects, and preparing them for the rule of Rome, will be fully understood.[5]

Means of securing a province.
Where Rome did not make use of this system she secured her hold upon a country by a mixture of policy and force. To win over one tribe at all events, or to play one prince against another, were easy devices, which hardly ever failed of success. The want of unity in uncivilised races made conquest easy[6]; and traitors were never wanting, when there was none of that national unity which would make treason seem a crime. Thus the Moschi were won over in

---

[1] The case of Juba, king of Mauretania under Augustus, is a remarkable one. He was a thorough Roman, and a trained man of letters ; Plut. *Jul.* 55. Cicero describes Ariobarzanes as ' Euseben et Philoromaeum,' *Ad Fam.* xv. 2. § 4 ; Agrippa and Herodes in Judæa seem to have been Roman citizens, and to have had the *ornamenta praetoria* and *consularia*, Dio. lx. 8.

[2] Strabo, xvii. 3. § 15.

[3] C. I. L. vii., p. 18 ; and Hübner's note. Henzen, p. 136.

[4] Church and Brodribb, *Annals*, p. 402 ; Marquardt, i. 150.

[5] See Strabo, iv. 5. § 3 ; Marquardt, i. 343 ; Boissière, *Hist. de la Conquête et de l'Administration Romaines dans le nord d'Afrique*, p. 415, for a discussion of a rationale of the system.

[6] Cf. Tac. *Agr.* 12.

Asia Minor[1]; Galgacus complains of the number of his
fellow-countrymen who served against him in Britain[2];
and Caesar availed himself of the friendship of the Remi
and Aedui in Gaul.[3] Similarly the mutual jealousies of
the petty princes of an invaded country were dexterously
made available for Roman ends. So we find the Romans
in Britain upholding a wife against her husband, and sending troops to support her when in difficulties.[4] But these
were merely temporary expedients; and once thoroughly
established in a country, Rome secured herself there by
very different measures. Wherever, owing to the natural
difficulties of the country, or the exceptional spirit of the
people, repression was necessary, there was a chain of
'fortresses with military garrisons.'[5] We find these for Forts.
instance among the Silures in Britain,[6] and Tacitus commends the promptitude with which they were established in
newly-conquered districts of the same province by Agricola.[7]
There was also a line of these along every frontier; for
example (not to mention more important but more familiar
instances) on the northern border of Gallia Narbonensis in
the time of Caesar.[8] Colonies again, when planted in a Colonies.
newly-conquered country, were really nothing but such
fortified outposts on a larger scale. This is the account
which Cicero[9] gives of Narbo Martius (Narbonne) in
Southern Gaul; and Tacitus[10] says much the same in his
brief and pointed manner of the colony of Camulodunum

[1] Tac. *Ann.* xiii. 37. [2] Tac. *Agr.* 32.
[3] Caes. *B. G.* v. 54, vii. 54. [4] Tac. *Ann.* xii. 40 ; *Hist.* iii. 45.
[5] Tac. *Ann.* xiv. 33. [6] Ibid.
[7] Tac. *Agr.* 20, 22. [8] Caes. *B. G.* vii. 7.
[9] Cic. *pro Fonteio*, v. § 13 : ' Est in eadem provincia Narbo Martius,
colonia nostrorum civium, specula populi Romani ac propugnaculum
istis ipsis nationibus oppositum et objectum.' The same metaphor
occurs Cic. *de Leg. Agr.* ii. 27. For τὰ φρούρια in Spain, see App.
Hisp. 38.

[10] *Ann.* xii. 32 : ' Colonia Camulodunum valida veteranorum manu
deducitur in agros captivos, subsidium adversus rebelles, et imbuendis
sociis ad officia legum.'

2

in Britain. The natives themselves regarded them quite
in this light, and hated them as the 'headquarters of
tyranny'[1]; and that their hatred was sometimes not without
good cause appears from the detestable oppressions practised by these same colonists of Camulodunum.[2] More
important perhaps than any of these measures were the
great military roads which it was the first object of Rome
to drive across a conquered country. These magnificent
causeways, raised considerably above the level of the
ground, and with a deep ditch on each side of them from
which the earth that formed them had been dug, were in
themselves eminently defensible, and enabled troops to be
massed on any given point with security and despatch.
The great Egnatian way, running from Dyrrhachium to
Thessalonica, 'that military road of ours,' as Cicero[3] calls
it, 'which extends through Macedonia to the Hellespont,'
was completed very shortly after Rome had possessed herself of Macedonia, and is still the main avenue of communication in those countries.[4]

Roads.

Besides these definite and tangible measures Rome secured
her position by the attractions of commerce and a higher
material civilisation. The Roman trader was ubiquitous.
He even preceded the Roman arms; thus we find him in
Africa before the Second Punic War, and crossing the
Great St. Bernard and paying toll to the barbarians before
either end of the pass was secured by Roman troops[5]; and
wherever the Roman arms were carried, the merchants
followed in crowds.[6] The immense and permanent diffusion
of Roman citizens over the world which Rome had conquered was one of the chief agencies at work in levelling
differences and establishing a sort of unity between its

---

[1] Tac. *Agr.* 16.   [2] *Ann.* xiv. 51 ; cf. *Ann.* i. 59.   [3] *De Prov. Cons.* 2.
[4] Mommsen, iii. 263.   [5] App. *Hisp.* 4 ; Caes. *B. G.* iii. 1.
[6] Mommsen, iii. 260 ; Finlay, i. 47 ; Diod. v. 26 ; Duruy, iii. 257.
Appian (*Mith.* 28) speaks of the 20,000 Italians destroyed by the
generals of Mithridates at Delos and other Greek places,

heterogeneous parts. So again the higher civilisation of Rome exercised an immense attraction upon backward races.[1] The Romans quite understood this; and an interesting and characteristic passage of Tacitus[2] shows us Agricola of set purpose introducing the Britons to the pleasant luxuries of their conquerors. 'All this in their ignorance they called civilisation, when it was but a part of their servitude.'

If a Roman province was conquered and secured in some such way as this, how was it organised after conquest? One of the first objects of the Romans was to put an end to all leagues and combinations which might prove dangerous to their rule. In this they only followed that rule of *divide et impera* which had proved so successful in Italy. Political leagues like that of Achaia came to an end, though afterwards allowed to exist for certain purposes (Paus. 7, 16, 10); and if the Romans still permitted the 'community of Sicily'[3] and the 'confederacy of Lycia'[4] to exist, it was because they were devoid of political significance. To break up a province as far as possible into a number of isolated units was the tendency of the earlier period. It is only under the Empire that we find anything of the nature of a provincial parliament; and even then it is easy to exaggerate the significance of those shadowy assemblies. Even before Rome had fully taken over a country and subjected it to her rule, we find her at work destroying any national unity it might possess, subdividing it and isolating its different parts. Thus Macedonia was broken up into four confederacies without right of intermarriage, and no one was allowed to hold landed property in more than one of

First organisation of a province.

'Divide et impera.'

---

[1] This is illustrated by the case of the Ubii; see Tac. *Hist.* iv. 28.

[2] Tac. *Agr.* 21.

[3] Cic. *in Verrem*, iii. 63; Mommsen, *Provinces*, i. 259.

[4] σύστημα Λυκίας. See Marquardt, i. 219. The Lycian League was destroyed by Claudius; see Freeman, *Federal Government*, pp. 162-169. The Amphictyonic Council held meetings in the time of Pausanias; Paus. *Phoc.* viii. 3; Finlay, i. 67; Tozer's Strabo, p. 241.

the confederacies.[1] Illyria was treated in much the same fashion.[2] The later divisions introduced by Rome for purposes of jurisdiction, the *conventus* or circuits, tended, whether intentionally or not, to the same result. These divisions were quite apart from race distinctions, and must have contributed not a little to confuse and even obliterate these distinctions. Thus Strabo[3] writes : ' The places situated next to these towards the south and extending to Mount Taurus, are so intermixed, that parts of Phrygia, Lydia, Caria, and Mysia, running into one another, are difficult to be distinguished. The Romans have contributed not a little to produce this confusion, by not dividing the people according to tribes, but following another principle have arranged them according to jurisdictions, in which they have appointed days for holding courts and administering justice.'

The same ends were secured by the immense variety of rights and privileges that existed over the area of a single province. The towns might be either free towns or allied towns, or Roman colonies, or municipia with Roman or Latin right, or simply ordinary provincial towns without either special privilege or special disqualification. These differences of right would depend largely upon the attitude they had severally adopted while the Romans were engaged in military operations in the country. The differences of land tenure followed from the same cause. Some states had their lands taken from them for good ; to others they were, as the phrase went, ' restored.'[4] ' What could be more humane than the conduct of our ancestors,' exclaims Cicero, 'who very frequently restored their property even to foreign enemies whom they had conquered ?'[5]

---

[1] Livy, xlv. 29; Mommsen, ii. 508.

[2] Marquardt, *Organisation de l'Empire*, pp. 173, 174 (French tr.).

[3] Strabo, xiii. 4, § 12. Later on there was a recrudescence of the ethnic differences thus swamped.

[4] Cic. *pro Fonteio*, 1 ; cf. *Pro Balbo*, 18 ; Livy, 33, 34.

[5] *De Leg. Agr.* i, 6 : ' Quid enim illis clementius qui etiam externis hostibus victis sua saepissime reddiderunt ?' Cf. *in Verrem*, ii. 21, 37, iv. 54.

The Lex Agraria of 111 which regulated the tenure of the land and the payment of the taxes in the province of Africa is extremely puzzling from the number of tenures it establishes. The three main divisions are into *ager privatus ex jure Quiritium*,[1] that is, land assigned to Roman colonies or to Roman citizens individually ; *ager privatus ex jure peregrino*, that is, the land of free or allied towns, paying no taxes ; and *ager publicus populi Romani*,[2] that is, the land of conquered communities like Carthage, which became the absolute property of Rome. But this was not all. Some towns which had started with the same rights as the others, gained for this or that reason privileges to which the others were strangers. Immunity from taxation would be the chief of these, and adventurers like Antony[3] or good-natured emperors like Claudius[4] were far from unready to bargain away or present such privileges. It is obvious from all this how absolutely isolated and independent would become the the interests of each single town within a Roman province. From Rome a town might get everything, but from its neighbours nothing. The citizens of one town were not as a rule allowed to hold land within the territory of another ; and when we find a number of provincial towns co-operating for any purpose of common advantage, as, for instance, the Spanish municipia that combined their subscriptions to build a bridge over the Tagus,[5] the case is exceptional enough to excite attention. Such an instance of close intercourse, again, as that of the *hospitium* between different tribes in

---

[1] This land would be that of the colonies (C. Gracchus had powers for more than merely one; see Sall. *Jug.* 42) previously founded by C. Gracchus.

[2] This land would be that of the seven free cities, Utica, Thapsus, etc., which assisted Rome against Carthage. See this important law (commonly but erroneously called the Lex Thoria) in C. I. L. i. 90 and Mommsen's full discussion of it, ib. i. 96. Bruns, p. 74.

[3] For the traffic in such matters, of which Cicero accuses Antony, see *Phil.* i. 10, ii. 14, 17, 36, 38.

[4] Tac. *Ann.* xii. 58, 60 ; Suet. *Claud.* 25.

[5] C. I. L. ii. 760.

the north of Spain, of which there is epigraphic evidence,[1] is almost without a parallel. *Hospitium* with Romans,— that was another matter[2]; between Rome and the provinces the communication was easy and incessant; but between province and province, or between different parts of the same province, it was never, even under the Empire which could afford to be more liberal in this matter than the Republic, more than tolerated.

Adaptability of the Roman Administration.

But though in these respects Rome was inflexible enough, the great merit of her administration of the provinces is, on the whole, the pliancy and adaptability of it. ' Everywhere where the Roman conquest found a good municipal and financial organisation, it had remained content with it.'[3] The Romans were not cursed with the passion for uniformity; and, as Tacitus[4] said of them, 'they value the reality of Empire, and disregard its empty show.' The extent to

Illustrated by case of Egypt.

which they left the pre-existing arrangements unaltered in Egypt is an extraordinary proof of their wise conservatism. In the first place, they left the religion of the people quite untouched, local deities were recognised on the provincial coinage, and through Alexandria their cult spread over the whole Mediterranean world. Roman governors were not above associating themselves with their ceremonies, and devoutly listening to the miraculous statue of Memnon.[5] The arrangements of the Ptolemies remained the groundwork of the government; the Roman governor stepped into their throne, was in the eyes of the Egyptians a vice-king, and had none of the ordinary insignia of a Roman magis-

---

[1] Orelli, 150, 156.

[2] Willems, *Droit public*, p. 347 ; SCtum de Asclepiade, C. I. L. i. pp. 110-112 ; Bruns, 176.

[3] Egger, *Examen critique des historiens anciens de la vie et du règne d'Auguste*, p. 44.

[4] Tac. *Ann.* xv. 31.

[5] Cf. Boissier, *L'Empire Romain en Orient* (in *Rev. des Deux Mondes*, July, 1874), p. 114 ; and for the protection extended by Rome to foreign religions generally, Cic. *in Verrem*, iv. 51.

trate. The great peculiarity of Egypt was the subdivision of the land, and here, from the absolute necessity of definite and permanent arrangements in a country whose soil was annually submerged, the Romans were more than usually conservative. The main division was into three Epistrategiae—Thebais, Heptanomis, and Arsinoite, which were in fact Upper, Middle, and Lower Egypt. Each of these was divided into nomes; the nomes were again divided into toparchies, and the toparchies into κῶμαι and τόποι. Each of the three great divisions was under an equestrian ἐπιστρατηγός, to whom the minor magistrates were responsible. Originally there were thirty-six nomes; later on forty-seven can be pointed out, and there were perhaps more. Each nome had a town for its capital, but the town was only a part of the nome, and by no means the source of authority in it, as would have been the case in Greece, or other Roman provinces. The magistrate here was called by the Romans στρατηγός. These officers were native Greeks or Egyptians, appointed for three years by the imperial government, and were no doubt the channels through which the government reached the peasants. They received copies of the decrees issued by the prefect in Alexandria, and it was their duty to make these known to the inhabitants of their district. The copy of the decree issued by the prefect Tiberius Alexander, found in the Grand Oasis in 1820,[1] is prefaced by the following notice from the strategus: ' I, Julius Demetrius, strategus of the Oasis of the Thebais, have published the copy of the decree sent me by the prefect, Tiberius Julius Alexander, in order that you may know and enjoy its beneficent provisions.' There were also minor officials known as κωμογραμματεῖς, whose main business it was to look after the boundaries which the Nile was continually unsettling, but who also had duties connected with

---

[1] Selections from this decree, along with a shorter one of a previous governor, Cn. Vergilius Capito, are added at the end of the present chapter.

the taxation of their nome.[1]   The genuine Greek towns, such as Naucratis and Ptolemais, stood wholly outside the nome arrangements, and governed themselves on the usual Greek model with archons and boule. Alexandria however, the second city of the Empire, had too unruly a population to be allowed self-government, and was under a *juridicus Alexandriae* who was named directly by the emperor, the local senate being removed by Augustus. Its population consisted of three distinct races: firstly, Greeks with administrative and judicial magistrates of their own (ἐξηγητής and ἀρχιδικαστής); secondly, Jews, with an Ethnarch chosen by themselves, and a council of elders; thirdly, Egyptians as resident aliens or μέτοικοι.[2]   The prefect, being the direct servant of the Emperor, united in his person the duties of the legatus and procurator of the ordinary Imperial provinces. The procurator patrimonii (the private property of the Emperor) was called ἰδιολόγος.   This arrangement lasted to the time of Diocletian.   Egypt was prosperous in the early Empire; irrigation was carefully studied, through trade to the East encouraged.   Only in the second century did peasant and Jewish revolts lead to agricultural decay.

The Greek East.   It is unnecessary to point out the peculiarities of this administration.   The general difference in the administration of East and West illustrates the same marvellous readiness of Rome to adapt herself to existing circumstances. The incompatibility of Roman and Greek was a fact she

---

[1] See the decree of Cn. Vergilius Capito. ‘Let the imperial scribes, and the κωμογραμματεῖς and τοπογραμματεῖς in each nome, keep account of what is paid by the nome, in case any illegal exactions have been made, or anything else of the kind.   And if they do not, let them pay 60 (denarii?) over and above the sum they have thus failed to keep account of.'

[2] Numerous documents bearing on this administration of Egypt have been published by Mr. Flinders Petrie and Mr. Mahaffy.   See also E. Kuhn, *der Zustand Aegyptens*, ii. 454 ; Müller's *Handbuch*, iii. 553. Wilcken, *Observationes ad historiam Aegypti prov. Rom.*   Milne, *History of Egypt under Roman Rule.   Griech. Urkunden aus den Kgl. Museen zu Berlin* (B. G. U.).

early recognised ; it could not be stated more strongly than it is in the *pro Flacco* of Cicero ; and the policy of Rome was to leave the Greek cities very much to themselves, though no doubt always favouring the aristocratic element in them, as Sparta had done before her, at the expense of the democratic element. The Romans could not deal with Greek ecclesiae, and the contemptuous tone in which Cicero[1] speaks of the democratic assemblies of Asia is a faithful echo of the ordinary Roman feeling. But on the whole these towns remained wonderfully unchanged, and even under the Empire, as far as inscriptions go, a town like Tomi on the Black Sea might have appeared wholly independent and outside of Roman rule, if it were not for the occasional mention of the 'sacred rescripts' (ἱεραὶ ἀντιγραφαί) of the emperor.[2] This conservatism was very natural. The Romans would have given themselves an immensity of trouble, if they had insisted upon a uniform administration everywhere, without any proportionate advantage ; nor did they possess a large enough official class or civil service to enable them to dispense with the help of the municipal authorities. In the Greek cities of Asia Minor a municipal census had been regularly taken,[3] and it was natural that the Romans when they conquered the country should make use of it. In Egypt the immemorial survey of the country was the basis of their administration. They were indeed only too glad to be saved the enormous labours of the survey in at all events one country, and in the decree of Tiberius Alexander which has been preserved to us we find the governor assuring the Egyptians that no changes in that survey were meditated. It is worth adding that the peculiar Egyptian foot-measure was maintained under

---

[1] 'Graeculae contionis,' *pro Flacco*, 10, § 23 ; also 7, 8, 24 of the same oration.

[2] Perrot, *Mém. sur quelques inscriptions inédites des côtes de la Mer Noire, Revue Archéol.* 1874, p. 27.

[3] Appian, *B. C.* v. 4. For Sicily, cf. Cic. *in Verrem*, ii. 53-56.

their rule; just as in Gaul the *leugae* were not totally dispossessed by the Roman system of measuring by miles.[1]

Sicily.   A marked instance of their attitude to the existing arrangements of a province is that of Sicily. Here the Lex Hieronica, the judicial and financial arrangements established by the king who had been Rome's faithful ally, was maintained in its entirety. In particular the tithes which he had established were maintained as the regular tax; and the arrangements by which the dealings between the farmers and the middle men were controlled were carefully observed. These laws, though framed with the utmost care and even severity, were yet just, and, if they were observed, it was, according to Cicero, impossible for the farmer of the tithes to exact from the cultivator more than his due.[2] The Romans, when they made Sicily a province, took care that not only the king's laws should be maintained, but also that they should preserve his name[3]; and till the disastrous governorship of Verres, no praetor had violated its provisions.[4] Even the senatorial commission appointed during Verres' years of office to inquire into the taxation of his province, though they had at first intended to introduce reforms, ended by maintaining the law of Hiero in its integrity.[5]

Lex Provinciae.   But whether the Romans were assisted by such preexisting conditions or not, they in all cases made it their business to establish a norm of administration in any country of which they determined to make a province. A country was not thought to be really conquered till it had been bound down by Roman laws as well as overthrown by Roman arms. Cicero argues for the prorogation of Caesar's command in Gaul on the ground that the Gallic peoples had indeed been subdued, but not yet attached to

---

[1] Marquardt, ii. 216; Roth, *Geschichte der Leuga,* in *Jahrbuch des Vereins von Alterthumsfreunden im Rheinland,* xix. 1.
[2] *In Verrem,* iii. 8.   [3] Ib. iii. 6.
[4] Ib. ii. 60.   [5] Ib. iii. 7.

Rome by laws, by a fixed code of rights, by a certain peace.[1] If this policy was thus necessary for security, it was of course indispensable for the future government of the province. Directly after the conquest of a country, the Senate dispatched a commission of ten senators, whose business it was, in combination with the general, to settle its future government. Thus Plutarch[2] relates that Lucullus, after his campaign against Mithridates, had written a sanguine letter to the Senate. Whereupon just when he is in the midst of the dangers and difficulties which shortly afterwards beset him, 'the legates arrived for the settlement of Pontus, as if now entirely reduced.' They must have been unwelcome visitors, but notwithstanding, it appears that Lucullus with their assistance and advice did make arrangements which Pompey afterwards annulled.[3] It is not possible to say exactly how much power the legates and the general respectively had, but it is easy to understand that a successful and powerful general would settle matters pretty much at his discretion. That the Senate however gave their commissioners definite instructions as to the line of conduct they were to follow, appears from Livy's[4] account of the commission sent to assist Paullus in regulating the affairs of Macedonia. On the other hand, Caesar[5] seems to have settled the affairs of Gaul without any such interference on the part of the Senate ; and there is no mention of a commission to control the arrangements of Pompey in Asia Minor. The norm of administration thus established was called, in general terms, the ' law of the province ' (lex provinciae) ; but as applied to any particular province it would be named after its original

---

[1] Cic. de Prov. Cons. 8 ; cf. chap. 12 and 14.

[2] Plut. Lucull. 35 ; Reinach, Mithridate Eupator, p. 376. For the ten commissioners sent to Greece in B.C. 146, see Polyb. xxxix. 15, 16. For a similar commission in Asia in B.C. 129, Strab. xiv. 1. 38.

[3] Plut. loc. cit. 36.

[4] Livy, xlv. 18. See a discussion on this subject in Willems' Le Sénat, ii., pp. 703-706.   [5] Cf. Mommsen, v. 97.

author. Thus we find the Lex Pompeia in Pontus and Bithynia,[1] the Lex Mummia in Achaia, the Lex Rupilia in Sicily. Such arrangements were called 'lex' on the principle of delegated authority, which was inherent in the Roman constitution; if the Senate and people gave a man authority to make such arrangements they were law just as much as if they had been passed in the assembly. The Lex Rupilia, however, is loosely so called; for in this case there was no vote of the people to authorise Rupilius, but only a senatorial decree.[2] This law happens to be the best known to us of all such constitutions, owing to the fact of Cicero having had occasion to mention it in his indictment of Verres. If we ask ourselves what sort of points such laws would be needed to settle, it is obvious, a priori, that the financial and judicial arrangements would above all require to be determined. It was impossible to leave the property and persons of the subjects absolutely to the caprice of the different governors. The uncertainty and arbitrariness which was the great evil of the provincial administration under the Republic, would in this case have been aggravated a thousandfold. There does not appear, it is true, to have been an absolute obligation on the part of the governor to obey the lex provinciae; for Verres disregarded it; but Cicero's language makes it plain that such conduct was unprecedented and outrageous. As the law of Hiero had already settled the financial administration, the Lex Rupilia seems to have chiefly concerned itself with the administration of justice, and laid down minute regulations as to the courts in which actions between Sicilians and Romans, between Sicilians of the same town, and between a Sicilian of one town and a Sicilian of another,

---

[1] E.g., Plin. Ep. ad Traj. 79, and Hardy's note.

[2] Lex is here used in an ambiguous sense : a lex from the point of view of Romans implies the action of the comitia; to the province the lex is a lex data, a 'constitution' given by an external authority, whether by a magistrate, confirmed by the Senate, or by the comitia.

were to be tried.[1] Sulla's arrangements in Asia Minor, on
the other hand, seem to have been chiefly financial, and
referred to the apportionment of the tribute among the
different cities of the province. These arrangements were
of the character of a 'lex provinciae,' inasmuch as they
remained the model for succeeding governors, and were for
instance copied by Pompey and Flaccus.[2]   Under the
Empire the financial arrangements came before everything ;
and the first thing that was done with a new province was
to take a census in it.[3] In the Republican period the
Romans had not learnt to be so systematic, and the general
plan was to maintain the taxes, which the country had
previously paid, or, in some cases, to make a parade of
generosity by diminishing them.[4]   Such arrangements
would make part of the 'lex provinciae.' In any case one
innovation was always carried out, namely, the division of
the country into taxation-districts, each with a town for its
capital, whose magistrates were bound to pay over the
amount of taxation due from the district.[5] This would
imply little change in the cities of Greece and Asia Minor,
but it would mean a great deal in countries like Spain and
Gaul; and it helps to explain the immense attention paid
by the Romans to the building and enlarging of towns in
such provinces.

We are now in a position to see what the rule of the Essentials
Romans meant at first to the natives of the countries they of the
had subdued. The essentials of that rule were, broadly, Roman
three ;—the tribute, conscription, and the Roman law. In rule.
antiquity conquest meant essentially the power to impose a
tribute upon the conquered. To get your taxes paid for you
was the sufficient reason for the previous expenditure of

---

[1] Cic. in Verrem, ii. 13.   [2] Cic. pro Flacco, 14.   [3] Marquardt, ii. 206.
[4] This was done for instance in Macedonia ; cf. Livy, xlv. 29.   For
Asia, cf. Cic. ad Qu. Fr. i. 1. 11. For Numidia, in later times, cf. Merivale, ii. 367.   See G. C. Lewis, Government of Dependencies, p. 123.
[5] Marquardt, ii. 190.

blood and treasure. Caesar's account of pre-Roman Gaul makes it very clear that the stronger tribes exacted tribute from the weaker[1]; and it is put forward as the object of the migration of the Helvetii that they intended to make the states they conquered tributary. Athens had previously yielded to the fascinations of this advantage of the stronger ; and the Romans perhaps consciously put it before themselves as the end of conquest. A native regarded them, above all, as plunderers[2] ; and they in their language currently and without arrière pensée spoke of the provincials as *stipendiarii*.[3] If we find Cicero in Cilicia begging the Senate for reinforcements, it is that he may secure the provinces 'in which are comprised the revenues of the Roman people'[4] ; and if he advocates the appointment of Pompey to the charge of the Mithridatic war, it is because that war is 'formidable and dangerous to our tax-payers and allies,' and because ' the surest and largest revenues of the Roman people are at stake.'[5] In his famous letter to his brother Quintus, Cicero defends the taxes imposed on Asia on the ground of their necessity for the expenses of the administration ; and later, under the Empire, the large standing army obviously necessitated a large tribute. ' There can be no peace without troops, no troops without pay, no pay without tribute,' says Cerialis in that curious speech in which he, or rather Tacitus[6] through his mouth, seeks to justify the Roman rule in Gaul.

The tribute.

---

[1] Caes. *B. G.* i. 36, 44, v. 27.

[2] Tacitus probably does not mistake in the speeches he puts into the mouths of Arminius, Galgacus, Caractacus. Cf. esp. *Agric.* 30, 31 ; *Ann.* xii. 34.

[3] Tac. *Ann.* iv. 20, xv. 25 ; Vell. Pat. ii. 37-39, 97.

[4] Cic. *ad Fam.* xv. 1. Cf. Dio, 37, 20 (of Pompey), χώρας προσόδους τε συχνὰς τοῖς Ῥωμαίοις ἀπέδειξε. Yet Cicero (*de imp. Pomp.* 14) says the provinces, except Asia, scarcely paid the expenses of their defence.

[5] Ib. § 6. For the way the *payers* regarded those revenues, *pro Flacco*, § 19.

[6] *Hist.* iv. 74. Cf. Caes. *B. G.* v. 22 ; Strabo, iv. 6, § 3 ; Tac. *Agric.* 13, 15, 31 ; *Ann.* xv. 6. The passage from Cicero's letter to his

But there were some peoples so poor and backward as to The levy.
be unable to pay tribute; and on these the blood-tax only
was imposed.[1] These levies of troops in the provinces
existed of course under the Republic; Caesar mentions
them for instance as held by him in Gaul, and the main
strength of Cicero's army in Cilicia was its non-Roman
element[2]; but, in the main, the practice of using provincial
troops almost to the exclusion of Italian did not establish
itself before the Empire. Warlike nations like the Batavi
would be well content to serve under the conquering eagles,
but by other peoples it was felt as a grievous burden.
What do you expect of your submission, Civilis asks the
Treviri, beyond a hateful service, everlasting tribute, the
rod, the axe, and the passions of a ruling race?[3] The recruiting officers were sometimes not above acting as did
Falstaff in a like position, and picking out for service rich
and elderly men, who would redeem themselves by a heavy
bribe.[4] This was bad enough, but if their conduct was
often as detestable as it is described to us in the same
chapter of Tacitus, it was no wonder that the levy was, to
some at all events of the subject races, more odious even
than the tribute.[5]

Another result of conquest was the introduction of the Roman
Roman law and polity. In a case which Tacitus describes, laws and polity.
their immediate application to a quite barbarous people
has an almost grotesque effect. 'The Frisians . . . gave
hostages, and settled down on territories marked out by Cor-

---

brother, referred to, runs as follows : ' Id autem imperium cum retineri
sine vectigalibus nullo modo possit, aequo animo parte aliqua suorum
fructuum pacem sibi sempiternam redimat atque otium.' *Ad Qu. Fr.*
i. 1., 11.

[1] *Tac. Hist.* iv. 12, 17.

[2] Cic. *ad Att.* vi. 5. A levy in Macedonia is mentioned ; Cic. *Phil.*
x. 6. These, however, would be auxiliaries, not legionary troops.

[3] Tac. *Hist.* iv. 32 ; see also Caes. *B. G.* vii. 77 ; Tac. *Agr.* 13, 15.

[4] Tac. *Hist.* iv. 14.   [5] Cf. *Ib.* iv. 71.

bulo, who at the same time gave them a senate, magistrates, and a constitution.'[1]   It was the Roman policy to introduce an aristocratic, or rather timocratic constitution everywhere, modelled on that of old Republican Rome ; and of course wherever the Romans went, they took their law with them. At first some latitude was allowed. The free and allied towns for instance were permitted, with more or less restriction, 'to use,' as the phrase went, ' their own laws '; but such classes of towns are gradually diminishing, and passing into Roman municipia, or are allowed the title of Roman colonies ; and, as the franchise becomes more and more widely extended, the Roman law comes to be the only law over the whole Empire.[2] From the first, to all provincials but the specially privileged, the decisions of the Roman governor and his subordinates constituted the law ; and it is well known that the governor commonly incorporated into his edict the law as laid down by the urban praetors at Rome. The part which Roman law, constitutional and civil, played in civilising and organising the subject races, was fully understood by the ancients ; and the mark which it has left on later history is uneffaced, and perhaps ineffaceable.

Moral aspect of the Roman rule.

The question as to the right or wrong of the Roman rule is not one to be settled off-hand. Modern opinion, on the whole, condemns a policy of conquest and annexation ; but it must be remembered that war was the normal state of things between two peoples in antiquity, unless there was a special agreement to the contrary, and that conquerors were, perhaps, hated, but not condemned by popular opinion as wicked.[3] Moreover, as has been already remarked, the

[1] Tac. *Ann*. xi. 19.

[2] See, for fuller discussion, p. 219 ff. For a long time the provinces had their own law, Holm, *Gesch. Sicil.* iv. 770. But the tendency was to uniformity. Dio, 37, 20, ἔς τε ἀρχὴν μίαν συνετάχθησαν καὶ νόμους ἔλαβον, ὥστε τὸν τῶν Ῥωμαίων τρόπον πολιτεύεσθαι.

[3] ' In ancient times it was necessary to be either anvil or hammer ' (Mommsen).   See Caesar's speech in Dio, 38, 39.

conquests of the Romans were, at first at all events, not deliberate, but were partly forced on her, and partly arose naturally out of the circumstances. Our own experience in India shows how difficult it is to stop the process of conquest once begun ; and moral indignation is out of place if it condemns all conquest merely as such. The practical question is, whether the conquered country had a free, national prosperous life before its conquest, and whether or not that conquest has given it a life more worth having than the old one. We justify our rule in India, where we are certainly aliens and interlopers to a greater degree than the Romans were in any of their provinces, by pointing to the peace and security we have given it, by dwelling on the endless petty wars and detestable tyrannies of its innumerable princes before our rule existed. In fact we say that the previous state of things was so bad that our rule is a desirable substitute. The Romans would have said, and did say, pretty much the same about their own rule [1] ; and it is quite impossible to give a fair judgment of that rule unless we have some clear idea of the state of things which it replaced. In attempting to give some account of the pre-Roman conditions in the different provinces, I by no means profess to be exhaustive, but only to put together the most necessary materials.

The country with which, from this point of view, we are best acquainted is Gaul. Caesar supplies us with a good deal of information, which can be eked out with occasional notices from Strabo. The point which comes out most clearly is that till the Romans conquered the country it was never free from petty wars.[2] The contest between

Necessity of an examination of pre-Roman condition of the provinces.

Pre-Roman Gaul.

---

[1] *Bellum Alex.* 65 : 'Tamen praeferendum existimavit quas in provincias regionesque venisset, eas ita relinquere constitutas ut domesticis dissensionibus liberarentur, iura legesque acciperent, externorum hostium metum deponerent.'

[2] Caes. *B. G.* vi. 15 : 'Hi, cum est usus atque aliquod bellum incidit (quod fere ante Caesaris adventum quotannis accidere solebat) . . .'

the Arverni and Aedui in particular had been so obstinate
and prolonged that at last the Arverni sought to crush
their rivals by calling in German mercenaries from across
the Rhine. This had led to the settlement of 120,000
Germans on Gallic soil; and it had not even benefited
the Arverni and their allies; for the German king Ariovistus had established himself among the Sequani. ' In
a few years all the Gauls will be driven from their country,
and all the Germans will have crossed the Rhine,' is the
substance of Divitiacus' appeal to Caesar. Ariovistus
had imposed a tribute upon the Aedui; and if Caesar can
be trusted, that people had been reduced to a humiliating
and miserable vassalage. Besides having to pay a tribute,
they were robbed of their lands and compelled to give
hostages with every circumstance of indignity. That
these ' hostages ' so often mentioned were in fact prisoners,
or rather slaves who were treated with great harshness,
might be conjectured, and is proved by another passage of
the same writer. Once begun, the stream of Germans
across the Rhine was incessant. Sometimes they came
in small detachments; sometimes whole nations at once.
Caesar puts the number of the Usipetes and Tencteri
at 430,000; and if we merely consider the fact of his
having destroyed and repelled these invaders, as he had
previously the still more numerous Helvetii,[1] the obligations
of Gaul to Rome will appear considerable. The Gauls
could not have resisted their invaders by their own strength,
owing to their lack of national unity. Caesar could never
have conquered Gaul if it had all resolutely united against
him; but the powerful combination that was formed against
him by the genius of Vercingetorix did not last; and it was
an easy task for him to beat his enemies in detail.

Cf. Strabo, iv. 1, § 2 ; Dio C. 37, 47 ; Tac. *Hist.* iv. 73 ; Coulanges,
Problèmes; D'Arbois de Jubainville, *Études sur le Droit Celtique.*
[1] Caes. *B. G.* i. ; Dio Cass. 38, 31.

Tacitus' description of the revolt of Civilis, a century later, gives an idea of the jarring jealousies and discords that were still rife among the Gauls, and ready to burst out directly Rome's heavy hand was removed.[1] And these tribal hatreds were not all. There were two factions, according to Caesar, in every city and every tribe. The nobles were as powerful as the feudal barons of a thousand years later, and the common people were little better than slaves.[2] What with debt, the burden of taxation, and the violence of the nobles, they did indeed in many cases voluntarily resign their freedom, and attach themselves as slaves to some powerful master.[3] This was accompanied by a low material and moral civilisation. There were no roads worth mentioning till the Romans made them ; and if it had not been for the immense facilities provided by the unrivalled river-system of the country[4] there could have been but little trade. The country was so little opened out that the mountaineers regularly exacted toll from the merchants who crossed their passes. It was impossible, for instance, to cross the Great St. Bernard[5] (and the same probably applies to all the Alpine passes, as it applies to the Pyrenees[6]) without paying a heavy blackmail to the natives ; and the Veneti of North-western Gaul laid similar burdens upon the commerce of the Channel.[7] The so-called 'towns' (oppida) of Gaul were as a rule nothing but wretched villages, as were also the 'towns' of Spain.[8] Vienna (Vienne) for example, afterwards the capital of the Allobroges and one of the chief cities of Gaul, had been, so Strabo tells us, nothing but a village, and owed all its magnificence to the Roman rule[9] ; and a French authority states

---

[1] Tac. *Hist.* iv. 69.

[2] Caes. *B. G.* vi. 13 : 'Plebes paene servorum habetur loco.'   [3] Ib.

[4] Strabo, iv. 1, § 14, iv. 3, § 3 ; Merivale, i. 198, 242.

[5] App. *Illyr.* 17 ; Caes. *B. G.* iii. 1.   [6] Plut. *Sert.* 6.

[7] Caes. *B. G.* iii. 1.   [8] Strabo, iii. 4, § 13.

[9] Strabo, iv. 1, § 11. On the other hand, Toulouse was apparently rich and splendid. Dio Cass., frag. 90 ; 38, 32.

as his opinion that the rise of a prosperous middle class in Gaul was due entirely to Rome. The general barbarism of the Gallic peoples outside the 'old province' is strongly asserted by Cicero,[1] and seems confirmed by the practice of human sacrifices, which Caesar[2] and Strabo[3] mention. Strabo adds that 'the Romans put a stop to these customs ;' just as we in India have put a stop to Suttee and Juggernaut.

Pre-Roman Spain. We are not equally familiar with pre-Roman Spain ; but some of the same points come out clearly. Just as in Gaul, the different tribes were continually at war ; and the necessity of constant preparation for self-defence made agriculture impossible, and neutralised the natural fertility of the country.[4] Another great evil was the brigandage which the physical features of the country made so easy that not even the Romans could wholly root it out, though they did an immense deal in that direction.[5] How wholly savage some of the races of the peninsula were appears from Plutarch's story of the miserable cave-dwellers on whom Sertorius played so clever a trick.[6] But the chief source of weakness in the country was, again, the absence of anything like national unity. 'The settlement of the Grecians amongst these barbarous nations may be regarded as the result of the division of these latter into small tribes and sovereignties, having on account of their moroseness no union amongst themselves, and therefore powerless against attacks from without. This moroseness is remarkably prevalent amongst the Iberians, who are besides crafty in their manner, devoid of sincerity, insidious, and predatory in their mode of life ; they are bold

---

[1] Cic. de Prov. Cons. 12.
[2] Caes. B. G. vi. 16.   Cf. Pliny, 30, 1, 13 ; Suet. Claud., 29.
[3] Strabo, iv. 4, § 5.
[4] Ib. iii. 3, § 5.   Contrast this passage with Caes. B. C. i. 85 ; Tac. Hist. ii. 67.
[5] Strabo, iii. 4, § 13 ;   msen, iii. 233.   [6] Plut. Sert. 17.

in little adventures, but never undertake anything of magnitude, inasmuch as they have never formed any extended power or confederacy. If they had had but the will to assist each other, neither could the Carthaginians by making an incursion have so easily deprived them of the greater part of their country, nor before them the Tyrians, then the Kelts, now called the Keltiberians and Berones, nor after these the brigand Viriathus, and Sertorius, nor any others who desired power. On this account the Romans, having carried the war into Iberia, lost much time by reason of the number of different sovereignties, which they had to conquer one after another; in fact it was nearly two centuries, or even longer, before they had subdued the whole.'[1] Of the great number of different races in the country none showed the capacity of developing a high type of civilisation by itself. The 'unmitigated barbarism' which Dean Merivale[2] ascribes to them is perhaps too sweeping an expression if we remember what Strabo tells us of the Turdetani[3]; but it certainly seems that the stimulus of Phoenician or Greek or Roman civilisation was needed to enable them to make great and permanent progress. Under Roman rule Spain was exceptionally fortunate. The country was as a rule well governed[4]; it enjoyed profound peace from the time of Augustus till the end of the Antonine age[5]; and it assimilated the Roman civilisation perhaps more readily than any other province. South-eastern Spain was wonderfully rich and prosperous, and studded with cities which enjoyed an intense and vigorous municipal life.[6]

[1] Strabo, iii. 4, § 5 ; Vell. ii. 90.   [2] Merivale, ii. 157.
[3] Strabo, iii. 1, § 6 ; cf. Mommsen, ii. 385. See Marina, *Romanentum und Germanenwelt* (1900), E. Philipon, *Les Ibères* (1909).
[4] Mommsen, iii. 233.
[5] Caes. *B. C.* i. 85 ; Tac. *Hist.* ii. 67.
[6] Much of our evidence as to the municipal arrangements within a Roman province comes from Spain. I refer particularly to the Lex Salpensana and Malacitana of the Flavian period, and the Lex

Pre-
Roman
condition
of other
provinces. It is not worth while to go through the other provinces in equal detail. But it may be pointed out that Britain, like Gaul and Spain, was harassed by incessant wars[1]; that there was no national feeling in the country to inspire courage and union against Rome, and that the standard of civilisation was a very low one.[2]   Illyria was rendered insecure by brigandage[3] till the Romans put a stop to it, and had been a perfect nest of pirates.[4]   Numidia had been exposed to the predatory excursions of the Moors[5]; just as Egypt had been to some extent to those of the Ethiopians.[6] To Egypt the Roman rule was a relief. She exchanged a master who was both incompetent and despotic for a master who was despotic but competent. In either case the rule was that of foreigners ; and it would be absurd to suppose that the mass of the Egyptians entertained any sentimental feelings with regard to the few last vicious and feeble representatives of the line of the Ptolemies. Cyprus is also an interesting case, the islanders welcoming Cato who came to take possession of the island, in the hope that they would in future be friends and allies of Rome instead of slaves. (Dio C. 39, 22). Asia Minor, protected against the pirates and the barbarians, would have been well off under Roman rule if it had not been for the tax-gatherers and the usurers. ' Let Asia consider this,' says Cicero, ' that no calamity of foreign war or intestine discord would have been wanting to her if she were not protected by this Empire.'[7] Rome put an end to riots in the towns,[8] and to brigandage in the

---

Ursonitana of Caesar. For pre-Roman Lusitania, see Dio Cass. 37, 12; walled cities in pre-Roman Spain, App. *Hisp.* 41 ; for coinage, Zobel de Zangroning. Head, *Num. Chron.* for 1882, p. 183 ; *Hist. Num.,* p. 1 *sq. ;* Heiss. *Descr. gén. des monnaies anciennes de l'Espagne.*

[1] Caes. *B. G.* v. 11.   [2] Strabo, iv. 5, § 2.
[3] *Bell. Alex.* 42.   [4] Mommsen, ii. 218.
[5] *Bell. Afr.* 97.
[6] Strabo, xvii. 1, §§ 12 and 53 ; Mommsen, *Provinces,* ii. 275.
[7] Cic. *ad Qu. Fr.* i. 1, 11.
[8] Cic. *ad Qu. Fr.* i. 8 : ' Nullas esse in oppidis seditiones.'

country.[1] She exacted a tribute it is true, but then, says Cicero, the Asiatics paid tribute before, and some of them more than they do now.[2] It was no loss to the country that it should be rid of its petty kings; Roman rule at its worst was better than that of a Pharnaces.[3] ' In the whole peninsula of Asia Minor the Roman conquest had nowhere suppressed a truly independent, rich and powerful political life, because nowhere had it met with such a life.'[4] Where such a life did in some measure exist in that country, it was not national but municipal, and Rome interfered to a very slight extent with the internal affairs of the towns.

We are now in a better position to discuss some of the charges brought against the Roman rule. ' From Mummius to Augustus the Roman city stands as the living mistress of the dead world, and from Augustus to Theodoric the mistress becomes as lifeless as her subjects.'[5] ' The extension of equal rights to all the subjects of a common master was after all a very poor substitute for national independence or for full federal or municipal freedom.'[6] By a 'dead world' I understand a world without any active political life, without self-government, and without ambition; a world which had peace and material prosperity perhaps, but no freedom and no self-respect. The second passage implies an answer to an objection. Does not, it might be urged, the extension of the franchise through the period of the Republic and the early Empire provide an object of ambition, and a means of securing independence ? Maybe, we are answered, but that is 'a very poor substitute for

(marginal note: Moral aspect of the Roman rule.)

---

[1] Ib. : ' Sublata Mysiae latrocinia.' Cf. Polyb. iii. 3 (on result of Galatian War), ἀπέλυσαν τοὺς ἐπὶ τάδε τοῦ Ταύρου κατοικοῦντας βαρβαρικῶν φόβων.

[2] Cic. ad Qu. Fr. i. 1, 11.   [3] Bell. Alex. 41.

[4] Perrot, Quelques inscriptions des côtes de la Mer Noire, p. 30.

[5] Freeman, Essays, 2nd Series, p. 336.

[6] Ib., p. 321. This passage refers directly to the Empire; but it opens up several large questions which apply to the Roman rule as a whole.

national independence, or for full federal and municipal freedom.' Let us consider this last point first. Ideally no doubt it would be a very poor substitute; but practically and as a matter of fact was it a substitute for anything of the sort? Where was the national independence which Rome destroyed? In Macedonia, perhaps, alone of all her conquests. There was no nation, we have seen, in Spain, none in Gaul, none in Britain, none in Asia Minor. It is impossible not to lament the extinction of Macedonia, but it must at the same time be remembered that Rome had not provoked the struggle, and it may be questioned whether the Macedonian government had enough vitality left, if quite exempt from Roman interference, to defend its subjects from the perpetual encroachments of the barbarians, as Rome defended them.[1] If then the Roman rule did not in the great majority of cases destroy national independence— there being none to destroy—still less did it destroy ' municipal freedom.' It is plain matter of fact that where they found municipal arrangements existing, the Romans let them alone and even encouraged them; and where they did not exist they made it their first object to introduce them. The amount of independence enjoyed by these towns was considerable, and all the evidence goes to prove that the life that went on in them was a busy and active one; that their elections aroused a genuine political interest; and that their magistrates were conversant with affairs, and trained by the experience of public life. The municipal arrangements, though terribly perverted by Constantine and his successors, were on the whole both successful and permanent; and, after the cloud of barbarism was passing away, may have influenced the establishment of the ' free towns' of the Middle Ages.

These municipal arrangements form one element in the

---

[1] Cic. *pro Font.* 20. The foreign policy of Macedonia was in this period execrable. Such crimes as the sack of Cios and Abydos do much to alienate our sympathies : Polyb. xv. 21, Liv. 31, 7.

answer to the question, Were the provinces dead and stagnant, or on the contrary alive and vigorous in their life ? But it may be said that after all municipal life is very different and very inferior to national life; and that if the provinces had the one, they in no sense possessed the other. Now national life in the strict sense they had not. Those ties of like blood, like speech, like interests, like traditions, which go to build up a modern nation, hardly existed under Rome. But those feelings which are the precious part of national unity, the self-respect which springs from the consciousness of being part of a great and powerful whole, the loyalty and the patriotism it evokes, can exist apart from unity of place or even of blood. ' I indeed think that both he and all municipal citizens have two fatherlands, the one of their birth and the other of their citizenship,' says Cicero.[1] The liberal policy of Rome gradually extended the privileges of her citizenship till it included all her subjects ; and along with the *Jus suffragii* went of course the *Jus honorum*. Even under Augustus we find a Spaniard consul at Rome[2] ; and under Galba an Egyptian Jew was governor of Egypt.[3] It is not long before even the emperor himself is supplied by the provinces.[4] It is easy to comprehend therefore how the provincials forgot the fatherland of their birth for the fatherland of their citizenship. Once win the franchise, and to great capacity was opened a great career. The Roman Empire came to be a homogeneous mass of privileged persons, largely using the same language,[5] aiming at the same type of civilisation, equal among themselves, but all alike conscious of their superiority to the surrounding barbarians. The Gauls of Provence and the Spaniards

[1] Cic. *de Legg.* ii. 2.   Cf. the remarks which Dio puts into the mouth of Maecenas ; lii. 19.

[2] Cornelius Balbus, 40 B.C.   [3] Tiberius Alexander ; Tac. *Hist.* i. 11.

[4] Trajan and Hadrian were natives of Italica in Spain.

[5] Claudius took away the franchise from a Greek who could not speak Latin (Suet. *Claud.* 16).   For further instances to illustrate this point, see Duruy, iii. 384, note.   Valerius Max. ii. 2, 2.

of Baetica were more Roman even than the Romans themselves. If we are to be so indignant with the Roman rule,
we ought to be still more indignant with our rule in India.
Political freedom and self-government is no more possessed
by the Hindoos than it was by the provincials; and the
Hindoos are worse off in that there is no prospect open to
them of rising to high office, or to the vice-royalty, while
corresponding prospects were open to the subjects of Rome.
If then there was, speaking broadly, no conscious inferiority
to make the provincials regret the past, but every reason to
make them look forward to the future, it would be a great
mistake to regard them as so many mean-spirited slaves
who had not the courage to resist their masters. They did
not feel themselves to be slaves; and what with their share
of local independence and their hopes of the Roman franchise,
they were not slaves. Moreover, though it is possible to
make too much, it is also possible to make too little of the
peace and material prosperity they enjoyed under Rome.
It was the first duty of a Roman governor to protect his
province from inroads from without. Caesar, though so
busy with his conquests in further Gaul, yet found time to
protect the frontier of Illyricum from the Pirustae[1];
Gabinius was reproached for not properly defending Syria
against the pirates; and Suetonius blames Tiberius for
allowing Moesia, already a corn-growing province, to be
raided by Dacians. It is one of the heaviest charges which
Cicero brings against Piso that he had not protected his
province against the Thracians.[2] The chaos into which the
administration fell in the later years of the Republic caused
neglect in this as in other matters; but with the Empire
we see the custody of the frontiers made a point of the first
importance. All such impediments to trade, as those in
Gaul and Spain already mentioned, were removed; and
with the clearance of the Mediterranean from pirates came

[1] Caes. *B. G.* v. 1.
[2] Cic. *in Pis.* 40; Dio Cass. xxxix. 56; Sueton. *Tib.* xli.

an immense development of commerce.[1] The Roman occupation of Egypt gave a great impulse to the trade with India. ' I was with Gallus,' says Strabo, ' at the time he was prefect of Egypt, and accompanied him as far as Syene and the frontiers of Ethiopia, and found that about 120 ships sail from Myoshormos to India, although in the time of the Ptolemies scarcely any one would venture on this voyage and the commerce with the Indies.'[2] So the district of Batanea (Haouran), now almost impassable for European travellers, was covered with posts, and rendered perfectly secure under the rule of Rome.[3] Everywhere within the charmed circle of the Roman dominion was peace ; sometimes, it is true, secured by stern measures, as in parts of Britain[4] and in the valley of Aosta[5] ; but as a rule the sternness was reserved for the barbarians without, and the peace was only a blessing to the provincials. No progress was possible to countries distracted by petty wars which could never lead to a decisive issue. Agriculture and all the arts became impossible. Outposts of civilisation, like the Greek cities on the Black Sea, must have welcomed the Roman rule as that of friends and deliverers. Ovid shows us how miserable had been the condition of Tomi before

---

[1] Strabo, iii. 2, § 5. 'Pacatum volitant per mare navitae,' says Horace, *Od.* iv. 5. Cf. *Mon. Anc.* 25 ; Suet. *Aug.* 98.

[2] Strabo, ii. 5, § 12 ; cf. xvii. 1, § 13.

[3] Boissier, *L'Empire Romain en Orient*, p. 119.

[4] 'Solitudinem faciunt, pacem appellant '; Tac. *Agr.* 30.

[5] The Salassi had been long a source of trouble from their raids upon travellers over the Alps. In 143 B.C. they had been defeated by Appius Claudius, but soon afterwards renewed their old habits. In 35 B.C. Antistius Vetus attacked them unsuccessfully, but in 34 B.C. Messala checked them for a time. In 25 B.C. Terentius Varro Murena conquered them and sold 30,000 into slavery. The remnant gave no further trouble, and the colony Praetoria Augusta (Aosta) secured peace. An inscription (Dessau 6732) shows that the Salassi were not exterminated, but that certain of them were admitted to the new colony. Dio Cass. xlix. 34, 38 ; liii. 25 ; Livy, *Ep.* 135. Suet. *Aug.* 21.

the Empire asserted itself against the barbarians in that region; and its ruins and inscriptions show us its prosperity half a century later.[1] The material condition of the provinces, partly no doubt for selfish reasons, was well looked after. Parts of Algeria now wholly barren were fertile and populous, owing to their unsurpassed system of irrigation.[2] Their roads and bridges are indeed still the most durable memorials of their Empire.

But it must be allowed that these praises apply in strictness only to one period of the Roman rule, a period of about 200 years from Actium. The next section will show how far these duties were performed by Rome under the Republican government, and will seek to point out the main causes of the maladministration in the provinces, which made that government equally mischievous and impossible.

Egyptian Decrees (C. I. Gr. 4956-7).

1. Of 49 A.D. The governor of the Theban Oasis publishes a copy of a decree received from the Egyptian prefect Capito relating to the abuse of liberae legationes and other exactions:

Καὶ πάλαι μὲν ἤκουόν τινας δαπάνας ἀδίκους καὶ παραλογηθείσας ὑπὸ τῶν πλεονεκτικῶς καὶ ἀναιδῶς ταῖς ἐξουσίαις ἀποχρωμένων γείνεσθαι, καὶ νῦν δὲ ἐν τῇ τῶν Λιβύων μάλιστα ἔγνων ὑποθέσει, ὅτι ἀναλίσκεταί τινα ἁρπαζόντων ἀδεῶς τῶν ἐπὶ ταῖς χρείαις ὡς ὑποκείμενα εἰς δαπάνας καὶ ξενίας αὐτῶν τὰ μήτε ὄντα μήτε ὀφείλοντα εἶναι, ὁμοίως δὲ καὶ ἀνγαρειῶν ὀνόματι. διὸ κελεύω τοὺς διοδεύοντας διὰ τῶν νομῶν στρατίωτας καὶ ἑκατοντάρχας καὶ χιλιάρχους καὶ τοὺς λοιποὺς ἅπαντας μηδὲν λαμβάνειν μηδὲ ἀνγαρεύειν εἰ μή τινες ἐμὰ διπλώματα ἔχουσι, καὶ τούτους δὲ στέγῃ μόνον δέχεσθαι τοὺς διερχομένους, ὑποκείμενον δὲ μηδένα μηδὲν πράττειν ἔξω τῶν ὑπὸ Μαξίμου σταθέντων· ἐὰν δέ τις δῷ ὡς δεδομένον λογίσηται καὶ εἰσπράξῃ δημοσίᾳ, τοῦτον τὸ δεκάπλουν ἐγὼ ἐκπράξω οὗ αὐτὸς ἔπραξεν τὸν νομὸν, καὶ τῷ μηνύσαντι τὸ τετραπλάσειον μέρος δώσω ἐκ τῆς κατακριθέντος οὐσίας. οἱ μὲν οὖν βασιλικοὶ γραμματεῖς καὶ κωμογραμματεῖς καὶ τοπογραμματεῖς κατὰ νομὸν πάντα ὅσα δαπανᾶται ἐκ τοῦ νομοῦ, εἴ τινα εἰσπέπρακται παραλόγως ἢ ἄλλο τι, ἀναγραφέσθωσαν καὶ ἐν ἡμέραις ἑξήκοντα ἐπιδότωσαν. . . . ὃ δὲ ἂν παρὰ τὸ δίκαιον λελογευμένον ἢ πεπραγμένον ᾖ, τοῦτο διορθώσομαι.

2. A similar decree from Tiberius Julius Alexander, Egyptian prefect in 69 A.D. The governor refers to the numerous complaints of official

---

[1] Perrot, op. cit., p. 21.   [2] Boissier, *L'Afrique Romaine*, 136 seq.

oppression with which he has been assailed since his arrival in Alexandria, and expresses the hope that the reign of Galba will prove auspicious for the province. He then turns to particular regulations :

ἔγνων γὰρ πρὸ παντὸς εὐλογωτάτην οὖσαν τὴν ἔντευξιν ὑμῶν ὑπὲρ τοῦ μὴ ἄκοντας ἀνθρώπους εἰς τελωνείας ἢ ἄλλας μισθώσεις οὐσιακὰς παρὰ τὸ κοινὸν ἔθος τῶν ἐπαρχειῶν πρὸς βίαν ἄγεσθαι, καὶ ὅτι οὐκ ὀλίγῳ ἔβλαψε τὰ πράγματα τὸ πολλοὺς ἀπείρους ὄντας τῆς τοιαύτης πραγματείας ἀχθῆναι μετ' ἀνάγκης, ἐπιβληθέντων αὐτοῖς τῶν τελῶν· διόπερ καὶ αὐτὸς οὔτε ἤγαγόν τινα εἰς τελωνείαν ἢ μίσθωσιν οὔτε ἄξω, εἰδὼς τοῦτο συμφέρειν καὶ ταῖς κυριακαῖς ψήφοις τὸ μετὰ προθυμίας ἑκόντας πραγματεύεσθαι τοὺς δυνατούς· πέπεισμαι δὲ ὅτι οὐδ' εἰς τὸ μέλλον ἄκοντάς τις ἄξει τελώνας, ἢ μισθωτούς, ἀλλὰ διαμισθώσει τοῖς βουλομένοις ἑκουσίως προέρχεσθαι, μᾶλλον τὴν τῶν προτέρων ἐπάρχων αἰώνιον συνήθειαν φυλάσσων ἢ τὴν πρόσκαιρόν τινος ἀδικίαν μειμησάμενος.

ἐπειδὴ ἔνιοι προφάσει τῶν δημοσίων καὶ ἀλλότρια δάνεια παραχωρούμενοι εἴς τε τὸ πρακτόρειόν τινες παρέδοσαν καὶ εἰς ἄλλας φυλακάς, ἃς καὶ δι' αὐτὸ τοῦτο ἔγνων ἀναιρεθείσας, ἵνα αἱ πράξεις τῶν δανείων ἐκ τῶν ὑπαρχόντων ὦσι καὶ μὴ ἐκ τῶν σωμάτων, ἑπόμενος τῇ τοῦ θεοῦ Σεβαστοῦ βουλήσει κελεύω μηδένα τῇ τῶν δημοσίων προφάσει παραχωρεῖσθαι παρ' ἄλλων δάνεια, ἃ μὴ αὐτὸς ἐξ ἀρχῆς ἐδάνεισεν, μηδ' ὅλως κατακλείεσθαί τινας ἐλευθέρους εἰς φυλακὴν ἡντινοῦν εἰ μὴ κακοῦργον, μηδ' εἰς τὸ πρακτόρειον ἔξω τῶν ὀφειλόντων εἰς τὸν κυριακὸν λόγον. . . .

ἔγνων δὲ καὶ πρότερον τὴν ἄμετρον ἐξουσίαν τῶν ἐγλογιστῶν διὰ τὸ πάντας αὐτῶν καταβοᾶν ἐπὶ τῷ παραγράφειν αὐτοῖς πλεῖστα ἐκ τῶν νομιζομένων τελῶν· ἐξ οὗ συνέβαινεν αὐτοῖς ἀργυρίζεσθαι, τὴν δὲ Αἴγυπτον ἀνάστατον γείνεσθαι, καὶ νῦν τοῖς αὐτοῖς παραγγέλλω μηδὲν ἐξομοίωμα ποιεῖσθαι μηδὲ παραγραφειν ἄλλαξ ἢ ἄλλο τι τῶν καθόλου χωρὶς τοῦ κρεῖναι τὸν ἔπαρχον, κελεύω δὲ τοῖς στρατηγοῖς μηδὲν παρὰ ἐγλογιστῶν παραλαμβάνειν χωρὶς τῆς ἀδείας ἐπάρχου. καὶ οἱ ἄλλοι δὲ πραγματικοὶ ἐάν τε εὑρεθῶσι ψευδὲς ἢ παρὰ τὸ δέον παραγεγραφότες, καὶ τοῖς ἰδιώταις ἀποδώσουσιν ὅσον ἀπῃτήθησαν, καὶ τὸ τρίτον ἀποθήσουσιν εἰς τὸ δημόσιον. . . ,

περὶ δὲ τῶν ἀρχαιοτέρων ὑποθέσεων ἐνκειμένων ὑμῶν, αἷς πολλοὶ ἤδη ἐντεθνήκασι καὶ πολλάκις οὐδὲν πλέον περιεποίησαν πλὴν ἀργυρισμοῦ τῶν πραγματικῶν καὶ τῆς τῶν ἀνθρώπων ἐπηρείας, περὶ τούτων Καίσαρι Σεβαστῷ αὐτοκράτορι γράψω μετὰ τῶν ἄλλων ὅσα αὐτῷ δηλῶ, τῷ μόνῳ δυναμένῳ τὰ τοιαῦτα ὁλοτελῶς ἐκκόπτειν· ὡς ἐπ' ἐκείνῳ ἀνάκειται τῆς πάντων ἡμῶν σωτηρίας ἡ διηνεκὴς εὐεργεσία καὶ πρόνοια.

CHAPTER III.

The Period of the Republic.

Section I. *Historical Outline.*[1]

THE great struggle against Hannibal left the Senate the all but undisputed government of Rome. Originally a mere consulting board, assessors of the king or consul, the Senate had become the supreme executive body. That the government solely by the assembly and the magistrates should by experience be found wanting was as inevitable at Rome as at Athens. Rome was more fortunate than Athens in that she could develop a new organism to meet the need. The growth of the power of the Senate was all the more natural and legitimate the less it possessed strict legal standing-ground. But the fatal dualism thus introduced into the constitution—the Assembly governing *de jure*, and the Senate governing *de facto*—made all government after a time impossible. The position of the Senate being, strictly speaking, an unconstitutional one, it was open, in the absence of any official department or ministry charged with the supervision of provincial affairs, for any demagogue to bring matters of foreign policy or administration before an Assembly which was without continuity, without special knowledge, and in which there was no debate. Now, if

---

[1] In this sketch I have attempted to give an account of the different modes of appointment to provincial governorships ; of the duration of the governorships ; and of the authority of the Senate. The power and duties of the governor, and his subordinates; the amount of control exercised over the governor. The misery of the provinces and its causes require a separate treatment.

the Senate governed badly, the Assembly 'could not govern at all' (Mommsen); and there could be, in the long run, but one end to the constant struggle between the two sources of authority.

In the epitome of Livy, between a mention of the subjec- The first tion of Illyria (229 B.C.) and of the war against the Cisalpine provinces. Gauls (225 B.C.) occurs the brief statement: 'The number of praetors was increased to four.'[1] Now we know that a revolt against the new Roman authority took place in Sardinia in the year 226 B.C. We are therefore enabled with tolerable certainty to put the commencement of regular provincial government in the year 227 B.C. Whether before this date Sicily and Sardinia were governed by quaestors under the superintendence of the consuls, as Mommsen[2] supposes, cannot be proved; but is not improbable, as Rome had a more or less permanent hold on parts at all events of the two islands for some years past. The names of these two first provincial praetors are known. They are—C. Flaminius, the same man who afterwards fell at Thrasymene, for Sicily; and M. Valerius, a man not otherwise known, for Sardinia. The same authority which tells us this tells us also that these two praetors cast lots for their provinces.[3] Each had one or more quaestors given him (in Sicily at all events later on there were two quaestors), who were charged with the management of the income and expenditure. The praetorships were annual, for no better reason than that the city praetorships were annual; and of course the quaestors were changed along with their superiors. The next provincial governments were Hither and Further Spain, which were established in the year 197 B.C. Experience had taught the Romans the

[1] *Epitome*, xx.; Klein, *Die Verwaltungsbeamten*, etc., pp. 11, 199; *Staatsr*. ii. 180.

[2] Mommsen, ii. 209.

[3] Solinus, 5. 1 : 'Utraque insula in Romanum arbitratum redacta iisdem temporibus facta provincia, cum eodem anno Sardiniam M. Valerius, alteram C. Flaminius praetores sortiti sunt.'

mistake of annual governorships in such a country as Spain, and a special law had assigned two years of office to the praetors sent to that country[1]; but the competition for command in the provinces was too great for the law to be maintained, and the principle of annually changing the governors grew into a constitutional maxim.[2] With these two new provinces went two new praetors, and the total number was now, therefore, six. Here for the present stops the election of the new praetors; and it becomes therefore necessary to inquire how the new functions[3] established in the period between the settlement of Spain and the reforms of Sulla were discharged. The matter was managed by prorogation. After the urban praetors and the consuls had held their year of office in Italy, they were sent for a year to a province assigned to them by lot.[4] Thus every year, besides the two consuls and the six praetors, there would be two ex-consuls and six ex-praetors available for foreign service. As there was in law no difference between a magistracy in Italy and one in the provinces, there was nothing to prevent this arrangement; and as the Senate could prolong a man's term of office in a province for a year, or could refuse to do so, it practically had a very large control over the provincial appointments.

Lex Sempronia.

These arrangements were a natural enough growth, and in no way an affair of legislation; but there was one very important law passed during this period, which remained in

---

[1] *Lex Baebia*, cf. Livy xl. 44: Praetores quattuor post multos annos lege Baebia creati, quae alternis quaternos iubebat creari; so interpreted by Mommsen.

[2] Yet after Sulla, at any rate, the governor remained in power until the arrival of his successor without formal prorogation. Willems, *Sénat*, 2, 572.

[3] Five new provinces — Macedonia, Africa, Asia, Narbonensis, Cilicia; and the presidency of the new standing court *de Repetundis*, which had been established 149 B.C.; Mommsen, iv. 120.

[4] Cf. Nep., *Cato* 2: Sorte provinciam nactus Hispaniam (after his consulship); the same passage suggests that an ex consul might refuse the governorship of a province.

force for the following century. This was the *Lex Sempronia* of C. Gracchus, so often mentioned by Cicero.[1] It was to the effect that the Senate should each year decide before the election of the consuls what provinces they were to govern. It did not deprive the senators of their power to decide what the provinces for the consuls of the current year should be, but by obliging them to decide this point *before the elections* it sought to prevent favouritism in one case and unfairness in another, and thereby to deprive them of means of influence.[2] As it turned out, the Senate had no difficulty in making use of the law for their own purposes; and when, for instance, they expected the election of Caesar, they took care to provide beforehand that he and his colleague should have the unimportant province of the roads and forests.[3]

The position of the Senate had been steadily deteriorating during this period. Even during the Second Punic War we find the comitia assuming the functions of the executive, and appointing generals against Hannibal[4]; and when the Senate wished to declare war against Philip, the comitia at first positively refused its assent.[5] As every measure to have legal force had in the last resort to come before the comitia,[6] the Senate had to manœuvre in every possible way to win the comitia over to their views. They were only able, for instance, to prolong Flamininus' command in Macedonia by the help of the tribunes.[7] The

Position of the Senate.

---

[1] Cic. *de Prov. Cons.* 2 and 7; *pro Balbo*, 27; *de domo sua*, § 24; *ad Fam.* 1, 7, § 10.
[2] Mommsen, iii. 355.
[3] Suet. *Caes.* 19, provinciae minimi negotii; cf. also Dio Cass. 36, 37; Merivale, i. 172; Mommsen, iv. 203.
[4] Mommsen, ii. 277, 286 (Flaminius and Varro).
[5] Livy xxxi. 6.
[6] Caesar, *B. C.* i. 6, complains: 'In reliquas provincias praetores mittuntur: neque exspectant quod superioribus annis acciderat, ut de eorum imperio ad populum feratur.'
[7] Livy xxi. 28; Plut. *Tit.* 70; Mommsen, ii. 432.

assembly was not long in dropping any feelings of awe or respect it may still have felt in regard to the Senate ; it only needed hardihood and a certain contempt for tradition to overturn a system of tacitly usurped and tacitly acknowledged authority [1] ; and when the Gracchi, however good their motives, had set the example, inferior demagogues were quick to follow it. The worst of this was that the government of the Senate was so bad and so unequal to the ever-increasing charges of the state, that there seemed good and reasonable ground for interference. The conduct of the Jugurthine war, for instance, was so shameful that it is hardly wonderful that the people should have angrily set its authority aside, and directly appointed Marius to the conduct of the war.[2]   But this action, though legal, was yet in the highest degree unconstitutional, and was far from being justified by any superior capacity for affairs possessed by the Assembly.   It was, however, to a certain extent practically justified by the circumstances; but when shortly afterwards the Assembly gave Marius the command in Asia, though Sulla had been already appointed, and though Marius was a private person, it is obvious that it was using its powers simply for party purposes : and of that there could be but one outcome.   Such interferences, however, were in this period still rather the exception than the rule ; the people had not yet completely banished the consciousness of their own incapacity.   On the whole the Senate was left to conduct matters of foreign policy and finance, and the executive generally.   The Senate still resolved on declarations of war, still settled new provinces by its commissioners, and still exercised control over its generals.   The state of things typified by the Vatinian and Manilian laws did not yet exist in this period ; but forces were at work of which it was the natural development.

[1] Warde Fowler, *City State*, p. 229 et seq.

[2] Sallust, *Jug.* 62, 73.   The comitia assigned Numidia to Marius, though the Senate had given him Gaul.

The next great step in the legislation about the govern- Sulla's
ment of the provinces was made by Sulla. He raised the Laws.
number of praetors to eight ; and made a law that provinces
should in future be governed not by consuls and praetors,
but by proconsuls and propraetors,[1] a particular province
being assigned to a proconsul or a propraetor, according as
it needed more or fewer troops.[2] This would make ten
magistrates every year eligible for provincial command ;
and there were at this time ten provinces.[3] These governorships were made strictly annual ; and there was a clause
to the effect that the governor must leave his province
within thirty days after the arrival of his successor.[4] Thus
it became rare for the comitia to give a man direct military
command[5]; and as the prorogation to the provincial
governorships still remained, strictly speaking, in the hands
of the Senate, Sulla meant no doubt to make a man feel
that he owed his appointment to it, and not to the Assembly.
In this then, as in his other laws, it appears that Sulla's
chief aim was the rehabilitation of the senatorial authority.
But the Senate could not be restored to what it had been ;

[1] Mommsen, iv. 121-2, deduces the existence of this law from the
custom after Sulla's time. But the custom was not uniform, and we
have no positive information as to the Lex Cornelia. Willems, *Le
Sénat*, ii., p. 578, holds that he has proved that the consuls at any rate
were not compelled by law to stay their year in Rome. It only grew
gradually to be the custom. Id. *Droit publique*, p. 256.

[2] Livy, xli. 8, says of Sardinia : ' Propter belli magnitudinem provincia consularis facta est.' In Macedonia the proconsul Piso was
succeeded by the propraetor Q. Ancharius; Marquardt, i. 381, note 3.
The most obvious difference between the proconsul and propraetor
was that the former had twelve, the latter only six fasces; Marquardt, i. 381.

[3] Sicily, Sardinia, the two Spains, Macedonia, Asia, Africa, Narbonensis, Cilicia, and Cisalpine Gaul ; Mommsen, iv. 123.

[4] Cic. *ad Fam.* l. c. 9, iii. 6 and 10; Mommsen, iv. 124. Other
clauses limited the amounts which provinces might spend on laudatory
deputations.

[5] The comitia gave command on special occasions, as in the cases of
Pompey, Caesar, and others ; but the ordinary practice was the other
way.

and though Pompey's legislation ten years afterwards did not disturb these particular arrangements, the Senate yet The extra-failed to draw any particular advantage from them. In ordinary fact the Senate had already practically nullified Sulla's com-mands. policy and stultified themselves, when seven years earlier they had given Pompey the command against Sertorius, though he had previously held no curule magistracy what-ever.[1] In so doing they not only violated Sulla's laws but every rule of the constitution, and had no right to be sur-prised if the tables were before long turned upon them, and the comitia imitated their own lawlessness. It was not many years before Pompey received, this time from the comitia, the conduct of the Pirate War, and shortly after-wards of the Mithridatic War, in each case with powers which transcended the strict republican limits altogether. The Vatinian Law giving Caesar Gaul for five years, and the Trebonian Law giving Pompey Spain for five years, followed in the same track; and when Pompey further governed Spain from Rome by his legates[2] it became obvious that the foreign conquests had brought a strain to bear upon the constitution which at last destroyed it.

Pro-vincial Apart from these extraordinary commands, it had already com-become the custom for the great majority of governors to mands stay longer than the strict year in their provinces. The com-monly Senate did not send them their successors when the year pro-was out, and so they stayed where they were, like soldiers longed. on guard, till relieved. So we find Verres three years in Sicily[3]; Fonteius three years in Gaul[4]; Q. Cicero three years in Asia.[5] In fact, Cicero's example shows that a governor had to take a great deal of trouble not to stay longer than his year in his province; and he was able to leave it when he did, not because a successor was sent him,

---

[1] Mommsen, iv. 292.   [2] Plut. *Pomp.* 53 ; Dio C. 39, 39.
[3] Cic. *Div. in Caec.* 4.   [4] Cic. *pro Font.* 10.
[5] *Ad Qu. Fr.* i. i.   Murena was in Asia from 84 to 82 B.C. Lucullus from 74 to 66, Servilius Isauricus in Cilicia from 78 to 75 ; see Mar-quardt, i. 384, note 5.

but by leaving one of his officers as his representative. The simple reason of this state of things was that two consuls and eight praetors were not enough for fourteen provinces.[1]

The provincial appointments had by this time to a large extent become a matter of intrigue. The constitutional arrangement was that the Senate should assign what the provinces were to be for a given year, and that then those eligible for such commands should divide them amongst themselves by lot, the consuls casting lots when designate, the praetors while their year of office was going on.[2] But if an ambitious man wanted a particular province, there was a much simpler way of going to work. Lucullus wanted to be appointed to the province of Cilicia. Now the influential tribune of the year was Cethegus; and the person influential with Cethegus was his mistress Praecia. So Lucullus made friends with Praecia, and induced her to use her interest with her lover. She did so; and a law was passed, giving Lucullus what he wanted.[3]

Jobbery practised in regard to such appointments.

The last important law affecting the appointments to the provinces before the *Leges Juliae* was a law of Pompey's, passed in the year 52 B.C., and arranging that provinces should only be given after five years' interval. That is, instead of a man being sent directly to his province after his year of office was over, on the first of the next January, he had to wait five years before becoming eligible.[4] This was primarily intended as a blow against Caesar, as it obviated the difficulty the Senate would otherwise have had in giving

Pompey's arrangement of the five years' interval.

---

[1] Marquardt, i. 385. In 50 B.C. there were five consular provinces —two Gauls, two Spains, and Syria; and nine praetorian—Cilicia, Sicily, Sardinia, Macedonia, Asia, Africa, Crete, Cyrene, Bithynia.

[2] *In Verr.* iii. 95: ' Quas ob res, quid agis, Hortensi ? Consul es designatus: provinciam sortitus es.' Marquardt, i. 382.

[3] Plut. *Lucull.* 6. Cf. Suet. *Jul.* 11 : ' *Conciliato populi favore* tentavit per partem tribunorum ut sibi Aegyptus provincia plebiscito daretur.' The two consuls had also the right of interchange after allotment. Willems, *Le Sénat.* ii., p. 577.

[4] Suet. *Jul.* 28 ; Dio Cassius, xl. 56 ; *Staatsrecht,* ii. 219.

him a successor immediately on the expiration of his command, that is on March 1, 49 B.C.; but it also, for the next few years at all events, would enable the Senate to control the provincial appointments pretty much at its pleasure.[1]

Caesar's arrangements.

When Caesar had attained supreme power this law was treated as a dead letter, though probably not repealed; and Augustus afterwards reverted to the five years interval.[2] Remembering how his own power had been attained,[3] Caesar took care to limit the tenure of a praetorian province to one, of a consular province to two years.[4] Other arrangements of his were to raise the number of praetors to sixteen[5] and of quaestors to forty, half of whom (both praetors and quaestors) were to be nominated by himself. He assigned all the praetorian provinces, the consular ones being still left nominally to the Senate.[6] He could also nominate honorary praetors who would be eligible for provinces; he decided which province should be assigned to whom; and he had the right of recall.[7] Above all, he was probably given pro-consular power throughout the whole Empire.[8] Lastly, to obviate possible opposition from the Senate, its numbers were raised from 600 to 900, the new members being all men devoted to his interests.[9]

Section II. *The Governor.*

The governor of a Roman province united in his single person civil and military authority. He was commander-in-

---

[1] Dio, xl. 30.

[2] Dio Cassius, xlii. 20, liii. 14; Marquardt, i. 382. Willems, *Le Sénat*, ii. 598.

[3] This is the way Dio Cassius, xliii. 25, puts it.

[4] Cic. *Phil.* i. 8, ii. 42, iv. 3, viii. 9; Merivale, i. 392.

[5] At first from 8 to 10; then to 14; afterwards to 16. Dio Cassius, xlii. 50, xliii. 47 and 51; Suet. *Jul.* 41.

[6] Of course without sortition. τάς τε ἡγεμονίας τὰς ἐν τῷ ὑπηκόῳ τοῖς μὲν ὑπάτοις αὐτοὶ δῆθεν ἐκλήρωσαν, τοῖς δὲ δὴ στρατηγοῖς τὸν Καίσαρα ἀκληρωτὶ δοῦναι ἐψηφίσαντο. Dio Cassius, xlii. 20.

[7] Mommsen, iv. 480, 534.   [8] *Ad Att.* ix. 17, § 1; Dio Cassius, xli. 36.

[9] Cic. *ad Fam.* xiii. 5, § 2; Suet. *Jul.* 47, 76, 80; Dio Cassius, xliii. 47; Watson, *Cicero's Letters*, p. 495.

chief and supreme judge, and (though this was the special business of the quaestor) largely interfered in matters of finance. The special feature of the Roman system was its union in one single head and hand of functions which modern states take care to separate. In this way their system produced men of the most extraordinary and varied capacity. The Romans, one would think, expected more from human nature than it could give, but nevertheless they often got what they expected; on the other hand, the strain was too excessive for ordinary men, and tended to put them out of the field. The Romans could not avail themselves of the services of the majority of competent men, who may make good specialists but nothing more, so easily as we can. Therefore a Roman governor was either a wonderful success, or a gigantic failure; and the opportunities of harm possessed by a vicious and incompetent administrator were beyond calculation.[1]

The first business of a Roman governor was to publish his edict. Cicero wrote his at Rome[2]; and it was the custom for it to be made known in the province before the governor entered upon his office. The urban praetors exactly in the same way issued their edict on entering upon their office at Rome: the difference was that at Rome the edict was controlled by and had to adapt itself to the body of civil law, of which the Twelve Tables long remained the nucleus; while in the province it was only controlled by the lex provinciae and the local codes, to neither of which unfortunately was the governor absolutely obliged to conform.[3] In theory each new governor might issue a completely new edict; but in practice it was not so, partly

---

[1] Cic. *pro Mur.* 30: duae sunt artes quae possint locare homines in amplissimo gradu dignitatis, una imperatoris, altera oratoris boni. But the same man was often both at Rome.

[2] Cic. *ad Fam.* iii. 8, § 4.

[3] For the difference between law and edict, see Cic. *in Verr.* i. 42; Mommsen, *Stadtrechte von Salpensa und Malaga*, p. 390 et seq.

because each governor would in this way have given himself a great deal of unnecessary trouble, and partly because
by any great innovations he would have been sure to injure
the web of complicated interests in his province, and so
make enemies, and court an accusation. Great part of the

The
gover-
nor's
edict.
edict was traditional, and passed on from praetor to praetor
without change; ' *edictum tralaticium* ' Cicero calls it[1]; and
in this way a regular code of law was built up in the
provinces, just as the urban praetors built it up at Rome.
The regulations of the lex provinciae would be largely
copied into the annual edicts. The Lex Rupilia for instance
had allowed each city to use its own laws, at all events
in certain cases; and this provision had been regularly
copied into edict after edict, and was even, in form, maintained by Verres.'[2]   In the same way we know from Cicero
that it had been one of Aquilius' arrangements that no slave
in Sicily should be allowed the use of weapons; and this too
was copied in all successive edicts.[3] Moreover these provincial edicts were, in many points of civil law, largely
modelled upon the edicts of the urban praetors. As regards
the law of inheritance, Cicero informs us that not only
previous praetors of Sicily, but even Verres himself, had
transferred word for word into their edicts the regulations
accustomed to be issued at Rome[4]; and in that famous
passage which is the chief source of our knowledge for this
subject he says that all points which his edict does not
definitely mention, he will settle according to the 'urban
edicts.'[5]   The edict of a particularly good or famous
governor would become a model for his successors; we find
Cicero for instance largely copying from that of the incor-

---

[1] Cic. *ad Att.* v. 21, § 11 ; *ad Fam.* iii. 8, § 4.   See also Roby's
Digest, clxxviii. ; Muirhead, *Roman Law*, p. 262.

[2] Cic. *in Verr.* ii. 27.

[3] Ib. v. 3.

[4] Cic. *in Verr.* i. 46.

[5] Cic. *ad Att.* vi. 1, § 15 : dixi me de eo genere mea decreta ad edicta
urbana accommodaturum.

ruptible Scaevola. A governor would give some idea of what his government was going to be by the nature of the edict he issued; all edicts for instance would deal largely with the treatment of the publicani, and if the edict unduly and scandalously favoured them, as did that of Verres,[1] the unfortunate provincials would know what to expect. The edict, again, dealt with the whole question of usury and debt; Cicero fixed the rate of interest recoverable under his jurisdiction[2]; and its provisions would therefore largely concern not only the Roman bankers (negotiatores) in the province, but the different towns and states, all of which were as a rule deep in debt to these extortioners. A good governor would insert a clause in his edict to prevent the cities ruining themselves by extravagant expenditure on the complimentary deputations sent to Rome in honour of his predecessors[3]; and above all, nothing would so clearly distinguish a good and liberal governor from one of the opposite character as the amount of independence he left to the cities of his province.[4] Cicero seems to have allowed them an unusual amount of autonomy, while Verres overrode them in every particular.[5]

Directly the governor arrived in his province, the former governor, even though still in the country, became by right a private person. He had no authority to do any official act, and Appius' conduct in holding a court of justice after Cicero's arrival was so unusual as to have the character of a slight, which Cicero takes credit to himself for not resenting.[6] The new governor could absolutely change and abolish the old one's acts. Thus Appius complained of the changes introduced by Cicero,[7] and Pompey annulled the arrangements of Lucullus.[8] It was an almost unheard-of

Relation between incoming and outgoing governor

---

[1] Cic. *in Verr.* iii. 10 ; cf. *ad Fam.* iii. 8, § 4.

[2] Cic. *ad Att.* vi. 1, § 15. [3] Cic. *ad Fam.* iii. 8, § 4.

[4] Cic. *ad Att.* vi. 1, § 15, v. 21, § 11. [5] Cic. *in Verr.* ii. 13.

[6] Cic. *ad Att.* v. 17 ; *ad Fam.* iii. 6 and 8. Gabinius refused to receive his successor. Dio Cass. xxxix. 60.

[7] Cic. *ad Att.* vi. 1. [8] Plut. *Lucull.* 36.

thing for a governor to reverse a judicial decision of his predecessor, but there was nothing positively to prevent it, and Verres in fact did it.[1] The want of continuity thus inherent in the administration was a great evil. That one governor should undo the arrangements of another was satisfactory enough if it was a Cicero undoing the arrangements of an Appius; but it was not so satisfactory when the case was reversed; and in any case the uncertainty introduced into life must have been, to the provincials, hateful and mischievous.

Distribution of a governor's time.

The duties of a governor were, as has been already said, partly military and partly civil; the Romans knew nothing of a separation of judicial and executive functions.[2] It is possible to make out from Cicero's letters how a governor who stayed only the strict year in his province spent his time. Cicero entered his province at Laodicea on July 31, 51 B.C. After spending a few days in hearing complaints and redressing grievances, he proceeded to Iconium, which he reached Aug. 24. There he reviewed the army, and started at its head southwards, reaching Tarsus Oct. 5. He then immediately set out to chastise the hostile tribes of Mount Amanus, bringing the campaign to a successful conclusion by Dec. 17. After spending the few remaining days of the year at Tarsus he returned to Laodicea on Jan. 5, and administered justice there till May 7. On that day he set out again for Cilicia proper (his province extended far beyond Cilicia), reached Tarsus on June 5, and remained there administering justice and winding up his affairs till July 17. On Aug. 3, 50 B.C., he embarked at Side in Pamphylia.[3]

Whatever may have been the exact parts of the year employed upon the discharge of the different civil and

[1] Cic. *in Verr.* ii. 28.

[2] For a general sketch of the duties of a governor, see Cic. *ad Qu. Fr,* i. 1, and Ramsay, *Church in the Roman Empire,* p. 208.

[3] Watson, pp. 152, 156, and his references,

military functions,[1] in provinces needing an army there was always this double work for the governor to discharge. Caesar in the midst of his dangers and conquests found time to hurry off to Hither Gaul to hold the circuits after each campaign[2]; and his civil appears to have been as successful as his military administration. The weight and authority which the possession of military force in his own person must have given a civil administrator is obvious enough ; but that was a doubtful advantage, for the fault of the Roman system was not that the governors had too little authority, but too much.

As commander-in-chief, besides directing the levies[3] and calling out, in case of need, any Roman veterans that might be living in the province,[4] the governor had an immense source of influence, and could inflict a great deal of misery by the power he possessed of quartering his troops for the winter in any town of the province he pleased. This was what the provincials dreaded more than any other oppression, and they were willing to bribe the governor with a round sum to be exempt from such formidable visitors. *Military duties.*

But it was in his capacity as supreme judge that the proconsul must have impressed himself most strongly upon the minds of the provincials. Under the Empire the provinces were divided into *conventus* or districts for judicial purposes, corresponding to our ' circuits.' Thus there were four circuits in Baetica, three in Lusitania. In the republican period the word is hardly yet used in this technical sense, but from the first a certain number of towns were set apart as convenient centres, ' where the praetor was *Jurisdiction.*

---

[1] In Sicily the praetors went round their circuits administering justice in the summer, as then the harvest was being got in, all the labourers were at work, and the tax-payers could not conceal their real property. (*In Verr.* v. 12 and 31.) But in less peaceful provinces the summer would commonly be taken up with military operations, and the winter devoted to the administration of justice.

[2] Caes. *B. G.* i. 54. vi. 44, viii. 4 and 46.

[3] *Bell. Alex.* 50.   [4] Cic. *ad Att.* vi. 18.

accustomed to make a stay, and hold a court.'[1]   To these centres the Roman citizens dwelling in the neighbourhood resorted at fixed intervals, so as to form a ready-made body of jurymen, from whom the praetor might appoint fit persons to try the several cases brought before him. It was one of the complaints brought by Cicero against Verres that he repeatedly passed over these capable and respectable persons,[2] and appointed judges from his own good-for-nothing retinue.   To these centres the cases that had arisen in a large surrounding district were brought.   Cicero did most of his judicial work at Laodicea, assigning one month to the cases of the district of Cibyra and Apamea, and two months to the cases of Synnada, Pamphylia, Lycaonia, and Isauria.[3]   For Cyprus he sent a special judicial officer, as the Cypriots, in virtue of some agreement or custom, could not be summoned away from their island.

In all cases the praetor presided, except where he delegated his authority to his subordinates; but he was assisted, and no doubt to a certain extent controlled, by his assessors, —always apparently Romans settled in the province,[4]—

---

[1] *In Verr.* v. 11, § 28 : ' Ex iis oppidis in quibus consistere praetores et conventum agere soleant.' The phrase ' forum agere ' is also used in the same sense, Cic. *ad Att.* v. 16 and 21, § 9, vi. 2. For further details as to the Conventus, see Holm, *Gesch. Sic.* iv. 753 ; Schulten, *De Conventibus civium Romanorum ; Staatsrecht*, ii. 209 ; Lewis, *Government of Dependencies*, ed. Lucas, 118 : Ramsay in *Classical Review*, iii. 176. They are only proved for Spain, Sicily, Illyricum and Asia, but probably occurred in most provinces.

[2] Cic. *in Verr.* ii. 13, 34 : 'Selecti e conventu aut praepositi ex negotiatoribus nulli.'

[3] Cic. *ad Att.* v. 21, § 9.

[4] In the S. C., giving freedom and immunity to Asclepiades for his services in the war against the pirates, one clause especially privileges him either to be tried by the laws of his own country or, if he preferred it, ' before Roman magistrates, with Italians for jurymen.' The Latin ' apud magistratus nostros Italicis judicibus ' is in part a supplement, but can be taken for certain, as the Greek exists in full : ἢ ἐπὶ τῶν ἡμετέρων ἀρχόντων ἐπὶ 'Ιταλικῶν κριτῶν.   C. I. L. i., p. 110.   See Hitzig,

whom he appointed to try the case along with him.[1] There was, however, nothing to prevent a governor deciding a case simply on his own authority, but it would be an unusual and excessively unpopular proceeding, and even Verres hesitated before he made up his mind to incur the odium of such an act. On this occasion the Roman knight who was counsel for the defendant refused to conduct the case before Verres alone, and indignantly left the court.[2]

It must not be supposed that all cases arising in the province came before the praetor. The free and allied towns had their own laws, and lay, by right, wholly outside his jurisdiction, and a *conventus* was seldom held in one of them. Thus a charge of sacrilege was brought by a Samian against a Chian, and tried by Chians. The number of cases that came before the praetor as compared with those that came before the local courts would depend upon the arrangements of the *lex provinciae* ; upon the amount of liberty claimed by the towns ; and last, but not least, upon the inclination of the governor to respect those liberties. So the people of the little town of Bidis in Sicily had apparently a right to settle legacy cases by their own municipal law, but Verres ignored the right.[3] Another right granted to the Sicilians was that no man should be forced to give security to appear in any court (forum) but that of his own district. It would of course have been ruin to a poor man to have to leave his business, and make a

Jurisdiction.

Die Assessoren der röm. Magistr. und Richter, 1893, Mommsen, *Strafrecht*, 138-140. Bruns, p. 176.

[1] A passage of Cicero, *ad Att.* ii. 16, § 4, indicates that the governor was assisted in his judicial decisions by a body of legal advisers, just as in military matters he commonly asked the advice of his officers. The ' consilium ' mentioned in this passage may perhaps be a similar body to that mentioned *pro Balbo*, 8 and 17, whose authority was necessary to legalise a general's bestowal of the franchise ; see Warde Fowler, *City State*, 230. Such a body would help in maintaining senatorial control over provincial governors.

[2] Cic. *in Verr.* v. 9.   [3] Cic. *in Verr.* ii. 22, 24, 25.

journey, and appear in a court held at the other end of the island. This right too Verres disregarded.[1]   In those provinces in which there were numbers of Roman colonies and municipia, the jurisdiction of the governors and of the towns existed side by side, each keeping no doubt within its accurately defined limits.   The *lex Rubria*, by which Caesar organised the municipia of Cisalpine Gaul, empowered the municipal magistrates to decide all civil cases where the money involved did not exceed 15,000 sesterces.[2] The *lex Julia Municipalis* contained a similar provision,[3] and not improbably allowed the duumvirs *criminal* jurisdiction over slaves.[4]   This *lex Julia* was probably the norm for the municipal charters of Roman and Latin towns in the provinces ; and in the law of Malaga published under Domitian we find the following clause: ' In the case of money demanded in the name of the municipium from any citizen (municeps) or settler (incola), if the sum is not less than 1,000 sesterces, and not so great as to [come within the jurisdiction of the proconsul, let the duumvir or prefect decide about it.[5]]'   It appears then that the more important civil cases and the great mass of the criminal cases would regularly come before the Roman governor, and the minor civil cases, the ordinary law business of daily life, before the duumvirs of the towns of Roman constitution, or the other local magistrates of non-Roman towns ; while the difficulties of having two different codes of law existing side by side gradually disappeared, as the provincial towns adopted the Roman law in preference to their own,[6] and so

[1] Cic. *in Verr.* ii. 15, 40.

[2] The existing fragments of the *Lex Rubria* are printed ; C. I. L. i., p. 115.   Other fragments discovered in 1880 mention 10,000 sesterces, probably referring to another class of suits, *Hermes,* xvi. 27.

[3] This can be made out from § 116 of the law ; C. I. L. i., p. 119.

[4] This is a conjecture of Mommsen, but is supported by the analogy of the *pro Cluentio,* 64-66.

[5] § 69 of the *Lex Malacitana ;* C. I. L. ii., p. 260 (No. 1964).   The words in brackets are the certain supplement of Mommsen.

[6] Cic. *pro Balbo,* 8.

paved the way for the bestowal upon them of the regular municipal constitution.

In the performance of his judicial functions, the governor was armed with absolute powers. In theory, though no doubt this was much mitigated in practice, the provinces were perpetually under martial law. The governor was, in the first place and before all, commander-in-chief, and the rods and axes which had to be laid down on his return to Rome attended him everywhere throughout his province. So he could punish with imprisonment or death ; and no one, unless he were a Roman citizen, would in strictness have a right of appeal. This was perhaps the chief advantage of being a Roman citizen in the provinces, and the one most coveted by the provincials. In civil cases, however, it appears that sometimes a second trial was allowed by a new governor, on security for double the amount at issue being deposited by the appellant.[1]

The governor had also large powers in the matter of finance. It was the quaestor who kept the accounts; but it depended mainly upon the governor whether the sums transmitted to Rome were large or small[2]; and it was in his power to remit[3] and probably to impose taxation. Above all, his dealings with the farmers of the taxes were most important for the welfare or misery of his province. In Cicero's opinion the right management of these gentry was the prime difficulty of a governor. It was dangerous and troublesome to quarrel with them ; and on the other hand, if they were left to their own devices, there was no hope for the provincials.[4] There are indications that Cicero himself was not resolute enough to control them as he

Finance.

[1] Cic. *pro Flacco*, 21, and for the subject in general Reid *Municipalities*, 479.

[2] In Sicily, for instance, this would depend upon how the tithes were sold ; and the whole of the Verrines shows the influence the governor had in this respect.

[3] Cic. *in Verr*. iv. 9 ; *ad Fam*. iii. 7.

[4] *Ad Qu. Fr*. i. 1, 13.

should have done [1]; just as he was certainly too indulgent to those other harpies of the provinces, the Roman bankers.

Absolute nature of the governor's authority.
The authority possessed by the governor was then, in its reference to the provincials at all events, essentially absolute. It was recognised to be such by the Romans themselves [2]; and the restrictions which they sought to put upon his action shows this in a clear light. It was apparently illegal, or at all events invidious, for a governor to buy anything in his province ; and to obviate the necessity of his doing so, he was provided with everything that he could be supposed to want at the public expense.

It is commonly said that the governors were not salaried in this period, and in the strict sense they were not. In theory the provincial, like the urban magistrates, were sufficiently compensated for their labours by the glory of being allowed to serve their country. But, besides that they had no expenses of maintenance or travel, the sums allowed them for the expenses of the administration were on so lavish a scale that it was easy to save largely out of them, and probably few governors acted like Cicero in refusing to keep what thus remained over, either for himself or his retinue (Cic. *ad Att.* vii. 1, § 6). The *vasarium* or outfit of Piso, governor of Macedonia, was 18 million sesterces.[3]

Why was this ? 'Because they thought it a theft, not a purchase, when the seller could not sell at his own price. And they knew very well that if a provincial governor wanted to purchase something that was in another man's

---

[1] Cic. *ad Att.* vi. 1, § 16 ; vi. 2 and 3. Such phrases as 'cumulate publicanis satisfactum,' 'publicanis in oculis sumus,' 'publicanos habeo in deliciis,' are significant.

[2] Cic. *ad Qu. Fr.* i. 1, 8.

[3] Cic. *in Pis.* 35: 'Nonne sestertium centies et octogies, quod, quasi vasarii nomine, in venditione mei capitis ascripseras, ex aerario tibi attributum, Romae in quaestu reliquisti ?' Cf. also *ad Fam.* v. 20, 9. Me omnem pecuniam quae ad me salvis legibus pervenisset Ephesi apud publicanos deposuisse ; id fuisse H. S. xxii. milia.

possession, and was allowed to do so, it would come to this, that he would get whatever he pleased, whether it was for sale or not, at whatever price he chose to give for it.'[1] The same thing is illustrated by the story Cicero tells of the conduct of Lucius Piso, when praetor of Further Spain.[2] He had lost his gold ring; so he sent for a goldsmith, while seated on his tribunal at Corduba, and weighed him out the necessary amount of gold. He then ordered the man to set up his bench in the forum, and there and then make the ring in the presence of every one. This was affectation no doubt, but affectation is not often so significant. The fact is that in his province the governor was a king; the praetor of Sicily indeed lived in Hiero's palace.[3] Cicero takes credit to himself that he did not, like other governors, make difficulties about admitting anyone to audience, and employed no chamberlain whose intervention it was first necessary to secure.[4] He speaks exactly as a Louis XIV. might have spoken. A formidable and impressive figure must a governor, even a good one, have been to the provincials, holding in his hands as he did the issues of life and death, and all-powerful for worldly weal and worldly woe. They familiarised themselves with that austere figure later on, when better protected against its will. They even came close enough to it to discover that if the sword was of steel the rest of the figure was sometimes of clay; but they never became quite insensible to the spell, in this period so strong, of the

> Heart-quaking sound of *consul Romanus*.

SECTION III. *The Governor's Subordinates.*

1. The provincial quaestors were perhaps originally instituted with the idea of lessening the power of the

The quaestor.

---

[1] Cic. *in Verr.* iv. 5; cf. Lewis, *Government of Dependencies* (ed. Lucas), 272, note 1; *Codex Theod.* iii. 6, 1.
[2] Ib. iv. 25.　　　　　　　　　　[3] Ib. v. 12.
[4] Cic. *ad Att.* vi. 2, § 5; cf. *ad Qu. Fr.* i. 1, 8, § 25.

governor by subducting from it all financial functions.[1]
In Sicily were two quaestors, and one in every other
province. We do not certainly know their full number
before Sulla[2]; but only that he raised it to twenty;
and Caesar after him to forty. When the quaestor left
Rome he took with him the chest containing the money
which was to supply all the expenses of the administration, and into which the taxes of the province were
paid: of all these at the end of his term of office he had
to render account.[3] He had his own jurisdiction, corresponding to that of the aediles at Rome[4]; or the governor
could if he pleased delegate to him his judicial authority
Thus we find young Caesar sent round Baetica by his
praetor for the admistration of justice.[5]   The quaestor
also had military duties, partly connected with the levying
and equipment of troops,[6] and partly with the direct
leadership of men, at all events in times of emergency.[7]
Cicero left his quaestor as governor of the province, in the
interval between his own departure and the arrival of his
successor.[8]   The quaestors were not directly appointed by
the governors, but assigned to the different provinces by
lot.[9]   Caesar and Pompey were guilty of a considerable ir-
regularity when they directly appointed their quaestors without the previous observance of this form.[10]   Though their
appointment was of this fortuitous character, the Romans

---

[1] This is Mommsen's view, ii. 210.

[2] Mommsen, iv. 112-3, note, 123, note.   Tac. *Ann*. xi. 22, gives a sort
of history of the quaestorship.

[3] Cic. *in Verr*. i. 14 ; Mommsen, *Staatsr*. i. 677.

[4] Gaius, i. 6 ; Marquardt, i. 390.

[5] Suet. *Jul*. 7 (Cic. *Div. in Caec*. 17 ; for similar custom in Sicily).

[6] Plut. *Sert*. 4.   [7] Cic. *Phil*. x. 6.

[8] Cic. *ad Att*. vi. 6, § 3.   See also the case of Cassius in Syria
(*Fam*. xv. 14) and of P. Cornelius Lentulus in Asia, 43 B.C., Cic. *Fam*.
xii. 14, 15.   See Sall. *Jug*. 103 ; Mommsen, *Staatsr*. i. 16; ii. 223.

[9] Marquardt, i. 388, and his authorities.

[10] Cic. *ad Att*. vi. 6, § 4 ; *Phil*. 2, § 50; *Fam*. ii. 15; *ad Qu. Fr*.
i. 1, § 11.

laid great stress upon the almost paternal relationship which existed or should exist between the quaestor and his superior.[1] This was natural enough, considering that the quaestors were always quite young men at the outset of their career ; but it had important practical consequences. It was, for instance, an impossible impiety for a quaestor to give evidence against the consul or praetor under whom he had served in a province.[2] At the same time it was expected of him that he should exercise some sort of control upon a tyrannical superior[3] ; and the governor was accustomed to take his advice in important matters.[4] On the other hand, his superior could quash a legal decision of his,[5] and could even (though this would be an extreme course), if he chose, dismiss him.[6]

2. There were as a rule three legates in a consular, one in a praetorian province. Their appointment was an indefeasible privilege of the Senate, which could vary their number at pleasure, and in special cases increase it to ten, and even fifteen.[7] The governor would, however, let the Senate know whom he wished appointed, and as a rule no doubt his request would be complied with. The governor generally proposed relatives or friends for the office ; they were his subordinates and he was responsible for them. If they proved incompetent he dropped them ; if the contrary, they received a district to look after, with the fasces but without the axe, possessing jurisdiction in civil cases but not in criminal. If a legate won a victory it was the governor who received the credit of it, as the legate could not take his own 'auspices.'[8] The harm an

The legati.

---

[1] Add to Marquardt's references, Pliny, *Epist.* iv. 15.

[2] Cic. *Div. in Caec.* 18, 19.

[3] Ib. 10, and for a case where a quaestor hesitatingly took up arms against his chief, Dio C. 42, 15.

[4] Cic. *in Verr.* v. 44.   [5] Cic. *Div. in Caec.* 16.

[6] Cic. *in Verr.* iii. 58.

[7] Caesar had ten legati in Gaul, Cicero had four in Cilicia. Pompey, when invested with the cura annonae, had fifteen (*ad Att.* 4, 1).

[8] Summarised from Marquardt, i. 387, and his authorities.

ill-disposed legate could do was very considerable; Verres
was nearly as mischievous when legate, as he was when
praetor [1]; and if the provincials complained, the governor
refused to decide the matter himself, as not within his
jurisdiction, but referred them to Rome.[2]

The
comites.

3. The comites were something like our attachés or
secretaries of legation, young Romans of birth who were
taken into the provinces to learn the business of administration. So Cicero took with him his son, his nephew, and a
relation of Atticus. Catullus was a *comes* of C. Memmius
in Bithynia. The comites were chosen by the governor,
who was responsible for their good behaviour. They were
supported at the public charge, and their number could be
controlled by the Senate.[3] A position as comes gave a man
a good opportunity of looking after any property he might
possess in the province [4]; or was accepted with the undis-
guised motive of making a little money. Catullus' object
in expatriating himself to Bithynia seems to have been
nothing more respectable,[5] and Cicero apparently transgressed use and wont when he refused to divide the £8,000
saved from the allowance made for administration, among
his subordinates.[6] Their influence in the province may be
gathered from the epithets applied to them by Horace [7];
and on the other hand from the remark of Cicero, that
Verres' retinue did Sicily more harm than would have been
done by a hundred troops of fugitive slaves.[8]

The
prefects.

4. Besides other minor officials, the dragomans, inter-
preters, bailiffs, lictors, architects [9] (meaning rather what

---

[1] Cic. *in Verr.*, Act i. 4 ; i. 16.   [2] Ib. i. 19.

[3] Marquardt, i. 391, and his authorities.   [4] Cic. *pro Caelio*, 30.

[5] Catullus, ix. 9, 13, xxviii. 6, 9 ; Ellis' *Commentary*, p. l.

[6] Cic. *ad Att.* vii. 1, 6.

[7] ' Stellasque salubres Appellat comites '; Horace, *Sat.* i. 7, 24.

[8] Cic. *in Verr.* ii. 10.

[9] Marquardt, i. 393; also occurring among the attendants of a colonial
commission ; ib. 429 ; see Cic. *de Leg. Agr.* ii. 12 and 13. Under the
Empire, at all events, local talent is used ; see Pliny, *Epist.* x. 49.

we should call engineers), there were also the prefects. Strictly speaking, these were three in number, and all of a military character[1]; but the prefecture, for which Scaptius asked Cicero, and which Cicero refused to give to any Roman negotiator, seems to have had judicial duties connected with it. The L. Volusius whom Cicero sent to Cyprus to administer justice[2] was not a legate, for we know the names of Cicero's four legates from another passage,[3] but probably a praefectus, and it was for the post which he held that Scaptius asked. Roman moneylenders asked for these appointments for the sake of the small military force that went with them, and which enabled them to put the screw on procrastinating debtors.[4] And no doubt most governors were laxer in giving them than was Cicero.

SECTION IV. *The control of the Governor by the Senate.*

Besides the fact that in the great majority of cases a governor owed his appointment to the Senate, there were a number of ways in which the Senate could control and influence his action. The Senate supplied him with the money for his troops,[5] and it was their decision which settled how large a force his was to be. Cicero, for instance, complained to the Senate of the insufficient number of troops provided him.[6] A governor was expected to keep up a regular correspondence with the Senate,[7] and was liable to

---

[1] Sociorum, castrorum, fabrum, are the three military *praefecti*, but there were others, Marquardt (Fr. tr.), ii., p. 579.

[2] Cic *ad Att.* v. 21, § 6 ; vi. 2 and 3 ; *Staatsr.* i. 223, 224.

[3] Cic. *ad Fam.* xvi. 4, § 8.

[4] Cic. *ad Att.* v. 21, § 10. Such *praefecti* are quite different from the prefects of islands, and other small appointments to which it was not worth while to send a regular governor. These latter were directly appointed by the Senate with full powers ; there was, for instance, a prefect of the Balearic Islands under Nero (Orelli, 732).

[5] Plut. *Pomp.* 20.

[6] Cic. *ad Fam.* xv. 2.   [7] Cic. *in Pis.* 16.

have his policy altered or overridden at its decree. A governor setting out for his province usually received its definite instructions, especially with regard to the conduct he was to follow with allied states or princes [1] ; and on his return had to give in his accounts to the Senate,[2] besides leaving one or more copies in the province.[3] The Senate could also bestow or refuse the coveted honours of the triumph or *supplicatio* [4] ; and a governor's arrangements needed its confirmation to be valid.[5] Any extraordinary illegality on the part of a governor could be met by its special decree [6] ; and it was not apparently in the power of a governor to make requisitions of ships or money without its consent.[7]

**Ineffi-
ciency
of the
senatorial
control.** Here are the elements of an efficient control ; yet in practice the senatorial supervision was absurdly inadequate. The Senate was called to two tasks at once, either of which singly would perhaps have exceeded its powers,—the management namely of the provinces, and the struggle against the democracy. Just when the utmost watchfulness, concentration, and unanimity were needed for foreign affairs, the Senate was distracted and divided by the party politics of Rome. The instinct of self-preservation made it turn chiefly to what seemed most nearly to concern its own welfare ; and the reins of empire began to slip from its slackened grasp. The unauthorised raid of Manlius Vulso upon Galatia shows this at an early date ; later on comes Gabinius' impudent entry into forbidden Egypt.[8] The

---

[1] Caes. *B. G.* i. 35; Cic. *ad Fam.* xv. 2, § 4; for exceptions see Dio, xxxviii. 41.

[2] Cic. *in Pis.* 25. [3] Cic. *ad Att.* vi. 7

[4] Cic. *de Prov. Cons.* 7 ; *in Pis.* 19.

[5] Mommsen, iv. 502 ; Pompey's case; Dio, xxxvii. 20, xxxviii. 7, xxxix. 22.

[6] Cic. *in Verrem*, iii. 39.

[7] Cic. *pro Flacco*, 12.

[8] Cic. *in Pis.* 21. Other unauthorised expeditions : Lucullus against the Vaccaei, Dio, xxxviii. 41 ; Aemilius in Spain, Appian, *Hisp.* 81 ; Crassus in Parthia, Dio, xl. 12.

magistrates gained steadily upon the Senate. Caesar openly disregarded senatorial control. Extraordinary and prolonged commands followed one another in quick succession; and such commanders did not trouble themselves to send in reports or ask advice. Without continuous or efficient control the administration became a chaos. Cicero complains of the neglect at Rome of provincial affairs [1]; and in so far as they were attended to, they were made the stalking-horse by which one political party attacked another. To administer rightly the heterogeneous mass of Roman subjects needed unwearied diligence, and an organisation in thorough working order. The Senate was too much interested in the other game it had to play to give itself this enormous trouble; and notwithstanding disconnected efforts here and there, the governors were, if they chose, practically exempt from its control, especially in the last years of the Republic.[2]

SECTION V. *The control of the Governor by his Province.*

Apart from the definite protection of the law, it was a great advantage to a provincial to be under the patronage of some powerful Roman. The governor of the province would be careful of injuring persons thus protected: ' the Spanish governors felt that no one could with impunity maltreat the clients of Cato.' [3] It was a common thing for whole peoples to become the clients of the Roman generals who had first conquered them.[4] Thus we find a Fabius patron of the Allobroges [5]; the Marcelli of Sicily [6]; and the

Patrons and clients.

---

[1] Cic. *pro Plancio*, 26. Sed ita multa Romae geruntur ut vix ea quae fiunt in provinciis audiantur.

[2] Dio C. xlii. 20.   [3] Mommsen, iii. 33.

[4] Cic. *de Off.* i. 11, § 35 : ' Ut ii qui civitates aut nationes devictas bello in fidem recepissent, eorum patroni essent more majorum.' Mommsen, *Römische Forschungen*, pp. 340, 348, 361. So Marius was patron of Gaetulians, *Bell. Afr.* 35.

[5] Appian, *B. C.* ii. 4 ; Merivale, i. 216.

[6] Liv. xxvi. 32 ; Cic. *in Verr.* ii. 49.

elder Cato of Spain.[1]   This patronate was often hereditary ;
it was so for instance in the case of the Marcelli, the Fabii,
and the Minucii[2]; and in the inscriptions recording the
clientship of towns or individuals the relationship is often
acknowledged on both sides as valid for their posterity.[3]
The duty of a patron to his clients was recognised as clearly
as in the old days when both patron and client were Romans.[4]
In particular a patron was expected to further his client's
interests, if any business, legal or other, brought the latter
to Rome.   The patron of a provincial town was anxious to
secure its advantage [5]; and the tie must have been a close
and real one if Bononia was specially thanked by Octavian
for joining with the rest of Italy to take his side in the civil
war, regardless of the hereditary clientship between itself
and the Antonii.[6]

The
Roman
franchise.
But the protection of the patronage was shadowy and
unsubstantial compared with the privileges attached to the
possession of the Roman citizenship. The martial law
under which all other provincials lay did not apply to him
who could say with St. Paul, 'I am a Roman.' At least
four laws were passed to secure Roman citizens from the
rods and axes of the magistrate[7] ; and a lex Julia of 8 B.C.
punished the magistrate guilty of putting to death, torturing,
flogging or imprisoning a Roman citizen who had appealed,

---

[1] Cic. Div. in Caec. 20.   Under the Empire we find a patron of Narbonensis, Henzen, 6954 ; of Britain, Orelli, 366 ; and, not to mention
others, Caesar had been patron of Baetica.

[2] Minucius Rufus is mentioned as patron of the Ligurians ; C. I. L.
i., p. 73, No. 199 ; a position he owed to his father having conquered
the country.

[3] Cic. pro Flacco, 22 ; in Verr. iv. 41.   The common form in the
inscriptions is, ' eum cum liberis posterisque suis patronum coopta-
verunt ' . . . 'liberos posterosque eorum in fidem clientelamque suam
recepit.'

[4] Cic. in Verrem, ii. 47 ; Plin. Ep. iii. 4.

[5] Cic. ad Fam. xiii. 64.   [6] Suet. Aug. 17.

[7] A lex Valeria and three leges Porciae ; C. I. L. i., p. 71 ; also,
apparently, a Sempronian Law ; Cic. in Verr. v. 63.

by outlawry, or, in other words, 'interdiction from fire and water.'[1] Only a Roman citizen could appeal against a decision of the governor[2]; and the trial of Rabirius and the banishment of Cicero made it evident that not even a consul, acting with the authority of the Senate, could put a citizen to death without trial. It was a minor advantage that the harbour or octroi duties levied by a free town were not paid by Roman citizens[3]; and that they had the almost exclusive right to serve on provincial juries. The flagrant violation of all these rights by Verres is in Cicero's eyes perhaps his most atrocious crime, as it would be the one which would most surely rouse the indignation of the people of Rome. Cicero says that wars have been waged 'because Roman citizens were said to have been ill-used, or Roman vessels detained, or Roman merchants robbed[4];' and his indignation becomes scathing and terrible, as he relates how Roman citizens had been tortured, executed, even crucified by the orders of a Roman governor.

Unfortunately, though the whole of Italy gained the franchise in the first century B.C., it only gained it at the sword's point; and this great concession was not, for a long time, followed by similar indulgences to the provincials. Individuals here and there who had done Rome notable services were rewarded with the franchise all through this period; but Caesar was the first Roman statesman who thought of bestowing it upon a whole province. It was generally bestowed for military services. Marius, for instance, perhaps the first Roman general to give it without direct senatorial authority, rewarded his Gallic soldiers with it after his victory over the Cimbri near Vercellae. Sulla

---

[1] This was the crime of 'vis publica,' mentioned by Tac. *Ann.* iv. 13; see Church and Brodribb's note, p. 346.

[2] See Greenidge in *Classical Review*, x. 225; Coulanges, *Recherches*, pp. 35-38. For the case of Marcellus and the Transpadani, see Cic. *Att.* v. 11; Suet. *Jul.* 28; Appian, *B. C.* ii. 26; Plut. *Caes.* 29.

[3] Marquardt, ii. 263.   [4] Cic. *in Verr.* v. 58.

seems to have been liberal in this respect[1]; and Pompey claimed the acknowledged right of a Roman general to make it the reward of loyal service. The oration delivered by Cicero for Cornelius Balbus, as also that for the poet Archias, turn upon this question of the franchise. Apparently the claim of a general to bestow it, unless he was specially authorised by a previous law,[2] was in strictness invalid, and actions might be brought against the enfranchised person. But Cicero does not hesitate to assert that ' no one ever lost his action who was proved to have been presented with the franchise by any one of our generals.'[3] The advantages to Rome of being able to reward distinguished military service by so coveted a prize, are too obvious to need recommendation by the eloquence of Cicero[4]; more remarkable is the fact of its being made the reward for an accuser who had secured a conviction for extortion.[5] But Julius Caesar after all was the first to give it with a liberal hand. He enfranchised the soldiers of his Alaudae legion[6]; and, if Antony may be trusted, intended to give Sicily at all events the Latin right.[7] He also encouraged learning by enfranchising ' all professors of medicine at Rome, and all teachers of liberal knowledge.'[8] If this policy had been begun earlier, and carried out boldly by a succession of statesmen, some of the worst miseries under which the provincials in this period laboured would probably have been averted.

Provincial deputations. The provincial deputations so frequently mentioned in Cicero do not seem to have been of much consequence, unless they came for the express purpose of setting the law in motion against a governor. In one case we find it mentioned that a provincial deputation, sent for a quite different

---

[1] Cic. *pro Scauro*, passim ; *in Verr.* iv. 17.   [2] Cic. *pro Balbo*, 8.
[3] Ib. 23.   [4] Ib. 9, 13, and 21.
[5] Ib. 13 and 22.   This was a provision of the severe Lex Servilia.
[6] Suet. *Jul.* 24.
[7] Cic. *ad Att.* xiv. 12 ; *Phil.* i. 10 ; Holm, iv. 751.   [8] Suet. *Jul.* 42.

purpose, had attended the courts and there supported by their presence a former quaestor of the province who was undergoing trial.[1] But such cases must have been rare ; and in any case it does not appear that such demonstrations, even if permitted, could have been of practical assistance. Equally futile but more humiliating were the *encomia* which a province was wont to send after its governor, on his leaving the province. These were most eagerly sought for, perhaps most punctiliously exacted by the worst governors. Appius had his from the Cilicia which he had ' plundered and all but ruined[2] ;' and even Verres received one from Syracuse. The Senate knew very well what these forced praises were worth, and, Cicero hints, paid very little attention to the deputies who brought them.[3]

But if the laws had only been carried out there would have been little need of anything else to protect the provinces. From an early date there had been laws passed against extortion, and in these there was no lack of severity. The first of them was the Calpurnian Law passed in the year 149 B.C. ' Lucius Piso, tribune of the plebs, was the first to pass a law about extortion,' is Cicero's account.[4] ' The avarice of the magistrates gave birth to the Calpurnian laws,' says Tacitus.[5] The *Lex Junia*, which followed, passed between 149 and 124 B.C., is only known by its being mentioned in the *Lex Acilia*. This latter law, passed probably in the year 125 B.C., is more than once noticed by Cicero as having been exceptionally severe, and is probably the law of which considerable fragments still remain to us. Next followed the *Lex Servilia* of 111 B.C. Under this law were brought the two infamous accusations of Scaurus and Rutilius, the knights being then in possession of the juries. One of its provisions was that curious one already mentioned,

(margin note: Leges Repetundarum.)

---

[1] Cic. *pro Plancio*, 11 ; cf. Dio C. xlii. 16, Λογγῖνος δὲ, καταβοησάντων αὐτοῦ διὰ πρεσβείας τῶν Ἰβήρων, τῆς ἀρχῆς ἐξέπεσε.

[2] Cic. *ad Att.* v. 15. [3] Cic. *ad Fam.* iii. 8.

[4] Cic. *Brutus*, 27. [5] Tac. *Ann.* xv. 20.

that an accuser who secured a conviction should be rewarded with the Roman franchise. Sulla 79 B.C. passed a
law dealing with these cases, but nothing is known of its
contents except what may be indirectly gathered from the
notices we possess of the later Julian law. This *Lex Julia*
clearly laid down what requisitions a governor might make
upon his province. He could claim wood, salt and hay,
besides shelter when travelling, but was required to pay for
everything else.[1] It also followed the Servilian and Cor-
nelian laws in ordaining that, if the accused could not upon
condemnation restore what he had extorted, those who had
received any part of the proceeds from him might be
prosecuted for it.[2] It also expressly forbade provincial
governors to leave their province to enter a neighbouring
kingdom, unless specially authorised by the home government ; doubtless with a view of preventing such excursions
as that of Gabinius into Egypt.[3] It seems to have been
full of excellent provisions, and still stricter than any of the
previous laws on the same class of offences.[4]

The Lex Acilia.   But it is possible to go more into detail than this. We
possess a good part of the *Lex Acilia*,[5] from which at all
events the following points can be made out :

The persons liable to accusation are these—dictator,
consul, praetor, master of the horse, censor, aedile, tribune
of the plebs, quaestor, *triumvir capitalis*, *triumvir agris dandis
assignandis*, tribune of the soldiers.[6] None of these could
be accused while their term of office lasted. An accuser
could ask the praetor for a lawyer to plead his case, and
could refuse the lawyer offered. The necessary 650 jurymen
were to be chosen by the *praetor peregrinus* within ten days
after the passing of the law. They had to be of not less

---

[1] Cic. *ad Att.* v. 16.   [2] Cic. *pro Rabirio Postumo*, 4.
[3] Cic. *in Pis.* 21.
[4] Cic. *pro Rab. Post.* 4. A list of these laws in chronological order
is given by Mommsen, C. I. L. i., p. 54.   [5] Bruns, p. 59.
[6] Equites therefore were not liable ; cf. *pro Rab. Post.* 5.

census than 400,000 sesterces. No one who was or had been tribune of the plebs, quaestor, *triumvir capitalis*, tribune of the soldiers, to be chosen ; no present or past senator[1]; no gladiator, actor or convict ; no one under thirty or over sixty years of age ; no one living more than a mile outside Rome ; no father, brother, or son of one of the above-named magistrates, or of a senator. Twenty days after the accuser had given in the name to the praetor, one hundred were to be chosen by the praetor out of the 650 jurymen. No relation of the accused was allowed to be on the bench; and the praetor had to swear that he had chosen no man with any sinister motive. Then the praetor was to tell the accused that he might pick fifty out of the hundred jurymen ; and if the accused did not avail himself of this privilege the accuser might do so. The jury were to be told to estimate the damages ; which went on the principle of restoring the same amount as had been extorted, if extorted *before* this law ; but if *after* this law, a double amount. The money was to be got out of the man's goods or his bail, and lodged by the quaestor in the treasury, and then if claimed, paid over to the persons injured.[2] If not claimed within five years, the money was to remain in the treasury. The accuser, or that one of the accusers who was considered by the jury to have done most to secure the condemnation, was to be made a Roman citizen, he and his sons, and lineal posterity ; and to be incorporated in the tribe

[1] 'Quive in senatu siet fueritve.'

[2] The essence of these suits, as their name (*de repetundis*) denotes, lay in the restitution of wrongfully acquired property. In the trial of Verres the damages were laid at one hundred million sesterces (Cic. *Div. in Caec.* 5) ; in that of C. Cato at only 18,000 sesterces (*in Verr.* iv. 10) ; in that of Dolabella at three million sesterces (Cic. *in Verr.* i. 3 and 38). Even when quadruple (Gaius, iii. 189 ; Gell. xi. 18, § 10) of the original exaction was paid, Zumpt (de legibus jusdiciisque repetundarum, Berlin, 1847) thinks, and it is probable enough, that the whole sum was paid over to the provincials to make up for the great expenses of a prosecution ; cf. Tac. *Ann.* iv. 20 ; Plin. *Ep.* ii. 9 ; Cic. *in Verr.* i. 3, iv. 8 ; Mommsen, *Staatsr.* ii. 205 ; 516, note 4.

to which the condemned man had belonged. If such an accuser did not care to accept the franchise, still the right of appeal was to be given him, just as if he had been a citizen.

Facilities allowed to an accuser.   Exceptional difficulties might no doubt now and then be put in the way of provincials desirous to avail themselves of these laws[1]; and it is possible that none but very bad cases of extortion were tried under them; but it cannot be said that on the whole the task of the accuser was rendered unduly difficult. On the contrary, any possible trouble or danger of the provincials was lightened if not removed by the practice which Cicero,[2] Tacitus,[3] and Plutarch[4] notice of young Romans making their début in public life by one of these accusations. When Cicero is defending a provincial governor thus accused, he hints pretty openly that the accuser's motive was often nothing better than mere notoriety; and if the zeal shown in such cases was often as excessive as that which he ascribes to the accuser of Flaccus,[5] the suggestion was probably a well-grounded one. If an accuser wished to secure conviction he visited the province in person, and went about from town to town collecting evidence.[6] He was armed apparently with special powers, could subpoena any one to attend at the trial and give evidence, and if difficulties were made about the production of any municipal document could positively insist upon its being shown to him.[7]

Political importance of the judicia.   But though the laws were good enough, and though there was superabundant machinery to keep them effective, they yet in fact accomplished little or nothing. The reason of this was that the struggle of parties going on during all this period was fought out in the domain of the law-courts; the *judicia* were coveted as an instrument of political power.

[1] Cic. *in Verrem*, ii. 4, 11-12.   [2] Cic. *pro Caelio*, 30; *de Off.* ii. 16.
[3] Tac. *de Orat.* 43, fin.   [4] Plut. *Lucull.* 3.
[5] Cic. *pro Flacco*, 5, 8, 15.   [6] Ib.
[7] Cic. *in Verr.* v. 66.

The original arrangement was that the Senate supplied the judges for the courts, and that therefore a senator on his return from his province was, if accused, brought to trial before fellow-senators most of whom would in their turn some day command a province, and would then perhaps need for themselves the indulgence which their friend expected of them. Caius Gracchus, casting about for a weapon against the Senate, saw that he could wound them most effectually through the law-courts. He therefore passed a law to transfer the *judicia* from the Senate to the Knights. In the forty years between Gracchus' legislation and that of Sulla several attempts were made to admit the Senate at all events to an equal share of these privileges, but without effect.[1] Sulla summarily deprived the equites of all judicial authority whatever, and transferred it wholly to the Senate (81 B.C.). This only lasted a decade; and then Pompey had the *Lex Aurelia* (70 B.C.) passed, which divided the whole body of jurymen between senators, knights, and *tribuni aerarii*. Lastly, Caesar (46 B.C.) excluded this third class, and divided the appointments equally between the Senate and the Knights.[2]

It is obvious that in these changes the interest of the provincials was not the main object in view. It is difficult to say whether they suffered most when the Knights were judges alone or when the senators alone. Cicero claims a decided superiority for the decisions of the Knights, and

The Senators and equites as judges compared.

---

[1] A *Lex Servilia* of this period divided them between both orders, but was either not passed or soon abrogated; Tac. *Ann.* xii. 60; Mommsen, iii. 376-77. Drusus contemplated a law to the same effect. Livy, *Ep.* 71.

[2] Dio Cass. xliii. 25; Vell. ii. 89. Augustus restored the trib. aerarii, and added a fourth decuria; Caligula added a fifth. Mommsen, *Staatsr.* iii. p. 335, thinks that Augustus did not restore the trib. aerarii, but formed three decuriae of equites, adding a fourth of lower census. Cf. Suet. *Aug.* 32. Ad tres iudicum decurias quartam addidit ex inferiore censu quae ducenariorum vocaretur, iudicaretque de levioribus summis.

contrasts their incorruptibility with the shameless venality of the Senate.[1] It is very possible that they were less accessible to bribes; but that did not of necessity make their possession of the courts an advantage to the provincials. These latter only exchanged the whips of the governor for the scorpions of the publicani. *Publicanus* and *eques* are in fact identical terms; and as long as the governor let the farmers of the taxes do exactly what they wanted, there was no fear of his being condemned on his return. On the other hand, if a governor endeavoured to protect the unfortunate provincials against their oppressors, he exposed himself to great danger. One of the best officials the province of Asia ever had, Rutilius Rufus, legate of the proconsul Mucius Scaevola, was condemned and banished *for extortion* (92 B.C.); and Lucullus lost his command through similar endeavours to control the publicani.[2]

Perhaps, however, the ten years' exclusive possession of the courts by the Senate after Sulla's and before Pompey's legislation were the black-letter years of the provinces. In these ten years fall the trials of Cn. Dolabella, C. Antonius, and Verres. The trial of the last was perhaps one of the immediate causes which brought about the *Lex Aurelia;* and it is possible that Cicero, when he published the five orations against Verres which he had *not spoken*, had this result in view.[3]

Section VI.   *The condition of the Provinces.*

'All the provinces are mourning, all the free peoples are complaining; all kingdoms remonstrate with us for our covetousness and our wrong-doing; on this side of the ocean there is no spot so distant or so remote that in these

[1] Pseudo-Ascon, *in Caec. Divin.* 8, says the Knights were better than the Senators; Appian, *B. C.* i. 22, says they were not; see Merivale, i. 63.

[2] Plut. *Lucull.* 20. But his military disasters must be also taken into account.

[3] Cf. Cic. *in Verr.* Act. i. 13, 15.

latter times the lust and wickedness of our countrymen have not penetrated to it. The Roman people can no longer withstand, I do not say the violence, the arms, the warfare of all nations, but their complaints, their lamentations, and their tears.' Such is the picture given by a Roman of one period of the Roman rule.[1] But they are the words of a great rhetorician on a great occasion, and it may be questioned how far they represent the literal truth. Unhappily there is too much definite evidence to leave any doubt, and other strong passages of the same author, where there can be no question of deliberate rhetoric, point in the same direction. When Cicero says that the 'mildness and self-denial' which he showed in Cilicia seemed 'incredible' to the provincials,[2] he indirectly passes the worst condemnation on the Roman rule. In the same spirit is that passage of his letter to his brother Quintus in which he speaks of the cities receiving in him 'a guardian, not a tyrant,' the households 'a guest and not a pillager.'[3] Even in writing a formal letter to the Senate, where, if anywhere, one might suppose unpleasant truths would be kept out of sight, Cicero speaks casually and by the way of the 'harshness and injustice of our rule.'[4]

There was, if Cicero may be trusted, a regular deterioration visible in this rule. It was much better in the earlier years of foreign dominion than it was in his own generation.[5] The praises which Polybius gives to the incorruptibility of

Deterioration of the Roman rule.

---

[1] Cic. *in Verr.* iii. 87 ; cf. *pro Lege Manilia*, 22 : 'Difficile est dictu, Quirites, quanto in odio simus apud exteras nationes propter eorum, quos ad eas per hos annos cum imperio misimus, injurias ac libidines.'

[2] Cic. *ad Att.* v. 18 : 'Quibus incredibilis videtur et nostra mansuetudo et abstinentia.' Dio Cass. xxxvi. 39, L. Lucullus declined Sardinia : μισήσας τὸ πρᾶγμα διὰ τοὺς πολλοὺς τοὺς οὐδὲν ὑγιὲς ἐν τοῖς ἔθνεσι δρῶντας. Cf. Appian, *Mithr.* 23, on hatred of the Romans in Asia.

[3] Cic. *ad Qu. Fr.* i. 1, 2 : 'Cum urbs custodem non tyrannum, domus hospitem non expilatorem recepisse videatur.'

[4] Cic. *ad Fam.* xv. 1 : 'acerbitatem atque injurias imperii nostri.'
Cic. *in Verr.* ii. 22.

the first Roman governors of Greece confirm his views [1]; and it was very natural that the Romans should take some little time to be wholly corrupted by the seductive influences of absolute power and easily-acquired riches.[2] But from the first, if we except perhaps the philhellene tendencies which made educated Romans look tenderly upon Greece, there was little or no idea that Rome had duties to the provincials as well as rights. If a governor spared them, it was more often from his self-respect and feeling of what was due to his own dignity and character than from humanity.

Roman theory of their rule. The theory of the Romans as to the provinces was that they were the 'estates of the Roman people.'[3] Their importance for the State lay wholly in the revenues derived from them. The well-being of the inhabitants, except so far as it affected their tax-paying power, was not of much consequence; but the well-being of the land was of the greatest. To this was in part due the special attention paid by the Romans to tillage, to the building and maintenance of roads, and to the establishment of commercial centres. The claim advanced by Cicero[4] that the motive of the Romans was humanity was ill-grounded; but if the former motive, however selfish,[5] had been kept steadily in view, the provinces would have been well off.[6] It would be a great mistake to suppose that

---

[1] Polybius, vi. 56, xxxix. 17; but he admits a decline later on. See xviii. 35, xxxii. 11.

[2] Tac. Ann. ii. 54, states with force the view as to the corruption of the Roman character by foreign conquest.

[3] 'Praedia populi Romani,' Cic. in Verr. ii. 3; Holm, iv. 547.

[4] Cic. Div. in Caec. 5; in Verr. v. 44. Some have held that Cicero darkens the picture to bring out the contrast with his own beneficence. Cf. Hirschfeld's Aus dem Orient, p. 10; Zielinski (Cicero im Wandel der Jahrhunderte, pp. 4, 64), thinks that the Romans began provincial rule with the Scipionic ideal of a just protectorate, and that Sulla replaced it by the regular proconsular system.

[5] Passages which illustrate the selfishness of the motive are—Cic. in Verr. iii. 50 and 55; Pro lege Manilia, 6; De Leg. Agr. ii. 30, where Cicero shows that the tribute always ceased with war or other disturbance.

[6] See Marquardt, i. 398.

the misgovernment of the provinces was regarded with toleration either by public opinion or by the law. Unfortunately the men whose collective opinion was so meritorious, were not equally sound as individuals. The temptations were too strong and the control too imperfect for the average man not to yield to the one and to take advantage of the other.

The governor as possessing the most authority with the least responsibility had it in his power to inflict the greatest amount of misery. The jobbery connected with the appointments told severely in the last resort upon the provinces. If a man paid heavily to get his province, he expected to recoup himself during his administration of it. But then he could not do that without exposing himself to a trial for extortion. The judges in such trials, however, were not above a liberal bribe: all that was necessary therefore was to make enough out of the province to have something to offer to them. Verres ruled Sicily for three years; and according to Cicero he boasted that the gains of the first year would be enough for himself, those of the second year for his friends and patrons, those of the third year, which was the most productive of all, for the judges.[1] So these trials were turned from a defence of the provincials into their worst scourge; and Cicero says that he expects deputations to the Senate to beg for their abolition.[2] In any case it was well understood that a man did not expatriate himself from the pleasures of Rome for nothing[3]; to obtain a province was the recognised means of setting a bankrupt on his legs again.[4] So regular were the extortions of the governor, that when Cicero was eccentric

(marginal note: Miseries inflicted by the governor.)

---

[1] Cic. *in Verr*. Act i. 14; cf. iii. 19, sub fin.

[2] Cic. *in Verr*. Act i. 14.

[3] Apparently the Romans regarded a provincial command as a great nuisance. ' Hujus molestiae ' is the phrase used by Cicero in writing to his brother (*ad Qu. Fr*. i. 1, 1); and when Cicero was himself in Cilicia he was always longing to be back in Rome again.

[4] Cic. *in Pis*. 6.

enough to abstain from them, the grateful people of Salamis told him that they had been able to pay their debts with 'the praetor's fund,'[1] with the money, that is to say, which had hitherto been yearly laid aside to conciliate their master's good-will. And even if the governor was himself well-intentioned, it was very difficult for him to resist the importunities of his dependents and acquaintances. The comites for instance came to the province to make money, and would regard any unusual rectitude or honesty in the governor as an eccentricity mischievous to their interests. Besides this he was continually being pestered by the letters of influential Romans, begging him to get in a debt for them, or to send them wild beasts for the shows,[2] or to exempt some lands of theirs in the country from the municipal taxes.[3]   It seemed as if a governor were sent to a province not in the interests of Rome or the provinces, but to carry out the wishes of a pack of spendthrifts and usurers in the capital.

Progresses.   If we wish to go more into details, the varieties of ill-usage endured by the provincials are so numerous as to be embarrassing.   Even when on his way to his province, and before he had yet actually reached it, a Roman governor might if he chose be a burden to the cities through which he passed.   Some of Verres' worst enormities were perpetrated in Achaia,[4] though he was merely passing through that country on his way to Cilicia : and the immense credit which Cicero takes to himself for demanding little or nothing from the places through which he passed on his way to his province would be by itself a proof that other governors did not observe a similar moderation.[5]

---

1 Cic. *ad Att.* v. 21, § 11 : 'vectigali praetorio.'
2 Cic. *ad Fam.* viii. 4, 6.   3 Ib. viii. 9.
4 Cic. *in Verr.* i. 17.
5 Cic. *ad Att.* v. 10, 16, 21.   For the billeting of the governor, etc., on a journey within his province, see Cic. *in Verr.* i. 24, 25 ; *ad Att.* v. 9, 0, 16, 17 ; Livy, *Ep.* 92.

But it was not only the governor and his staff who had Lega-
tiones
Liberae.
the right to claim lodging and entertainment without paying
for it. If a senator could have a *legatio libera* granted him
by his fellow-senators, he could travel in the provinces in
this way, armed with the authority of a regular legate,
though without either duties or responsibilities, and for as
long a time as suited his convenience. Money-lending, and
in fact all business, being of a personal character, and
almost always managed directly by the principals, it was a
common thing for a senator to obtain one of these lieuten-
ancies in order to hunt up a debtor[1] or a legacy[2] in some
distant province. That these persons abused their authority,
and were burdensome and almost intolerable to the provincials, is expressly told us by Cicero.[3] Cicero himself did
his best to put an end to so disgraceful an anomaly, and
would have had a *senatus consultum* passed for their total
abolition, if a tribune had not interposed his veto. So he
contented himself with limiting their duration to one year,[4]
a period which Caesar afterwards extended to five.[5] It was
one of the benefits of the Empire that it almost got rid of
these vexatious and harassing appointments.[6]

Somewhat analogous but far worse mischiefs were caused Quarter-
ing of
troops.
by the billeting of troops in this or that city of a province
for winter-quarters. In his speech for the Manilian law
Cicero doubts whether more cities of the enemy have in

---

[1] Cic. *pro Flacco*, 34.   [2] Cic. *de Lege Agr.* i. 3, § 8.

[3] *De Lege Agr.* i. 3 : ' Hereditatum obeundarum causa, quibus vos
legationes dedistis, qui et privati et ad privatum negotium exierunt,
non maximis opibus neque summa auctoritate praediti, tamen auditis
profecto quam graves eorum adventus sociis vestris esse soleant.' Cf.
de Lege Agr. ii. 17.   Sometimes *negotiorum suorum causa*. Cic. *ad Fam.*
xii. 21.

[4] Cic. *de Lege*. iii. 8.

[5] Cic. *ad Att.* xv. 11.   The exact provisions of the lex Julia are not
really known. Willems, *Le Sénat*. i. 149, 150.

[6] See *Staatsr.* ii. 653.   The last we hear of them is under Tiberius
(Suet. *Tib.* 31), but there was substituted something of the same nature
called *commeatus*. See Suet. *Claud.*, 22.

late years been destroyed by arms, than friendly states by this system of quartering.[1] It is one of the special praises which Plutarch gives Lucullus, that he never once quartered his troops upon a friendly Greek city[2]; whereof, he adds, the soldiers much complained. Sertorius won the hearts of the Spaniards by not quartering his troops upon them[3]; and when others did so, they did it avowedly to punish a town[4] or to bribe their men.[5] It can easily be imagined what misery and shame might be inflicted by the excesses of a rough soldiery, bent upon making up for the fatigues of the campaign by a winter of idleness and debauch. In a law of 71 B.C. giving freedom to the people of Termessus in Pisidia, one of the provisions is that no Roman governor shall quarter troops upon them except by special authority of the Senate[6]; and rich towns in the province of Cilicia (and no doubt also in other provinces) regularly paid the governor large sums to be excused this terrible visitation. The people of Cyprus, for instance, paid 200 Attic talents (nearly £50,000).[7]

Other petty oppressions.

The petty oppressions of different kinds which the governor had it in his power to inflict were innumerable. It was apparently the practice in certain provinces to make requisitions of wild beasts for the Roman shows; and natives could be set to a compulsory hunt after them.[8] Still worse

---

[1] Cic. *pro Lege Manilia*, 13.　　　　[2] Plut. *Lucull.* 33.

[3] Plut. *Sert.* 6; and for the insolence of the soldiers quartered at Castulo, ib. 3.

[4] Caesar, *Bell. Civ.* ii. 18 (Varro).　　　　[5] Ib. iii. 31 (Scipio).

[6] C. I. L. i. 204: 'Nei quis magistratus prove magistratu legatus neive quis alius meilites in oppidum Thermesum maiorum Pisidarum agrum Thermensium maiorum Pisidarum hiemandi caussa introducito, neive facito quo quis eo meilites introducat quove ibi milites hiement, nisei senatus nominatim utei Thermesum maiorum Pisidarum in hiber-nacula meilites deducantur decreverit.' Bruns., p. 94.

[7] Cic. *ad Att.* v. 21, § 7. Plutarch, *Sert.* 24, speaks of Asia as βαρυνομένην δὲ ταῖς πλεονεξίαις καὶ ὑπερηφανίαις τῶν ἐπισκηνῶν.

[8] Cic. *ad Att.* vi. 1, § 20; *ad Fam.* viii. 9. In the long-run the beasts were almost exterminated, and districts rendered habitable which

was the common exaction of money from the cities under
pretence of its being a voluntary contribution towards the
expenses of the aedile at Rome. This is probably the
purpose for which Caelius begs Cicero to obtain for him
a sum of money from the cities of his province.[1] These
contributions were so regular a thing that they had a technical name (*aurum aedilicium*). Cicero speaks of them as
a 'severe and iniquitous tax[2];' and if we may argue from
one known case, as much as 200,000 sesterces was extorted
from a province by a single Aedile as its contribution to
the pleasures of the sovereign people.[3] Almost more
vexatious were the expenses incurred by the cities on
temples, statues, commemoratory festivals in honour perhaps
of the villain who had fattened upon their miseries.[4] The
deputations to Rome to sing the praises of such a governor
were another source of expense which an honest man like
Cicero would either abolish or greatly curtail, even at the
risk of offending his predecessor.[5] Then there were the
'compliments,' in reality compulsory presents, to the
governor on the occasion of the valuing of the corn which
a province had to supply[6]; and the numberless opportunities
of extortion which a governor possessed in virtue of his
supreme authority over the taxation.

But the collectors of the taxes were more formidable
even than the governor. The system of middle-men which

The
Publicani.

---

would otherwise have been too dangerous ; cf. Strabo, xvii. 3, § 15 ;
Mon. Anc., § 22. Augustus accounted for 3,500 African wild beasts ;
Titus showed 5,000 beasts in one day ; Suet. *Tit.* 7 ; cf. Spartian,
Hadr. 7 and 19 ; Pliny, viii. 24.

[1] Cic. *ad Att.* vi. 1, § 20. See also *ad Qu. Fr.* i. 1, § 9, where Cicero
says that he had as aedile refused a grant from Asia. From the same
passage it appears that the usual grant was 200 sestertia (about £1,600).

[2] 'Gravi et iniquo aediliciorum vectigali ;' Cic. *ad Qu. Fr.* i. 1, § 26.

[3] Cic. ib. ; cf. Mommsen, iii. 31.

[4] There was a festival called *Verrea* in Sicily ; Cic. *in Verr.* ii. 63.

[5] Cic. *ad Fam.* iii. 8, § 2.

[6] Cic. *in Verr.* ii. 38, 42 ; *in Pis.* 35.

the Romans had adopted saved trouble in the administration no doubt, but at a terrible expense to the provincials. In some provinces, for instance Spain, fixed payments had been introduced immediately upon conquest ; and for these therefore no middle-men were necessary. But in others, such as Sicily, Sardinia, and Asia, the chief tax was not a fixed one, but consisted in a tithe of the annual produce. There were variations in its amount ; and it seemed simpler and more convenient that the administration should be assured of a definite sum beforehand without being dependent upon the goodness or badness of the harvests. It became the practice to let out such taxes to a company of rich men,[1] perhaps invariably Roman knights,[2] for a period of five years. Such a society then paid over the lump sum at which the taxes had been let out to it, and sent some of its members to the province to act the part of tax-gatherers. If the harvests were good during the period they would gain largely on their original payment ; if they were bad they would nominally lose. Such contracts were therefore of a speculative character ; and indeed Mommsen regards the publicani as corresponding to the stock-brokers of a modern capital. But as a matter of fact they secured themselves with tolerable certainty against losses, at the expense of the tax-payers. Their power in the provinces was so great that even Cicero gives his brother Quintus a hint to advise the provincials not to insist too rigorously upon their legal rights against them, lest worse should befall them.[3] It is only too probable that they habitually and as a matter of course exacted more than their due,[4] and the control of the

---

[1] These companies, however, had many shareholders, who were not all necessarily rich men. For their occasional losses see ad Att. I. 18 ; 2, I. Cf. W. Warde Fowler, Social Life at Rome in the Age of Cicero, chap. iii. for publicani and money-lenders.

[2] Dio Cassius xxxviii. 7 : πᾶσαί τε γὰρ αἱ τελωνίαι δι' αὐτῶν ἐγίγνοντο.

[3] Cic. ad Qu. Fr. i. 1, 12.

[4] Cf. Appian, B. C. v. 4 : Τῶν δὲ ταῦτα παρὰ τῆς βουλῆς μισθουμένων ἐνυβριζόντων ὑμῖν καὶ πολὺ πλείονα αἰτούντων. Cf. St. Luke iii. 13.

governor, who alone had authority over them,[1] was wholly inefficient. If a governor kept them to their legal right their hatred to him knew no bounds[2]; and they could be exceedingly dangerous to him on his return to Rome, particularly when the *Judicia* were in their hands. Lucullus owed his recall to their determined ill-will,[3] and Rutilius his banishment. Therefore most governors acted like Verres, and shared the plunder with them. The law expressly forbade any governor to invest money in their societies; but Verres did so[4]; and even if the law was not thus impudently broken, the vast majority of governors were shamefully subservient to them.[5] The governor could do a great deal for them by forcing the cities of his province to pay up their arrears[6]; or by supporting them with military force[7]; and in the exceptional cases in which a governor from good or bad motives was unfriendly to their interests, he could apparently do them a good deal of mischief.[8] If a debtor could not or would not pay, they had legal power to put in their claim and take temporary possession of his property[9]; and, it is hinted, the actual measures they took were often far more violent and summary than this.[10] Besides the tithes, the customs' duties were regularly farmed to these middle-men, even in countries where all the other taxes were raised by the direct system. Such dues were paid in the Italian harbours till far into the life-

---

[1] Verres threatened to make them pay eight-fold if they exacted more than their due; *in Verr.* iii. 8, 10, 21, 47.

[2] Cic. *pro Plancio*, 13, illustrates this in the case of Scaevola.

[3] See p. 80. [4] Cic. *in Verr.* iii. 56.

[5] Cic. *in Verr.* iv. 41.

[6] Cic. *ad Fam.* ii. 13 ; *ad Att.* vi. 2, § 5 ; *pro Plancio*, 26. We find even Cicero condescending to apply to provincial governors, who were friends of his, to further their interests; *ad Fam.* xiii. 9, 65.

[7] Cicero, *de Prov. Cons.* 5, speaks of garrisons for their protection ; cf. Dio, xlviii. 43 : τοῖς τε στρατιώταις τοῖς συνεισπράσσουσί σφισι τὰ χρήματα.

[8] Cic. *in Pis.* 17.

[9] Cic. *in Verr.* iii. 11. [10] Ib.

time of Cicero, and were regularly collected by the publicani who had contracted for them. The complaints of their rapacity were great even in privileged Italy, and Cicero says he could not be ignorant of the fate of the allies in remote provinces when even in Italy he heard the complaints of Roman citizens.[1] They had the right of search[2]; and were in fact custom-house officers, the difference being that they were considerably stricter and more arbitrary than is possible for such officials now. Their interests were so much more directly involved that this is not at all surprising.

The miseries which the publicani inflicted might be inferred from the bitter hatred which was felt for them.[3] When Cicero wishes to give his hearers a strong impression of the loyalty and friendliness of the Sicilians, he tells them that 'they are so fond of our nation that they are the only people where neither a publican nor a money-lender is an object of detestation.'[4] The Romans fully allowed that this hatred was deserved. Livy tells us that the Senate actually gave up the working of some mines in Macedonia and other lands which brought in a great revenue, 'because they could not be managed without the publicani, and wheresoever there was a publican, there either the law was a dead letter, or the allies were no better than slaves.'[5]

The Negotiatores. The *negotiatores* or money-lenders were the complement of the publicani, though at times in conflict with them.[6] They also were often knights[7]; and held a similar, perhaps slightly inferior, social position. They could not be senators, as the law expressly forbade senators to engage in such

---

[1] Cic. *ad Qu. Fr.* i. 1, 33.

[2] Cic. *de Leg. Agr.* ii. 23 ; Marquardt, ii. 262, and his authorities.

[3] If direct evidence is wanted, see Plut. *Lucull.* 7 ; *Bell. Alex.* 70. Important passages on the farming system generally are : Cicero, *ad Qu. Fr.* i. 1, 12 ; Livy, xlv. 18.

[4] Cic. *in Verr.* ii. 3.   [5] Livy, xlv. 18.

[6] Cic. *in Verr.* iv. 20.

[7] Cic., *ad Att.* ii. 16.

business[1]; but were often the agents of senators who stayed at Rome and pocketed the profits of their shameful trade. That they were not looked down upon by public opinion is shown by a passage in which Cicero describes how a negotiator in Sicily was accustomed to entertain the governor and other officials of the province, apparently almost on a footing of equality.[2] They were in fact as a rule those knights or moneyed men for whom there was no room in the societies of the publicani. There was an immense amount of capital at Rome which could neither be absorbed by the only two recognised modes of employment for it in Italy—farming and money-lending—nor by investing it in a society of publicani. This surplus capital poured itself out upon the provinces in a golden stream, only to return to Rome in still larger volume before long. The men of business who settled themselves in the provinces after the soldiers had done their work were bankers, brokers, money-lenders, money-changers, anything in fact but legitimate traders. That in this period they seldom were, though under the Empire the word negotiator is no doubt more loosely used, and with a wider meaning.[3] The same man could not be publicanus and *negotiator* at the same time,[4] but there was nothing whatever to prevent his being both at different periods.[5] The amount of money invested in this way was so large that when the outbreak of the Mithridatic war dislocated all business operations in Asia, credit at Rome was seriously affected.[6] There were such numbers

[1] Senators were forbidden to undertake opera publica and vectigalia. They or their agents engaged in other negotia ; but it was difficult for them to leave Italy. See Willems, *Le Sénat.* i., pp. 201, 4.

[2] This was Cn. Calidius ; Cic. *in Verr.* iv. 20.

[3] No doubt they were something between bankers and money-lenders. For later meaning see Willems, *Droit. publ.*, p. 371.

[4] ' Distinguuntur publicani a negotiatoribus,' says Ernesti, and refers to Cic. *in Verr.* ii. 3 ; *pro Flac.* 16 ; *pro Lege Manil.* 7 ; *ad Att.* ii. 16. He does not, however, add the necessary qualification of the text. Vell., ii. 11 : per publicanos aliosque in Africa negotiantes.

[5] Cic. *pro Rab. Post.* 2 ; Suet. *Vesp.* 1.   [6] Cic. *pro Lege Manil.* 7.

of these bankers in Gaul that, according to Cicero, not a
single payment passed from hand to hand without the intervention of one of them.[1]   They were particularly numerous
and influential in Africa.[2]   Cato formed three hundred of
them into a council for the government of Thapsus[3]; and
they furnished the Pompeian generals with money.[4]   As
they had taken the losing side, Caesar made them pay
heavily for their mistake.   Their contribution was two
million sesterces; five million sesterces were required from
the Roman settlers of Adrumetum; and it is especially
noticeable that in each case the sum paid by the Romans
settled in the place was larger than that imposed on the
citizens themselves.[5]

These bankers had large dealings with private persons;
but they had also to do with foreign princes, and with
provincial towns.   P. Sittius, afterwards the well-known
condottiere in Africa, had dealings of this sort, in particular
with the king of Mauretania[6]; and Brutus and Pompey
had both lent money to the unfortunate Ariobarzanes.[7]
Similarly the Rabirius Postumus whom Cicero defended
had the king of Egypt among his debtors.[8]   But much
more frequent and important were their dealings with the
provincial towns.   What with the legal taxation and the
illegal exactions of the publicani, the towns of Asia Minor
(to take the instance with which we are most familiar) were
unable to pay their taxes.   There were two ways of raising
the money, by imposing a tribute upon their own citizens,
or by borrowing.[9]   Unfortunately the latter fatal course
was too often adopted, and the town fell into the hands of

[1] Cic. *pro Fonteio*, i., § 11.   [2] Sall. *Jug.* 65.
[3] Plut. *Cat. Min.* 59; Merivale, ii. 359.   [4] *Bell Afr.* 90.
[5] Merivale, ii. 367.
[6] Cic. *pro Sulla*, 20.   [7] Cic. *ad Att.* vi. 1, § 3.
[8] Cic. *pro Rab. Post.* 2; Suet. *Claud*, 16.
[9] Cic. *pro Flacco*, 9: 'In aerario nihil habent civitates, nihil in
vectigalibus; duae rationes conficiendae pecuniae aut versura aut
tributo.'

one of the numerous negotiatores, who were ever on the watch for such an opportunity. There was no law to regulate the rate of interest in the provinces, as there was in Italy, and it often rose to 24, 36, or even 48 per cent. The latter was the rate claimed by Scaptius from the Salaminians. The hopeless and miserable indebtedness brought about by such a state of things was not viewed with entire satisfaction at Rome, and in 58 B.C. a law was passed (*Lex Gabinia*) to make such loans to towns illegal. But the law was a dead letter; it was in one case at all events evaded by special senatorial decree,[1] and the unholy system was still in full force under the early Empire.[2] The sums owed were often very large. Nicaea in Bithynia owed eight million sesterces to a ward of Cicero's[3]; and it was worth the while of the people of Apollonia to bribe their governor with two hundred talents to avoid being obliged to pay what Cicero calls 'their just debts.'[4] A governor could do a great deal to relieve the cities of his province of old debts and to discourage them from contracting new ones[5]; but he more often preferred to give their creditors the support of his authority when they demanded payment. This might be done by comparatively gentle means, and ostensibly at all events by moral influence[6]; but more often, it is probable, by doing what Verres promised to do, namely by putting the lictors at the service of a creditor.[7]

The indebted cities were really in a state of absolute bondage to such creditors as these. A wealthy Roman negotiator in a little country town which owed him money was worse than an eastern tyrant. To read stories, such as those which Cicero hints at in the *pro Flacco*, of the ruin

---

[1] Cic. *ad Att.* v. 2, § 1.

[2] Tac. *Ann.* iii. 40: Galliarum civitates ob magnitudinem aeris alieni rebellionem coeptavere.

[3] Cic. *ad Fam.* xiii. 61 ; cf. ib. xiii. 56.   [4] Cic. *in Pis.* 35.

[5] Cic. *ad Qu. Fr.* i. 1, 8,

[6] Cic. *pro Murena*, 20.

[7] Cic. *in Verr.* ii. 29.

and shame thus brought upon the little towns of Asia, is enough to sicken the heart and fire the blood with idle though righteous indignation. Even in a well-known and prominent place like Salamis in Cyprus, five of the municipal senators were locked up and starved to death by that same Scaptius who sought to obtain a prefecture from Cicero, in order to enact again, if it seemed profitable, a similar tragedy.   And it is right to remember that Scaptius was but the tool of no less a man than Brutus.   An agent is not bound to have a conscience ; and it is impossible to acquit Brutus of a heavy share of guilt in this miserable business.   And yet it cannot be supposed that Brutus was worse than many other money-lenders, or even as bad.   With such facts as these in view it is no wonder that the negotiatores were detested in all the provinces, and that a revolt generally began by a massacre of them.[1]

The effects of war in Asia.

But all this was as nothing compared to the state of things caused by the Mithridatic and Civil Wars.[2]   The miseries of the people of Asia are proved by the enthusiasm with which they welcomed Mithridates, and by the terrible massacre of the Roman citizens of the province.[3] But their sufferings were all the worse in the end.   Their country was made the battle-ground of the contending armies ; the licentious and mutinous soldiers of Fimbria were let loose upon them to work their will unchecked ; and when Sulla had brought the campaign to a successful conclusion he imposed a fine of 20,000 talents upon their cities.[4]   Still worse than this was their lot in the Civil Wars.   Pompey and his lieutenants needed money, and made requisitions which had to be obeyed[5]: it was fortunate that Caesar proved a milder conqueror than they had

---

[1] Caesar, *B. G.* vii. 3, 42 ; Cic. *ad Att.* v. 21 ; vi. 1 ; Tac. *Hist.* iv. 15 ; and Vell. ii. 110 (Pannonia).

[2] Besides the instances mentioned in the text, Illyria seems to have suffered greatly from the civil dissensions ; *Bell. Alex.* 42.

[3] Appian, *Mith.* 61 ; Val. Max. ix. 2.   [4] Plut. *Lucull.* 4.

[5] Caesar, *B. C.* iii. 3, 31, 2.

reason to expect. The treatment they received from Brutus and Cassius, and afterwards from Antony, filled up the measure of their sufferings. Brutus made them pay over ten years' tribute in one year, and when Antony visited them after Philippi, he demanded a similar sum.[1] The unfortunate cities represented to him their absolute inability to pay it; and he with difficulty consented to its being changed into nine years' tribute payable in three yearly instalments. These incredible exactions proved too much even for the wealth of Asia,[2] broken and ruined as the country had been by a succession of the most terrible misfortunes ; and a universal bankruptcy followed,[3] which Augustus had to meet by a remission of taxes, and even by a general cancelling of debts.[4]

The condition of Greece was not much better. Athens Greece. in particular stood a long siege from Sulla, and when taken was treated with terrible severity.[5] There was such a massacre that very few of the original citizens survived. When, under Tiberius, Piso passed through the place on his way to Syria, he 'terrified the citizens of Athens in a bitter speech, with indirect reflections on Germanicus, who he said had derogated from the honour of the Roman name in having treated with excessive courtesy, not the people of Athens, who indeed had been exterminated by repeated disasters, but a miserable medley of tribes.'[6] Sulla also treated Boeotia with great severity,[7] and though the Greek cities found comparatively merciful masters in Caesar and Augustus, it was unfortunate that the great majority of

[1] Appian, B. C. v. 4 ; Marquardt, ii. 197.
[2] Cicero, pro Lege Manil. 6, illustrates that wealth.
[3] Dio. Chrys. i. p. 601 R ; Marquardt, ii. 400, note 5.
[4] Marquardt, ii. 199. To all the other misfortunes of Asia we may add (if it is possible to argue from the cities of Cilicia—Cic. ad Att. vi. 2, § 5—to the cities of Asia) that their own municipal magistrates plundered the local revenues.
[5] Finlay, i. 26 and 54 ; Vell, ii. 23.
[6] Tac. Ann. ii. 55. [7] Finlay, i. 54.

them took the losing side in the Civil Wars.[1]   Greece fell
rapidly into a state of decline, from which it did not
recover.[2]   The poor soil of the country needed a full population and all the advantages of peace and wealth to keep
it cultivated ; and even under the early Empire, Greece is
that part of the Roman dominions on which it is least
pleasant to dwell.[3]

Spain.

Even in the western half of the Empire the provinces
were badly off, though their sufferings were not to be compared to those of Greece or Asia.   Spain was alienated by
a succession of bad governors, and so was not unwilling to
throw in its lot with a rebel like Sertorius.   The account
of the governorship of Q. Cassius Longinus, which we
happen to possess, lets in a lurid light upon the possible
misdoings of a governor even in a province generally so
well treated as that of Spain.   It is significant, however,
that the citizens of Italica (Santiponce) made a plot against
him, in which part of his own army joined, and very nearly
succeeded in assassinating him.[4]   The Spaniards had still
enough of their high spirit left to make it dangerous
to oppress them ; and this, along with their fortunate
exemption from the publicani, contributed greatly to

Sicily.

the general good treatment which they enjoyed.   Sicily
seems to have been tolerably treated on the whole ; the
island had brought no accusations against its governors
before that against Verres.   But the three years of Verres'
rule were years of unexampled misery and wrong ; and

[1] Sparta was an exception, as it sent troops to Octavius.   Brutus
promised his soldiers the sack of Sparta and Thessalonica in the event
of victory ; Finlay, ib. ; App. *B. C.* iv. 118.

[2] Cf. the letter of Sulpicius to Cicero (*Fam.* iv. 5), with Polyb.
xxxvii. 9.

[3] That the circumstances of Greece were exceptional is to be borne
in mind in reading the strictures on the Early Empire in Finlay's first
volume.   See Mahaffy, *Greek World under Roman Sway*, ch. xii.

[4] Plut. *Sert.* 6 ; Dio Cassius xlii. 15, 16 ; *B. Alex.* 48, 64 ; Livy,
Ep. cxi.

Lepidus, the third member of the second triumvirate, did his best to follow in his footsteps. There is indeed no part of the Roman world where some infamous governor had not left his mark. ' There have been many guilty magistrates in Asia, many in Spain, in Gaul, in Sardinia, even in Sicily itself,' says Cicero.[1] A Gabinius ill-used Syria,[2] a Piso or a C. Antonius Macedonia.[3] And even if such a governor was exiled for extortion, he had it in his power to make the people who received him miserable.[4]

Such an administration as that which I have attempted General to describe could not in the nature of things be permanent. remarks Its machinery was bad, and its agents were worse. If a on the government can avail itself of men of high character and Republican capacity, an imperfect system can be made to work toler- administration. ably well; but there can be no hope when both the system and the men are equally wanting. The system had at least three cardinal faults :—the inadequacy of the senatorial control; the thoroughly bad and unscientific system of taxation ; and the annual change of governor. The imperfect execution of the laws intended to control the governor is hardly a fault of the system. The laws themselves were good enough, but men could not be found who could be trusted to carry them out honestly without fear or favour. It was indispensable that the interests of the judges and of the executive should be divorced from the interests of the governors, before reform was possible. Collision was at all events better than collusion of interests.

Events at Rome co-operated with the misgovernment of Incapa-city of the the provinces to put an end to the authority of the Senate. Senate. Sheer disorder and incompetence must, after a time, become intolerable to every one ; and the fact that it was

---

[1] Cic. *in Verr.* ii. 65 ; cf. vi. 48.   [2] Cic. *in Pis.* 21.
[3] Cic. *in Pis.* 40; Finlay, i. 38.
[4] *E.g.*, C. Antonius, Cicero's colleague, in Cephallenia ; Strabo, x. 2 : ἐν τῇ Κεφαλληνίᾳ διέτριψε καὶ τὴν ὅλην νῆσον ὑπήκοον ἔσχεν, ὡς ἴδιον κτῆμα.

not possible to take a sea-voyage without danger can hardly have been viewed with much patience.[1]   It was also becoming evident that the provinces could not much longer supply the taxation, unless they were better treated.   We find repeated hints in Cicero of the ' existing difficulties of the treasury,'[2] and those Romans who could look at all beyond the immediate present could not fail to perceive the dangers in store for them, unless their administration were in every part drawn together, strengthened, and held in control.   As the Senate had proved its absolute incompetence in the judgment of every one, was the Assembly to be the supreme executive body ?   That was still more out of the question ; and what then remained except a military despotism which should at all events secure peace and good management ?

The large commands.   The large and protracted commands, instances of which had long been frequent, pointed in this direction.   In theory the idea of each province as a separate and independent unit still existed ; it was a special favour when one governor admitted another into his province,[3] unless the step was dictated by military necessities.[4]   But such a system would not work in practice.   On special occasions we find several provinces grouped together under one command ; Greece for instance with Macedonia and Illyricum[5]; or Illyricum with Further or with Hither Gaul.   Pompey had all three Spanish commands, Lepidus, Narbonensis and Hither Spain.[6]   Military reasons would of necessity bring about this disregard of the traditional mode of regarding the provinces.   In so far as the Republican government discharged its paramount duty of protecting the provinces from external enemies, it did so by means of large com-

---

[1] Cic. *in Verr.* v. 25, 38 ; *ad Att.* xvi. 2.
[2] Cic. *de Prov. Cons.* 5 ; *pro Balbo*, 27.
[3] Cf. Cic. *in Verr.* ii. 29.   [4] Cic. *ad Att.* vi. 5.
[5] Cic. *Phil.* x. 11.
[6] Dio C. 43, 51 ; and for the wide commands of Brutus and Cassius, Vell ii. 62, App. *B. C.* 3, 63.

mands which violated both the letter and the spirit of the existing constitution. Pompey's command against the pirates involved the subordination to him of all governors into whose province the war might carry him, and he was permitted to appoint legates to represent him, each of whom in virtue of such appointment acquired the imperium.[1] This surely was change enough ; but when Pompey further ruled the province from Rome by means of legates, we see the regular imperial system in full bloom. The commands given to Caesar, to Crassus, and those proposed to be given by the Agrarian Law—which Cicero combated—to a commission of Ten,[2] were equally unconstitutional. The Senate saw its authority threatened by such commands, and regarded them with great jealousy,[3] while the democrats supported them on that account with all the greater zeal. The signal success usually attained by these commanders induced even moderate men to regard them as an unavoidable necessity.

With the rapid extension of the Roman dominion the need for a strong and compact military administration had become more and more pressing. At present there was no such thing as a Roman army, but only detachments of troops stationed in the different provinces, practically owing obedience only to the governor, and without organic cohesion of any kind. The necessity for re-organisation betrayed itself here perhaps more clearly than in any part of the system, and the need was recognised by Augustus. But in every part of the administration the same phenomena were visible. The provinces had been governed without any definite scheme or purpose, in accordance with the pressing needs of the passing hour, and anxious deliberation for the future could be no longer delayed. One of those critical

(margin note: Necessity of reform in the army.)

---

[1] Plut. *Pomp.*[25. [2] Cic. *de Leg. Agr.*
[3] Cic. *pro Leg. Manil.* 9, where in defending Lucullus' recall he says : ' Vestro jussu coactus qui imperii diuturnitati modum statuendum vetere exemplo putavistis ' ; cf. Cic. *Phil.* xi. 7, 8.

points had arrived at which long-existent forces finally and overpoweringly assert themselves, and from which must date a new departure.[1]

[1] The provinces facilitated the introduction of the Empire, because they made it possible to obtain men and money without the authority of the Senate. The Pompeian soldiers in Africa set the precedent of selecting their own imperator (Vell. Pat. ii. 54), and after Caesar's death the quaestor of Asia took it upon himself to offer the revenues of Asia to Octavian as his successor, though he had no office (Nic. Damasc. *Vita Caesaris*, 18, in *Frag. H. Gr.* iii.).

CHAPTER IV.

The Period of the Early Empire.

JULIUS CAESAR had shown a capacity for rising to the needs The policy of his time which makes us all the more regret his untimely Julius death. Such radical and beneficent reforms as that of the Caesar; abolition of the tithes in Sicily and Asia; such comprehensive measures as his *Lex Julia Municipalis;* such practical improvements as those involved in the survey which he ordered, and in his reformation of the Calendar; all these and many more were the work of eighteen months of Empire. He had shown a wise economy in his restriction of the corn largesses, and an unexpected conservatism in his dealings with the law courts. Above all, his immense system of colonisation, along with his liberality in the bestowal of the franchise and his treatment of the Senate, especially in the incorporation of provincial members, shows how fully he had grasped the idea of an equally-privileged and homogeneous Empire ; and how he sought on the one hand to send Rome into the provinces, and on the other hand to bring the provinces to Rome.

Augustus with his narrower intellect was not equally of Augustus. capable of taking advantage of his unexampled opportunity. He regarded it as his duty to follow out the lines of his adoptive father's policy; but he had a talent for details rather than a genius for great combinations, and he deserted his guidance just where he should most closely have followed it. An examination of the measures which the two emperors either proposed or carried out, in so far as they affected the provinces directly or indirectly, is indispensable for an understanding of the period.[1]

Julius saw that one great cause of the misery of the provinces lay in the iniquitous system of taxation. He therefore, besides remitting for the present half of the taxation of Asia, abolished the tithes altogether; and did the same probably also in Sicily.[2] This meant an immense change, for besides that definite sums known beforehand were substituted for an ever-varying tithe, the publicani, except for the customs' duties and other indirect taxes of minor importance, were done away with. Augustus maintained this arrangement; and though we still hear complaints of the publicani under his successors, their opportunities for wrongdoing were greatly diminished, and a great decline sets in from the position of consideration and social dignity which, in the eyes of the Romans at all events, they had formerly enjoyed.

The Census. Of still greater importance in respect of the taxation was the census. The great fault of the taxation of the earlier period had been its irregular and arbitrary character. This largely proceeded from the want of any definite register of property which would make a fair apportionment possible. And if this was injurious to the provincials, it was also a fatal impediment to good government that it was impossible to calculate the revenue with any exactness beforehand. But to take a census implied immense and continued preliminary labours. The only country which had been

---

[1] Mr. Arnold had intended somewhat to modify this estimate of Caesar and Augustus. He, however, illustrated Caesar's virtues by certain quotations—his eloquence (Vell. Pat. ii. 36); his unfailing foresight (Dio Cass. xxxi. 4); his clemency (Vell. Pat. ii. 56); and the uselessness of killing him when another master was certain to take his place (Vell. Pat. ii. 72; Suet. *Caes.* 86; Gardthausen, *Augustus*, i. p. 29; Holm, *Greece*, iv. 740.)

[2] Dio Cass. 42, 6 (for Asia); Bouché Leclercq, *Manuel*, p. 235, note 2. The statement as to Sicily is rather an inference. It does not seem to be positively stated anywhere.

adequately surveyed before the Romans took the work in hand was Egypt; and here the Romans were content to leave well alone. But in the other, particularly the Western provinces, the work had to be done from the beginning; and in the hurry and confusion of the last years of the Republic it could not be even considered. But with the accession of Caesar came a momentary rest and lull; and Caesar seems at once to have put his hand to this great work. His *Lex Julia Municipalis* settled the census arrangements for Italy.[1] It was to be taken in each municipium or colony by the chief municipal magistrates; and deputies sent with the result to Rome, fifty days before the day fixed for the conclusion of the census in the capital. If a man had houses in more than one municipium he could have his census taken at Rome; but all other Italians must have it taken in their own municipium. It is noticeable that nothing is said here of those smaller towns, *fora* or *conciliabula*, which along with *municipia*, *coloniae*, and *praefecturae* make up an exhaustive classification of the political units recognised by Rome. The fact was that they had no magistrates capable of taking the census—no *quinquennales* —and so for these purposes were no doubt attached to a neighbouring municipium.

There is here no question of a survey. The *agrimensores* had indeed done their work long ago in every part of Italy; and the whole country was thoroughly mapped out. But before a census could be taken in the provinces, the first surveys had of necessity to be made. A survey of the whole Empire was ordered by Caesar, and carried out by Augustus.[2]

---

[1] See § 142-158 of the Law ; C. I. L. i., p. 120. Bruns, p. 102.

[2] The evidence for the Augustan census of the provinces is summarised in Pauly-Wissowa s.v. *Census*, where references are given to the researches of Humbert, Unger, and Kubitschek. Our literary authorities, as Dion Cassius, Josephus, and the epitome of Livy, have evidence for the census in Gaul, Spain and Syria ; as to other parts the information is chiefly epigraphic. The governor in most cases

The Survey.

The necessary labours began between the year 49 B.C. and 48 B.C., and did not end till late in the reign of Augustus.[1] Zenodotus, entrusted with the survey of the East, terminated his labours in the year 31 B.C. ; Theodotus, to whom was given the North, in the year 25 B.C. ; Didymus, in the West, in the year 27 B.C. ; and Polycletus, who had the South, in the second or third year of the Christian era. Simultaneously the collection of geographical materials of every kind had been actively proceeded with ; and from them under Agrippa's supervision[2] had been made a map, the model of later ones such as that of Peutinger or those of the Itineraria.[3]

After the survey was completed, it was possible to take a census, so as to ascertain both the population and the paying power of the Empire. The main positive authority for this universal census is the *Monumentum Ancyranum*[4] ; but it is possible to point to several occasions on which a

The Census.

partial or local census was taken. We know that Augustus himself held a census (27 B.C.) in the three Gauls. Others were afterwards taken by Drusus (12 B.C.) and Germanicus (A.D. 14); and again later on under Nero (A.D. 61) and Domitian. In the case of Judaea again, the census was taken on its being united to the province of Syria (A.D. 6) the earlier, probably in 7-6 B.C. having been under Herod's authority. The same measure was carried out, notwithstanding its unpopularity, in other provinces immediately on their formation, for instance in Britain and Dacia.

---

was charged with the duty, employing equestrian officials and pro-curators for special districts. In the Eastern provinces at least there is evidence of a 14-year cycle anticipating the Indictions of the later Empire. *Cf.* Ramsay, *Was Christ born at Bethlehem ?*

[1] C. I. L. iii. Suppl., p. 122 ; Rushforth, 23 ; *Mon. Ancyr.* ed. Mommsen, pp. 166, 177.

[2] See Pliny, *N. H.* iii. 3, fin.

[3] See Teuffel, *Roman Literature*, § 406.

[4] § 8, but the reference is primarily at least to full citizens.

The census—as already hinted—was a much easier matter in the senatorial provinces, which already had for the most part something of the kind, than in the imperial provinces, where were few towns and little civilisation. Labours of great difficulty had to be carried out in these provinces, to make a census possible, but once started it was a regular business enough, carried out by imperial officials in *all* provinces—senatorial as well as imperial. These officials fall into three classes: 1. The district officers who made out the lists or, when this was done by the local magistrates, had a revising power. Such an official was called *adjutor ad census, censor*, or *censitor*. So we find the census of the free state of the Remi (Rheims) taken all by itself, and its censor named. The officials of the second class could not do the work of the whole province, and it had to be parcelled out. In this way is to be explained the curious inscription which calls a man *censitor provinciae Lugdunensis, item Lugduni*[1]—meaning that to a general supervision of the lists of the whole province, this official joined the special duty of taking the census in Lyons itself. Where the towns were not so large and important as this, one man could take the census in a considerable number. Thus we find one man— in this case nothing but a cavalry officer—taking the census of forty-four civitates in Africa.[2] No such officials inter- fered with whatever towns of Roman or Latin constitution there might be in the province. In all such, whether colonies or municipia, the *quinquennales* (so called because, though they only held office for one year, there was always a five years' interval from one census to another) took the census themselves, and sent in the results to the provincial censor.[3] It will be noticed how closely these arrangements are copied from those of the *Lex Julia Municipalis*. 2. A provincial censor in each province, who can be pointed out

---

[1] Eph. Epigr. iv. 541. [2] C. I. L. iii. 388.
[3] See Marquardt, i. 486, for the Quinquennales, but, especially, Henzen, 7075, p. 423.

at all events in the three Gauls, Lower Germany, Tarraconensis, Lusitania, Gallaecia, Pannonia, Thracia, Mauretania, among imperial, and in Narbonensis and Macedonia
among senatorial, provinces. The lists of his province were
deposited in the archives of his capital, and a copy forwarded to Rome. These officials were at first always of
senatorial rank ; the first Roman knight who was entrusted
with the duty ('*primo umquam Eq. Rom. censibus accipiendis*'
runs the inscription) is probably not much earlier than the year
A.D. 200. These later equestrian censors are distinguishable
by being always called *procurator*, whereas the title of the
earlier provincial censor of senatorial rank was *legatus*.[1]
3. The supreme control lay with the emperor, to whom
were addressed petitions about the tribute, and who increased or diminished the payments. His minister for this
work was no doubt the one called *Magister a censibus* or
magister a libellis.[2]

The Bre-
viarium
Imperii.
With the materials gained mainly through the surveys
and the census, Augustus was able to compile that
Breviarium Imperii which Tiberius read to the assembled
Senate after the death of its author. ' This contained a
description of the resources of the State, of the number of
citizens and allies under arms, of the fleets, subject kingdoms, provinces, taxes direct and indirect, necessary expenses and customary bounties.'[3] A similar account is
given by Suetonius[4] and Dio. Cassius,[5] with the addition
that along with this Breviarium, and with the directions as
to his funeral, went another volume containing that ' Record
of his achievements ' (*Index rerum gestarum*) which we know
under the name of the *Monumentum Ancyranum*. In this
way a regular budget came into existence, which kept the
government regularly informed of its probable revenues,

---

[1] Henzen, 6944.

[2] See Rénier, *Mélanges*, pp. 46-70 ; Marquardt, ii. 210 et seq.
Dessau, 1454.

[3] Tac. *Ann.* i. 11.   [4] Suet. *Aug.* 101.   [5] Dio. lvi. 33.

and tended to check undue exactions. It was no longer open to a governor to send as much or as little from his province as he pleased. The regularity and method thus introduced into the administration enabled a largely increased amount of taxation to be obtained from the provinces without oppression. But it is not possible to regard with entire satisfaction the first beginnings of that perfectly organised and terribly effective machine of taxation which in the end destroyed the Empire and strangled the provincials in its iron grasp. These effects, however, though they perhaps then for the first time appeared in germ, took two centuries to become formidable; and meanwhile the arrangements of Augustus secured a regular and fairly equitable system. It is in these arrangements, impressive by their enormous scale, that Augustus best understood and carried out Caesar's design.

The system of transmarine colonisation commenced by Julius was actively carried out by Augustus. The objects of the system were to provide for the superabundant poor population of Italy, and to hold out a prospect to the soldiers after they had served their time. Caesar settled in all 80,000 Italians across the sea [1]; and in particular Corinth which the Republic had destroyed was colonised by Julius, who also formed the design, carried out by his successor, of resettling Carthage.[2] Augustus in the *Monumentum* records: 'About five hundred thousand Roman citizens served under my standard, of whom I sent back to their towns or planted in colonies more than 30,000.' [3] Again: 'I planted military colonies in Africa, Sicily, both Spains, Achaia, Asia, Syria, Gallia Narbonensis, Pisidia.' [4] The numerous colonies calling themselves by the title of *Julia Augusta* are among

Transmarine colonies.

[1] Suet. *Jul.* 42.
[2] Dio, xliii. 50 ; Plut. *Caes.* 60 ; Nicol. Dam., Vit. *Caes.* 12 (in *Frag. Hist. Gr.*, iii. 432), Tert. *Pall.*, 1, App. *Pun.* 136.
[3] *Mon. Anc.* § 3.
[4] *Mon. Anc.* § 28 ; the Sicilian colonies were perhaps intended to dehellenise the island (Holm).

those thus founded by Augustus. In the majority of cases these new settlers formed entirely new foundations, not settled in, but attached to existing cities, which were thereby raised to the rank of colonies.[1]   Unfortunately Augustus' arrangements seem to have been marked by a good deal of unnecessary and mischievous arbitrariness. Thus Nicopolis, founded in memory of Actium, was formed by compelling Epirots, Aetolians, and Acarnanians to desert their existing homes and settle in it whether they wished or not.[2]   On the other hand, it must be put down to the credit of Augustus that he paid for all lands on which he settled his colonists, both in Italy and in the provinces. According to his own account he was the first who ever did so. ' That I did, first and alone of all men who planted military colonies in Italy or the provinces.' [3]

The bestowal of the franchise.   In this way something was done to check the pauperism of Italy, to provide a future for the soldiers, and to Romanise the provinces. But it was all of little use if it did not go along with a liberal bestowal of the franchise. Otherwise the founding of these privileged colonies in the centre of an unprivileged district could only intensify the hateful feeling of legal inferiority, as mischievous to the Roman as to the provincial, which it should have been the object of a great statesman to do all in his power to eradicate. Julius had seen this clearly, and all the evidence goes to show that he had every intention of doing all that in him lay to put an end to this invidious and fatal difference between Rome and her subjects. It was by such extension of her franchise, and such incorporation of new elements that Rome had become great ; and every principle of statesmanship urged her to continue in the same path. Augustus, however, broke with those traditions. Partly from financial causes,

---

[1] This appears from a comparison of § 16 with § 3 of the *Mon. Anc.*

[2] Dio Cass. 51, 1 : τοὺς μὲν συναγείρας τοὺς δὲ ἀναστήσας τῶν πλησιοχώρων.   Pausan. 5, 23, 3 ; 7, 18, 8,

[3] *Mon. Anc.* § 16.

partly because the hope of the franchise was needed to induce provincials to serve in the army (*auxilia*), partly from that ultra-Roman sentiment which was both natural to him and diligently cultivated, he drew the line sharply between the conqueror and the conquered.[1] So the process was made a slow and gradual one, and only accomplished by Caracalla in the third century, when, but for the timid conservatism of Augustus, it might have been accomplished in the first. The number of citizens in the year 70 B.C. was 450,000,[2] in 28 B.C. it was over 4,000,000. This shows the immensity of its extension in that period of forty-two years, and a large share of this good work is to be ascribed to Julius. The *Monumentum Ancyranum* permits us to see in great detail what was the part played by Augustus. In the year 28 B.C. was taken the first census ; the number of Roman citizens was 4,063,000. A second was taken in 8 B.C. ; the number was 4,230,000. A third in A.D. 13 ; the number was 4,937,000.[3] That is to say, in forty-one years the increase was only 900,000, a number which can be explained entirely by the natural growth of population, and which compels us to suppose that the franchise was given very sparingly.[4]

The same tendencies appear in Augustus' treatment of the Senate. Julius had raised its numbers, had largely admitted provincials, and, in so far as he paid it any attention at all, appears to have aimed at making it representative of all classes of the State.[5] The same policy is shown

Augustus and the Senate.

---

[1] If the wise and liberal sentiments which Dio puts into the mouth of Maecenas were ever uttered, Augustus certainly paid no attention to them. For his dislike of extending the franchise see Suet. *Aug.* 40; Dio Cass. 56, 33 (one of his maxims left at death): μήτ᾽ αὖ ἐς τὴν πολιτείαν συχνοὺς ἐσγράφωσιν, ἵνα πολὺ τὸ διάφορον αὐτοῖς πρὸς τοὺς ὑπηκόους ᾖ. Still he did grant it at times ; see Suet. *Aug.* 47. Merita erga pop. R. allegantes Latinitate vel civitate donavit.

[2] Livy, *Epit.* 98.   [3] *Mon. Anc.* § 8.

[4] Under Claudius the number was 5,984,072 ; Tac. *Ann.* xi. 25.

[5] Suet. *Jul.* 41, 80.

by his creation at his simple will and pleasure of a number of new patrician families.[1] Augustus, though creating some new patrician families in 29 B.C.,[2] admitted no one into the Senate who did not possess at all events 1,200,000 sesterces (about £10,000); he entertained the idea of restoring it to its primitive number of 300[3]; and did at all events reduce it from the number at which it had been left by Caesar, to 600. He gave it a great deal of nominal power and dignity; and put this plutocratic assembly more in the forefront of the State than ever. He appears to have regarded himself as a reformer entirely in the conservative interest; and now that the comitia had been practically reduced to a nullity, the emperor and the Senate were left confronting one another as the sovereign powers of the State. But in reality the power of the emperor rested on something very real, the arms, namely, of his soldiers; and the power and dignity of the Senate on nothing but his will. Augustus, however, handed over to the Senate a large share of the administration; and Tiberius followed in the same track. The trials for extortion, the complaints and demands of the provinces, in fact the chief judicial and executive business, came regularly before the Senate. It is not long before it also became the chief legislative chamber. The last regular law was passed in the year A.D. 97,[4] and after that date the legislation of the Empire took the shape either of senatus consulta or of imperial edicts. It is not till the reign of Septimius Severus that a senatus consultum was passed for the last time.[5] But the elaborate make-believe

---

[1] Suet. *Jul.* 41.

[2] *Mon. Anc.* 8 : Patriciorum numerum auxi consul quintum iussu populi et senatus.

[3] Dio. liv. 14.

[4] Under Nerva; Gaius, 1, 157, 171 ; Ulpian, 11, 8; Dig. 47, 21, 3, 1. Mommsen, *Staatsr.* iii. 346 ; Karlowa, *Röm. Rechtsgeschichte*, i. 624.

[5] Ortolan, *History of Roman Law* (ed. Cutler, p. 293) ; and as late as the time of Caracalla Ulpian remarks: ' Non ambigitur senatum ius facere posse.'

of Augustus could not be concealed for long; he himself had to compel the possessors of the necessary census to enter the Senate against their will[1]; and the upshot of his policy was to give the Senate an outward dignity and apparent power which not only made it sometimes misunderstand its real position, but inevitably made it an object of jealousy and suspicion to a bad emperor. Tiberius, regarding it as a kind of religious duty to follow in his adoptive father's steps, imitated him in his treatment of the Senate,[2] and, in form at all events, referred to it all important matters. 'Caligula was the first emperor to show plainly his suspicion of it and aversion from it[3]; and after him every bad emperor regularly made a sacrifice of its best members. Claudius paid it a great deal of respect,[4] and on his accession Nero promised to observe the same policy.[5] But before long we find him vowing that he would be rid of it[6]; no important matter was referred to it[7]; and its members—men like Paetus Thrasea—were sacrificed to his insane jealousy. If we regard simply the interests of the senators themselves, Augustus' attempted rehabilitation of their authority does not seem to have been an unmixed advantage to them. The utter want of dignity and self-control which Pliny describes as characterising their meetings in the time of Trajan,[8] is what we should expect of an assembly which was the victim of a bad emperor and the spoilt child of a good one.

In some minor points Augustus partly imitated and partly deviated from Caesar's policy. He restored to the *tribuni aerarii* the place in the juries which Julius had taken from them; and the principle of the five years' interval between urban and provincial office again became the law.[9] Julius' brilliant idea[10] of codifying the undigested mass of Roman *Relation of Augustus' policy to that of Julius in other respects.*

---

[1] Dio. liv. 26.   [2] Tac. *Ann.* iii. 10, iv. 15; Suet. *Tib.* 30.
[3] Suet. *Calig.* 49.   [4] Suet. *Claud.* 12.
[5] Tac. *Ann.* xiii. 4.   [6] Suet. *Nero*, 37.
[7] Tac. *Hist.* iv. 9.   [8] Plin. *Ep.* iii. 20, iv. 25, viii. 14.
[9] Dio. liii. 14; Marquardt, i. 382.   [10] Suet. *Jul.* 44.

law does not seem to have made any impression on Augustus; and it was left to Hadrian to commence and to Justinian to complete the work. On .the other hand, he saw himself obliged, as Julius had been obliged, to maintain the ruinous and hateful system of corn largesses. Caesar had reduced the number of recipients to 150,000.[1] Augustus fixed it at 200,000[2]; and at that number it remained till the time of Alexander Severus. It would be superfluous to dwell upon the mischiefs of the system, as perpetuating and emphasising the invidious position of superior privilege enjoyed by the Roman mob, as destroying the agriculture of Italy, and as establishing a heavy drain upon the corn-producing provinces. But on the other hand, it must be remembered that the strength of the tie thus established between Rome and the provinces which fed her,[3] brought selfish motives into play on the side of equity and indulgence, and prevented even the worst and most careless of emperors from tolerating misconduct in the governors of the land which grew the 'sacred corn.'[4]

Organisation of the Army. There seems to have been no comprehensive plan left by Julius to assist Augustus in his organisation of the army. The great commander no doubt perceived the necessity of an organised defence of the frontiers, but preferred to settle for himself what these frontiers should be before defending

[1] Suet. *Jul.* 41. The number had been 320,000—figures which permit us to argue as to the population of Rome. Marquardt, ii. 115, puts this at 1,600,000.

[2] *Mon. Anc.* § 15.

[3] Tac. *Ann.* xii. 43. The necessity of the foreign supplies to Rome was so absolute that the shipowners were specially exempted from taxation (Tac. *Ann.* xiii. 51). Regular fleets, belonging to the State, the *classis Alexandrina* and *classis Africana*, brought the corn to Rome (Seneca, *Epp.* 77, §§ 1, 2; Aurel. Vict. *Epit.* 1, § 1; Suet. *Aug.* 98). This necessity obliged Octavian to come to terms with Sext. Pompeius (App. *B. C.* v. 72; Suet. *Aug.* 16). Vespasian had the idea of starving Italy into submission by holding Egypt; see Tac. *Hist.* iii. 8, 48, iv. 52.

[4] 'Annonae sanctae'; Willmanns, 1293; Orelli, 1810; Henzen, 5309, 5320, etc.; Boissière, p. 66, note 2.

them.[1] Thus the whole scheme must be taken to be the work of Augustus, assisted doubtless by the advice of Maecenas, and by the practical co-operation of Agrippa.[2] A famous passage of Tacitus gives the number of the legions in each province in the reign of Tiberius.[3] There were twenty-five in all, divided tolerably equally among the frontier provinces, with the exception that the Rhine was guarded by the extraordinarily powerful force of eight legions. The number of auxiliaries was about the same as that of the legions, and we are able to argue to a total force of about 320,000 men. Besides this, there were the three fleets which guarded the eastern and western coasts of Italy and the southern coasts of Gaul.'[4] Their respective stations were Ravenna, Misenum, and Forum Julii. There were, further, the troops stationed in Italy, of which the most famous were the praetorian guards, but these do not at present concern us.

For many years the Roman forces had been tending to the condition of a standing army. The continuous campaigns in the East or in the Gauls had not admitted of the men being disbanded for many years together[5]; and with the decay of the old martial spirit it had become more and more difficult and even impossible to attract men of any means or standing to the ranks. Marius had admitted the proletariate, and since his day military service had hardened

---

[1] Thus Caesar was preparing for expeditions against the Parthians and other eastern peoples at the time of his murder (App. *B. C.* ii. 110).

[2] For the value of Agrippa, see Dio, liv. 28 ; Duruy, iii. 285.

[3] Tac. *Ann.* iv. 5; cf. Josephus, *Bell. Jud.* ii. 16, 4.

[4] Ib. ; Suet. *Aug.* 49. The *praefecto Juliensium* mentioned in an inscription, Henzen, 6943 (if, indeed, it refers to Forum Julii, which Hirschfeld, *Gall. Stud.* i. 301 n., denies) was probably not a mere municipal prefect, as all his other titles are military, and as the place was of great military importance. Henzen supposes him to have been of the nature of a *curator*, assigned to the place by the emperor, with authority transcending that of the duoviri, and, I presume, specially responsible for the dockyards and arsenals.

[5] Merivale, iii. 45, 46, gives instances of this. For the difficulties connected with a large standing army, see Vell. Pat. ii. 81, 113, 130.

more and more into a regular profession. A civic soldiery is only possible where the campaigns are brief and toler-ably decisive, and not too far distant from home. It may be doubted whether any continental nation could raise its armies by conscription if, like England, it had to send its soldiers for a term of years to India. Augustus systematised and regulated these tendencies, and we are not wrong, therefore, in regarding him as the author of the standing army. The passage in Maecenas' speech, in which he gives his advice to Augustus about the army, is in reality a summary of what Augustus actually effected[1]; and there, as in the corresponding passage of Suetonius,[2] it is clearly brought out that the great change Augustus made was to define strictly the duration and the conditions of service.[3] The time of service was probably fixed at twenty years,[4] though in some cases the veterans were kept under the standards for a longer period. At its expiration a man was given his honourable discharge (*honesta missio*), received the promised bounty (3,000 sesterces), and was commonly en-franchised—he and any one whom he might marry—if not already a Roman citizen.[5] He was settled on land, of the quality of which there were frequent complaints, in remote and half-civilized provinces in the neighbourhood of the frontier he had helped to guard.[6] The great expenses of these bounties, though necessary to give the commander a hold upon his soldiers and to make them content with their position, could not be met without special measures.

---

[1] Dio Cass. lii. 27.   [2] Suet. *Aug.* 49.

[3] Χρόνον τακτὸν ἐστρατευμένους, says Dio, lv. 23. 'Ad certam stipen-diorum praemiorumque formulam.   Definitis . . . temporibus militiae et commodis missionum,' says Suetonius, *Aug.* 49.

[4] Twenty years in the legions, twenty-five in the auxiliary forces, twenty-six in the fleets, were the regular periods ; Bruns, p. 252   Cf. *Mon. Anc.* § 17 : 'Qui vicena plurave stipendia meruissent.' For longer periods, cf. Tac. *Ann.* i. 18 ; Suet. *Tib.* 48.

[5] Cf. the *diplomata* printed in Bruns, p. 274-6. A large number of such diplomata have been found in the different provinces.

[6] Tac. *Ann.* iv. 73 ; Vell. Pat. ii. 110.

Augustus accordingly instituted the military treasury (*aerarium militare*). 'In the consulship of M. Lepidus and L. Arruntius I paid 170,000,000 sesterces in the name of Tib. Caesar and myself into the military treasury which was established by my design to pay bounties to soldiers who had served twenty or more campaigns.'[1] This was the original endowment of the fund; but it was also supported by the proceeds of two new taxes, the tax of five per cent. on all legacies, except those left to near relatives or those of less value than 100,000 sesterces, and the tax of one per cent. on all goods bought or sold in Italy. Both caused great complaints, as their practical effect was to do away with the exclusive privileges Italy had hitherto enjoyed; but Augustus insisted, and in course of time both were extended to the provinces. Augustus appears to have made a hobby of his new treasury, and besides his own contributions to it received promises of subscriptions from foreign kings and peoples.[2] Other extraordinary sources of its revenue are sometimes mentioned. For instance, when Agrippa Postumus was banished his confiscated property was devoted to it.[3] Its administration was entrusted to three men of praetorian rank, appointed by lot, and serving for a term of three years.[4] In the third century these officials were chosen directly by the emperor.[5]

The *aerarium militare*.

In such ways, though not without difficulty,[6] sufficient money was procured to discharge these payments. But as the soldiers had also to be regularly paid, fed, and equipped, these sums by no means represented the one item of expenditure upon the army. But anything was worth paying for peace and security; and this the standing army secured for nearly 200 years. Nor are these the only services by which the army discharged the debit side of its account. Marius' canal in Narbonensian Gaul was the first of a great series of works by which the natural facilities of the pro-

Services of the troops.

---

[1] *Mon. Anc.* § 17. [2] Dio, lv. 25. [3] Id. lv. 32.
[4] Id. lv. 25. [5] Id. lv. 25. [6] Suet. *Tib.* 48.

vinces were improved. The soldiers were pioneers and road-makers as much as fighting men, and the spade and the sword were equally familiar to them. Drusus[1] and Corbulo[2] carried out similar works to that of Marius; and if the idea of making a canal between the Saône and the Moselle[3] had been carried out, it would have been a work of the most brilliant utility. Such works as these, or the building of amphitheatres,[4] or still more frequently the making of roads and bridges,[5] were ordered by the generals partly for the purposes of discipline, and partly with the conscious intention of improving the material condition of the province.[6] Less premeditated but not less welcome was the development of towns out of the legionary camps. The towns of Leon in Spain and Caerleon in England are two instances out of the multitude that might be adduced. Posted on the frontiers during their time of service, or settled on lands near it after their dismissal, the soldiers acted in both capacities as a centre from which Roman civilisation could extend itself. The army also acted as a medium for bringing the most different races of the world into close acquaintanceship. Tacitus is perhaps too uncompromising when he says that ' all that is sound in the armies is foreign,'[7] and that ' it is by the blood of the provinces that the provinces are conquered'[8]; but there can be no question of the immense foreign element in the army even from an early date. It was the general practice to post troops raised in one country in a far distant one. Thus we find Spaniards in Switzerland, Swiss (Rauraci) in Britain, Pannonians in Africa, Illyrians in Armenia.

It is noticeable that in all cases the troops were on the

---

[1] Suet. *Claud.* 1.   [2] Tac. *Ann.* xi. 20.
[3] Tac. *Ann.* xiii. 53.   [4] Boissière, p. 133.
[5] Tac. *Ann.* i. 20.   See Boissière, ' Musée de St. Germain ' in *Revue des Deux Mondes*, August 15, 1881, p. 742.
[6] To previous references add Suet. *Aug.* 18; Tac. *Ann.* xvi. 23; Dio Cass. xliv. 42.
[7] Tac. *Ann.* iii. 40.   [8] Tac. *Hist.* iv. 17.

frontiers. Rome did not find it necessary to keep garrisons in the interiors of her provinces, as we are obliged to do in India. The whole of Gaul was held by a single garrison of 1,200 men at Lugdunum [1]; the eight legions on the Rhine were designed mainly for the defence of the frontier against the Germans. Strabo tells us the same thing of Egypt ; the frontier had to be guarded against the Ethiopians, but there were hardly any troops in the interior [2] of the country. Not one of the 500 towns of Asia had a garrison.[3]   Such a state of things can be fairly put down to the credit of the Roman rule. It was partly no doubt due to the tremendous severity of her conquests,[4] but still more to the fact that she bestowed upon the conquered very positive advantages. She had the art of making her subjects emulate and copy her own civilisation. The peace which her arms secured put a spade in the hands of the peoples instead of a sword, and allowed the labouring millions to trade and dig, and bring the waste lands under tillage, without thought for their own defence. The provincials seem to have been generally disarmed, according to the advice which Dio puts in the mouth of Maecenas.[5] We find traces of a local militia here and there; for instance, in the law of the colony of Urso[6]; but the general principle was that enunciated by Maecenas, that the provincials should have all their fighting done for them by the Roman army. The result of this was that the provincials lost the military spirit, and without any kind of military organisation could make but a very imperfect resistance to the barbarians, once the troops on the frontier failed them.[7] Events so far proved

No troops within the provinces.

---

[1] Desjardins, *La Gaule Romaine*, p. 12; further aid could be drawn from the Rhine stations if needed.

[2] Strabo, xvii. 1, 53.   [3] Josephus, *Bell. Jud.* ii. 16.

[4] The cold and clear narrative of Caesar yet leaves a nightmare impression of the awful bloodshed by which his results were obtained. Cf. Merivale, ii. 74.   See also Vell. ii. 115.

[5] Dio, lii. 27.   [6] Cf. § 103 of the law, and § 89 ; Bruns, p. 122.

[7] The gallant resistance of Autun to the usurper Tetricus seems to

the Roman policy a failure, but before condemning it too
unconditionally it would be necessary to convince ourselves
that if arms had been put in their hands, the provinces
would have been secure from internecine discord.

Partition
of
provinces
between
Senate
and
Emperor.
But perhaps the most conspicuous of Augustus' changes
was the partition of the provinces between himself and the
Senate.[1] The principle of division was that those provinces
which enjoyed absolute peace, the older provinces, such as
Sicily, Narbonensis, and Asia, should be entrusted to the
Senate, while the frontier provinces, which needed military
force, went naturally to the commander-in-chief. In this
way Augustus pretended to relieve the Senate of the cares
and dangers of Empire, while leaving it its advantages, but
in fact secured himself the reality of power. The division
was an eminently natural one, and had been anticipated
under the Republic by the distinction made between consular and praetorian provinces. All new provinces, as
requiring, at first at all events, the presence of troops, came
as a matter of course under the emperor; and thus the
original number of twelve imperial, as compared with ten
senatorial provinces, was continually being increased. The
emperor reserved to himself the right of modifying these
arrangements if he thought fit. Thus Achaia and Macedonia were transferred by Tiberius from the senatorial to
the imperial category[2]; and again restored to their old
position by Claudius.[3] Moreover, the proconsular imperium
possessed by the emperor over the whole Empire enabled
him to interfere at will with the senatorial provinces. Thus

show that a good deal could have been done by the provincials if they
had had any sort of military organisation. (Cf. Eumen. *pro rest.
schol.* iv.)

[1] The authorities are Suet. *Aug.* 47; Strabo, xvii. 3, § 25; Dio,
liii. 12.   [2] Tac. *Ann.* i. 76.

[3] Suet. *Claud.* 25. Sardinia had been senatorial and became
imperial; C. I. L. x. 8023-4. Bithynia became definitely imperial
under Hadrian. For the case of Illyricum see Dio Cass. liv. 34;
Mommsen, *Staatsr.* ii. 239.

when Vologeses invaded Asia, the governor, Avidius Cassius, was directly appointed by the emperor[1]; and if a proconsul died during his year of office the emperor could directly nominate his successor.[2] The Senate of itself requested the emperor to appoint a proconsul to a province in which there was anything like a serious war to be apprehended; Tiberius appointed the proconsul to conduct the war against Tacfarinas[3]; and in exceptional circumstances a legate could be sent to assume the governorship of a proconsular province.[4]

The governors of the senatorial provinces were appointed in much the same way as they had been under the Republic. Pompey's arrangement of the five years' interval was usually maintained as the minimum[5]; but after Augustus' death we find it extended to ten or even thirteen years. These provinces were assigned by lot as under the old system[6]; as a rule, after the previous grades of aedile, quaestor, and the higher urban offices had been passed through; and were held only for a year. The two oldest consulars cast lots for the consular, the praetors also by seniority for the praetorian provinces. Two provinces, Asia and Africa, remained consular, and the appointments to these were the most dignified and the best paid; the

Mode of appointment to senatorial provinces.

---

[1] Zumpt, *Comm. Epig.* ii. 92. Dio Cass. 71, 1 (he may however have been governor of Syria, cf. Vulcat. Gall. *Avid. Cass.* v.).

[2] Orelli, 3651; an inscription of the time of Vespasian, part of which runs as follows : ' Proc. provinciae Asiae quam mandatu principis vice defuncti Procos. rexit.'

[3] Tac. *Ann.* iii. 32.

[4] Pliny was thus sent to Bithynia ; cf. Plin. *Ep.* x. 12, where he thanks Trajan for granting a relative the *proconsulship* of Bithynia.

[5] Suet. *Aug.* 36 ; but nevertheless, under Augustus the interval was irregular. See Mommsen, *Res gestae*, p. 170; *Staatsrecht* 2, 240; Hicks, *Ephesos*, p. 177.

[6] Suet. *Aug.* 47 : ' Ceteras proconsulibus sortito permisit.' Tac. *Ann.* iii. 71. The quaestor too by lot ; Suet. *Vesp.* 2 ; Tac. *Agr.* 6 and 42. Quaestors were only in senatorial provinces, cf. Gaius, 1, 6 : In provincias Caesaris omnino quaestores non mittuntur.

rest were praetorian. But whether the provinces were consular or praetorian, and whether the governors were men of consular or praetorian rank, in any case all governors of senatorial provinces were called indifferently proconsuls[1]; just as all governors of imperial provinces were called by the historians indifferently, though inaccurately, propraetors.[2] In outward dignity the proconsuls were far above the imperial legates; they had ten or even twelve fasces, whereas the legate had only five[3]; but they had little of the reality of power. As they had no military authority (except for the African proconsul up to the reign of Caligula, and special cases like that of Quirinius in Cyrenaica), they did not possess the power of life and death over any soldiers in their province. As too their office was usually annual[4] they made a very different impression to the imperial legate who scarcely ever stayed less than three, and sometimes as much as eight or ten or even more years in his province. It is no wonder, therefore, that Tiberius found a difficulty in inducing capable persons to stand for such appointments[5]; and if we still find traces of the old feeling which regarded a province as a prize,[6] it must have been rather for the salary connected with it than for any power or special profit to be obtained

---

[1] Cf. the passage of Suet. quoted in the above note; Perrot, De Galatia prov. Rom. p. 115; Dio Cass. liii. 13; Mommsen, Staatsr. ii. 221.

[2] Tac. Ann. xv. 22, where 'propraetors and proconsuls' is an exhaustive classification of provincial governors; Marquardt i. 409, note 4. The senatorial governors in theory had no one above them, the legates of imperial provinces were deputies of the emperor, who himself had proconsular power.

[3] 'Quinquefascalis dum agerem ;' Ephemeris Epig. i. 205.

[4] Cf. however Henzen 5425, procoss Asiae iii. (i.e., tribus annis continuis), and Mommsen, Staatsr., ii. 227, gives other instances. See Suet. Aug. 23. Praesidibus provinciarum propagavit imperium ut a peritis et assuetis socii continerentur.

[5] Tac. Ann. vi. 27.

[6] Ib. xv. 19; Hist. iv. 39; Dio Cass. xlii. 19.

from it. An ambitious man would rather covet a post as imperial legatus, and if a man wanted to become rich the surest way of doing so would be through a procuratorship.[1]

In theory the emperor was himself the governor of all his provinces; but as he could not be in twelve different places at once, he appointed in each a legate to represent him. The full title of such governors was *legatus Augusti pro praetore ;* and this is the way they are invariably designated in the inscriptions. They might be either of consular or praetorian rank ; and the provinces to which they were assigned were themselves also either consular or praetorian —an arrangement which was so far of importance that if consular legates had been sent to a province in the first instance, it was only very rarely that praetorian legates were substituted, and *vice versa.*[2] The provinces in which there was more than one legion, were always governed by consular legates ; and it became common, and would no doubt be welcome, to address such legates simply as ' consulares,'[3] thus clearly distinguishing them from the legates of praetorian rank.

The governors of Imperial provinces.

These legates were appointed directly by the emperor, and for as long a time as he pleased, and were sometimes even forbidden to go to their province, and ordered to govern by legates.[4] Dio makes Maecenas give the advice to Augustus not to let any legate of his rule a province less than three years or more than five ; for thus they would stay long enough to know their province thoroughly, not long enough to become dangerous.[5] And this was perhaps the generally observed rule[6]; Agricola, for instance, was three

---

[1] Suet. *Vesp.* 16 ; Tac. *Ann.* xvi. 17.

[2] Perrot, *Galatia*, p. 68. But see *Rhein. Mus.* xlv. 207, 208.

[3] So we find that after Augustus by consular and praetorian provinces are meant imperial ; by proconsular provinces are meant senatorial. Cf. Capitol. *M. Aurelius,* 22 ; Marq. i. 409, note 5.

[4] *Ann.* i. 80, vi. 27 ; *Hist.* ii. 65, 97 ; Suet. *Tib.* 63.

[5] Dio, lii. 23.

[6] This is Zumpt's opinion (*Comm. Epig.* ii. 87) and Mommsen's, see

years in Aquitania.[1] But the exceptions are very numerous. Galba governed Spain for eight years,[2] Flavius Sabinus was in Moesia for seven, and Poppaeus Sabinus for twenty-four[3]; and we find C. Silius legate in Upper Germany A.D. 14, and still there ten years afterwards.[4] Sometimes these appointments lasted even for life.[5] Tiberius in particular was famous for keeping his governors long at their posts.[6]

What constituted the vital difference between these legates and the proconsuls was not merely the longer duration of their power, but still more their possession of military force. The senatorial provinces being without troops counted for nothing in such a period of civil war as the terrible year of the three emperors (A.D. 69). 'The unarmed provinces with Italy at their head were exposed to any kind of slavery, and were ready to become the prize of victory,' says Tacitus.[7] The only exception to the rule that a proconsular was divorced from a military command was Africa ; and even here, in cases of special emergency, we find the governor appointed by the emperor. Still as a rule, in the reign of Augustus and Tiberius the proconsul of Africa disposed of troops, and yet was not selected by the emperor; a contradiction to the usual state of things which was sure before long to awake the susceptibilities of a jealous emperor.'[8] Caligula in fact, on his accession, at once put an end to it, took the troops from the proconsul,

The legate and the proconsul,

Res gestae p. 167, on P. Sulp. Quirinius, described on an inscription as for the second time legate of Syria.

1 Tac. *Agr.* 9.   2 Plut. *Galba*, 4.
3 Tac. *Hist.* iii. 75 ; *Ann.* vi. 45.
4 *Ann.* i. 31 and iv. 18.   5 *Ann.* i. 80.
6 Josephus, *Antiq.* xviii. 6 ; Suet. *Tib.* 41.
7 *Hist.* i. 11. Their unarmed condition is illustrated by *Hist.* ii. 81 and 83.
8 Cf. Cicero's expressions about Africa, *Pro Ligario*, 7: 'Africam, omnium provinciarum arcem, natam ad bellum contra hanc urbem gerendum.' Cf. Appian, *Pun.* 134 ; Caes. *Bell. Civ.* ii. 32.

and gave them to the legate whom he established by his side, with the exceptional title, explained by the exceptional circumstances, of *legatus Augusti pro praetore legionis*.[1] Henceforth the legate was continually encroaching upon his rival, whose position of superior dignity and inferior power exposed him to the most galling affronts. The legate felt that he was the emperor's man, and was sent there to assert his supreme authority in his own person. Caligula had made disputes inevitable. ' The patronage was equally divided between the two officers. A source of disagreement was thus studiously sought in the continual clashing of their authority, and it was further developed by an unprincipled rivalry. The power of the legates grew through their lengthened tenure of office, and perhaps because an inferior feels a greater interest in such a competition.'[2] Even if actual violence was not shown (Piso was put to death by Festus' order, A.D. 70),[3] the proconsul was always liable to the interference of the legate in the internal affairs of his own province. The emperors made it their special business to look after the roads both in Italy and in the provinces.[4] So if a road was wanted from the boundary of Numidia to a place far within the senatorial province, the legate was commissioned to superintend the making of it ; and his officers must have been constantly on the spot

---

[1] Tac. *Hist.* iv. 48 ; Mommsen, *Staatsr.* ii. 220 n. 3 ; *Ephem. Epigr.* iv. 536 (on a inscription of Simutthu, from which Mommsen infers that the proconsul retained some troops even after the appointment of the legate). Henzèn, 5463. L. Matuccio Fuscino leg. Aug. pr. pr. leg. iii. Aug.

[2] Tac. *Hist.* iv. 48.

[3] Tac. *Hist.* iv. 50.

[4] The epigraphic evidence on this point is very large. The following references may be given : Suet. *Aug.* 30 ; *Mon. Anc.*, § 20 (Flaminian road restored as far as Ariminum); Mommsen's *Res gestae*, p. 87 ; Kandler, *Inscr. nell' Istria*, No. 524 ; Bergier, i. 64-67, *De publ. et milit. imp. Rom. viis.* They also induced viri triumphales to undertake the work, C. I. L. i., p. 478, 6895 ; Wilmanns, 2, p. 79 ; Middleton, *Remains of Ancient Rome*, ii., pp. 352-358.

while his soldiers were engaged upon the work.[1]   The yearly tenure of the proconsul must also have gone far to put him into a subordinate position.   'Between this annual proconsul, this governor of a dozen months who put in an appearance at Carthage, and was scarcely arrived in his province before he was gone again, and this legate who on the contrary settled himself in Africa, and from his camp at Lambesis saw the proconsuls pass and disappear, what a difference in real authority, what inequality in power!'[2]

The imperial procurators.

If the legate was the emperor's man, still more was this the character of the procurator.   There were no quaestors in the imperial provinces, all the accounts being kept and money matters in general being managed by one of these officials.   But we also find them in the senatorial provinces.[3] While the whole field of finance was committed to them in their own proper provinces, moneys pertaining to the fisc were managed by procurators in all provinces alike without distinction.   They were practically independent of the senatorial governor.   'In any question of fiscal moneys which concerns the procurator of the prince, the proconsul will do best if he keeps clear of it.'[4]   Such taxes as the *vicesima hereditatium*, when applied to the provinces, were under the superintendence of a procurator, whose powers extended over several provinces at once[5]; and in a later period of the Empire there were procurators to manage every conceivable source of income.

These officials as constituted by Augustus had, properly speaking, no judicial authority.   But they began to presume

[1] E.g., the road from Carthage, the capital of the proconsular province, to Thevesta was made by the legate (A.D. 124), and in the inscription which commemorates it there is no mention of the proconsul ; Boissière, p. 254.

[2] Boissière, p. 252.   There were also sub-legates who were not propraetors.   See *Rhein. Mus.* xlvi. 1, xlviii. 246 ; *Staatsr.* iii. 282.

[3] See ante, p. 106.

[4] Dig. i. 18, 9 ; Marquardt, i. 414, note 4.

[5] Henzen, 6940, is a good instance ; Marquardt, ii. 305, for a full account.   Ramsay, *Church in the Roman Empire*, p. 56, note.

upon their position as the emperor's nominees from an early date. Under Tiberius a procurator of Asia was accused by his province, and the emperor supported the accusation, vehemently asseverating that the authority which he had given him extended only to slaves and to his own private moneys.[1] It was, however, doubtless found inconvenient in practice that officials entrusted with such important duties should not have wider powers; and at Claudius' request the Senate gave them authority[2] to decide suits,—a power which must have extended at all events to all cases connected with the fisc. In the imperial provinces it is possible to trace a similar process of encroachment. Here their position corresponding to that held formerly by the quaestors, legitimately gave them wide powers, which they took care to maintain and increase. 'A single king once ruled us; now two are set over us; a legate to tyrannise over our lives, a procurator to tyrannise over our property.' Such is the complaint which Tacitus puts into the mouths of the Britons.[3] The rapacity of a procurator goaded Britain into rebellion[4]; and when Galba was governor of Tarraconensis he was obliged to witness similar conduct on the part of his procurator, apparently without the power to check it.[5] It was so regular a thing for the legate and the procurator to quarrel, that Tacitus specially praises Agricola for having had no 'contention with his procurator' when he was governor of Aquitania; and so sharp was the dissension between Suetonius, the legate of Britain, and his procurator, that Nero sent a freedman to endeavour to arrange the difference between them. It is significant that the upshot was that a substitute was found, not for Classicanus, but for Suetonius.[6]

[1] Tac. Ann. iv. 15.
[2] Suet. Claud. 12. Claudius seems to have been a great patron of the procurators. Cf. Suet. Claud. 24, and Tac. Ann. xii. 60.
[3] Tac. Agr. 15. [4] Tac. Ann. xiv. 32.
[5] Plut. Galba, 4. As Galba sympathised with the Spaniards, it is to be supposed he would have done so if he could.
[6] Tac. Ann. xiv. 38.

The fact is that the procurator seems to have been designedly used, at all events by bad emperors, as a spy upon the legate, and, if need were, as an instrument against him. Being in theory nothing but the emperor's stewards,[1] and being wholly dependent upon his favour for success in their career, they were absolutely devoted to his interests. A legate might revolt against his master, a procurator never. It is the procurator who lets the emperor know of rebellious movements in his province,[2] and it is in the procurator that the emperor confides if he wants a legate put out of the way.[3] At least one instance occurs of a governor of senatorial rank being actually put to death by his procurator.[4] The whole tendency is for the authority of the procurator to extend and strengthen itself till he and the legate are left confronting one another as almost equal powers. That they could, in emergency at all events, dispose of military forces is proved by the appeal of the Romans of Camulodunum to Catus Decianus[5] ; and in times of disturbance we find them only too ready to try their hands at military measures.[6] It is not at all inconsistent with what has been said that in settled times and under good and capable emperors the procurators were obliged to maintain their proper subordinate position ; and had for instance to request a testimonial from the governor to the emperor on leaving the province.[7]

---

[1] See Hirschfeld, *Die Kaiserl. Verwaltungsbeamten*, p. 242, and Tac. *Ann.* xvi. 17.

[2] Tac. *Hist.* i. 12.

[3] Suet. *Galba*, 9: 'Nam et mandata Neronis de nece sua ad procuratores clam missa deprehenderat.'

[4] Tac. *Hist.* i. 7.

[5] Tac. *Ann.* xiv. 32. They asked him for military aid. He sent only 200 men. Tacitus' language implies that he could have sent more if he had chosen. Marquardt, ii. 518. Pliny, however, seems to imply that the procurator had no military forces in ordinary circumstances, *ad Traj.* xxvii., xxviii. Cf. Kenyon, *Greek Papyri in B. M.*, ii. pp. xxii and 286.

[6] E.g., the procurator of Corsica ; Tac. *Hist.* ii. 16.

[7] Pliny, *Ep.* x. 36.

Besides these officials of the imperial exchequer there were also a certain number of provinces ruled directly by a procurator, possessing the powers of an ordinary governor. Pontius Pilate was one of these minor governors.[1] These governorships were of a provisional character, and when the countries to which they had been applied had been thoroughly Romanised, or had lost the peculiarities which had made an exceptional treatment advisable, we find them organised like ordinary provinces. This happened for instance in the case of Thracia, Rhaetia, and Judaea itself.[2] Such provinces as these formed a class by themselves. In one passage Tacitus puts together a number of them,—' Mauritania, Rhaetia, Noricum, and Thrace, and the other provinces governed by procurators '[3]; and we are also able to point to procurators of Cappadocia,[4] of the Maritime Alps,[5] and of the Alps of Savoy.[6] It was however understood that these procurators were subordinate to the regular governor of the neighbouring province.[7] This subordination was natural enough, seeing that though they had some sort of military force, perhaps a few cohorts,[8] to protect their persons and assert their authority within the province, they yet had nothing that could be called an army, and could not defend their province against attack from without. So

---

[1] When Finlay, i. 36, argues to the irregular and arbitrary character of the government from the case of Pontius Pilate he does not seem quite to understand the exceptional character of these procurators. They were in fact governors, and we find the procurator of Judaea also called *praepositus*; Suet. *Vesp*. 4. They had the *ius gladii*. See Orelli, 3664, 3888; Mommsen, *Staatsr*. ii. 224. For the replacement of the procurator in Rhaetia and Noricum by legati see Mommsen in C. I. L. iii., pp. 588 and 707.

[2] Marquardt, i. 413. [3] *Hist*. i. 11.

[4] *Ann*. xii. 49. [5] *Hist*. ii. 12, iii. 42.

[6] ' Proc. Alpium Atrectinarum et Poeninarum '; Orelli, 3888; Mommsen, *Schweiz*, 6.

[7] See Zumpt, *Comm. Epig*. ii. 127, 133.

[8] Pontius Pilate certainly had troops, which would be very necessary in an unruly province like Judaea. See Philo, *ad Gaium*, 38.

under Claudius, when an incompetent procurator of Cappadocia raised auxiliary troops and ventured to meddle with
the very *crux* and mystery of Roman foreign policy, the
crown of Armenia, he was promptly recalled to his senses
by the arrival of a lieutenant with a legion from Quadratus
the governor of Syria. In this case it was the governor of
Syria who interfered; but as a rule it was the legate of
Galatia who was responsible for Cappadocia[1]; while Judaea
was under the special control of the governor of Syria.
Judaea however was annexed to Syria on the death of
its last king Agrippa[2]; and the constant inroads of the
barbarians compelled Vespasian to substitute a consular
legate with troops for the equestrian procurator in Cappadocia.[3]

Egypt.   The government of Egypt was analogous to that of such
provinces as these, but was in many points wholly exceptional.
Julius Caesar had deliberately abstained from making a
province of the country[4]; and when Augustus added it to
the Empire after Actium,[5] he subjected it to an altogether
exceptional treatment. The country was his private property, or rather the emperor's private property; it passed
as a matter of course, that is, from emperor to emperor.[6]
Augustus appointed a praefectus to represent him in the
province, somewhat·as in earlier times the urban praetors

[1] Perrot, *Galatia*, 98.   But this only lasted till Vespasian, ib. 61.

[2] *Ann.* xii. 23 (A.D. 41) ; and again put under a procurator from 44
to 70, when it became an entirely separate province.   See Marquardt,
i. 335.

[3] Suet. *Vesp.* 8 ; Perrot, ib.

[4] Suet. *Jul.* 35 : ' Veritus provinciam facere, ne quandoque violen-
tiorem praesidem nacta novarum rerum materia esset.'

[5] ' Aegyptum imperio populi Romani adjeci'; *Mon. Anc.* § 27
(30 B.C.).

[6] That is, it was patrimonium Caesaris, but not res familiaris.   See
Marquardt, ii. 249, 300 ; i. 284.   In 10 B.C. some alteration of the
status of Egypt seems to have taken place, and it became nominally a
province like the others, C. I. L. vi. 701, Aegypto in potestatem populi
Romani redacta.

had sent prefects to represent them in the municipalities of Italy.[1] This prefect was of equestrian, and not the highest equestrian rank,[2] sometimes even a freedman, and an appeal to the emperor lay against him. He was at the head of the financial, judicial, and military systems, making yearly circuits, controlling the movements of all troops and granting exemptions from taxation or liturgies. He had no definite term of office, and was assisted by a council of Roman citizens. An equestrian nominee of the emperor, *Dicæodotes*, went on circuit with him, represented him in his absence, and gave advice on technical matters. No senators were admitted into the province; and the greatest jealousy was shown of the smallest interference with it.[3] Not till the reign of Macrinus do we hear of a senatorial prefect of Egypt.

By the side of the prefect were two other high officials, the *idiologus*[4] or imperial procurator, and the *juridicus* of Alexandria.[5] The name of the former was that which had been held by the steward of the Ptolemies, and he served to keep a check on the financial activities of the prefect, employing *dioecetae* to administer domain lands. The latter was a municipal magistrate with very exceptional powers, appointed directly by the emperor, as Napoleon III. directly appointed the mayors of important French country towns.

---

[1] Other praefecti are those of islands already mentioned, of Mesopotamia under the later Empire, of Berenice in Arabia, and of some Ligurian peoples, cf. Marquardt, i. 413, and references. The praefectus in Egypt (with three legions, and after Augustus two) performed all the ceremonial functions of the kings ; Pliny, *N. H.* 5, § 57 ; Seneca, *N. Q.* 4, 2, 8, where the ceremonial casting of gold ornaments by the prefect into the Nile is described ; cf. Strab. xvii. 1, 12, τὴν τοῦ βασίλεως ἔχει τάξιν.

[2] *Ann.* xii. 60, ii. 59. His powers were great. Cf. *Hist.* i. 11.

[3] *Ann.* ii. 59.

[4] Marquardt, ii. 300. He is mentioned in the decree of Tiberius Alexander : πρὸς τῷ ἰδίῳ λόγῳ τεταγμένου. Cf. Strabo, xvii. 1, § 12, where Strabo describes him as only procurator a caducis.

[5] Henzen, 6924, 6925.

The reasons for the special jealousy of Egypt shown by Augustus and his successors were partly the great defensibility of the country, partly its immense importance as the granary of Rome. 'It was an accepted principle with our fathers,' says Pliny,[1] 'that our city could not possibly be fed and maintained without the resources of Egypt.' Egypt did in fact feed Rome for four months in the year.

The governor's subordinates. Of the subordinates of the governors, either in the senatorial or imperial provinces, it is not necessary to say much. The *juridici* that occur in different parts of Spain[2] and in Britain were assistants of the imperial legates, not appointed by the legates—for by Roman law a deputy could not appoint deputies—but directly by the emperor,[3] and they thus took the place of the republican quaestor as legal assistants of the governor. The legal council mentioned under the Republic as assisting the governor became a regular body under the title of assessors.[4] The comites still existed, and though doubtless under better control, are sometimes complained of in much the same terms as they were under the Republic.[5] The quaestors still performed their duties in the senatorial provinces; but were thrown

---

[1] Pliny, *Panegyr*. 31. According to Josephus, *B. J.* ii. 164, Africa fed Rome for eight months; cf. Juv. viii. 117. During the late Empire Egypt fed Constantinople, and Rome had to get corn elsewhere.

[2] E.g., the legatus et juridicus Asturicae et Gallaeciae (for references cf. Kuhn, *Verfassung* ii. 183). In this and probably in other cases the juridicus took the place of a procurator who had governed a special district in a province, and gradually received wider powers, sometimes conjoined with some military force, so that the district became practically an independent province.

[3] Henzen, 6487, 6489, 1178, C. I. L. xii. 3617, viii. 2747, and a complete list, Marquardt, i. 411, note. They occur only in imperial provinces, and are quite distinct from the juridici of Italy (instituted by M. Aurelius). For the whole subject, see Zumpt, ii. 40-55 ; Henzen, p. 113 of his indices, where are full references, and p. 297.

[4] Plin. *Ep*. x. 19. See an inscription given by Boissière, p. 241, note. Willems, *Droit Public*, p. 582, who quotes Cod. Just. 1, 51, 1, 2, 7 ; Savigny. *Droit public du* iv. *et* vi. *Siècle*, § 198-204.

[5] *Hist*. iv. 14 : 'Gravi quidem comitatu.'

into the shade by the rapid rise and great extension of the class of procurators. The cases which sometimes occur of subordinate governorships being given to centurions[1] are so obviously due to special circumstances as not to require a closer examination.

The great and beneficent change which resulted from Augustus' arrangements was the much stricter control in which the governors were now held. The emperors made it their business to keep themselves well acquainted with their Empire; of the eighteen years after the battle of Actium Augustus spent eleven out of Italy,[2] and the only two provinces which he had not visited were Africa and Sardinia.[3] It was not their interest to tolerate misgovernment or oppression. 'Everywhere it is the rule that the owner spares the soil, while the tenant exhausts it.'[4] Undisturbed by domestic politics they had leisure to devote their unwearied industry to the interests of the Empire as a whole.[5] The governors were regularly paid,[6] and consequently lost the excuses for exaction which they could have offered under the Republic. It was expected that the governors should regularly report to the emperor on any matters of importance that occurred in their province[7]; and the new imperial post would supply the means. The number of questions referred to his decision was constantly on the increase. At the end of the decree in which he

The emperor as supreme head of the provincial administration.

---

[1] A former *centurio primipilus* governed the Frisii; *Ann.* iv. 72. Furneaux suggested that he may have had the equestrian rank of procurator fisci; cf. *Rev. Archéol.* xv. 36.

[2] Duruy, iii. 230.

[3] Suet. *Aug.* 47.

[4] Boissier, *L'Opposition sous les Césars*, p. 20.

[5] Cf. Suet. *Vesp.* 21; Plin. *Ep.* iii. 5.

[6] Dio. lii. 23, liii. 15; Suet. *Aug.* 38; Marquardt, i. 416; Merivale, iv. 25; Madvig, *die Verwaltung und Verfassung des röm. Staats*, ii. 308. The proconsul of Africa had an income of a million sesterces.

[7] Euseb. *H. E.* ii. 2, παλαιοῦ κεκρατηκότος ἔθους τοῖς τῶν ἐθνῶν ἄρχουσι τὰ παρά σφισι καινοτομούμενα τῷ τὴν βασίλειον ἀρχὴν ἐπικρατοῦντι σημαίνειν, ὡς ἂν μηδὲν αὐτὸν διαδιδράσκοι τῶν γιγνομένων; Marquardt, i. 417.

regulates an immense amount of details connected with the
financial administration of the country, Tiberius Alexander,
prefect of Egypt under Galba, says he will not decide a
particular question himself, but ' I will write to the Emperor
the Augustus, and I will make known to him any other
points of consequence, as he alone can wholly eradicate
such abuses.'   Boundary disputes,[1] petitions for the right
of sanctuary,[2] petitions for the restoration of a temple,[3]
all such and many more were referred to his decision.
Such matters would previously have been settled in a
summary manner by the governor, and their reference to
Rome shows the tendency to limit and define his absolute
authority.   The extent to which Pliny when legate in
Bithynia refers to Trajan for directions is almost painful.
To strengthen and secure this direct and immediate control
of provincial affairs Augustus established an elaborate
postal system, by which he might be informed with the
greatest possible celerity of everything which occurred.
Such misgovernment as had been frequent under the
Republic was in part due to the remoteness of the governors
from Rome, and to the inadequacy of the communication.
The telegraph and the steamship have immensely strengthened the control which a modern country can exercise over
its dependencies.   Augustus made the best use of what
facilities he had, and everything points to the much readier
and speedier communication[4] between the provinces and
Rome.   And the emperor exercised this control not only
over his legates, but, in virtue of his proconsular power,
over the senatorial governors as well.   The emperor's will
overrode the edicts of the governors[5]; and where large
questions arose connected with the administration of a

---

[1] *Ann.* iv. 43.   Cf. Vespasian's letter to the Vanacini in Corsica;
C. I. L. x. 8038.
[2] *Ann.* iv. 14.   [3] Ib. iv. 43.
[4] For the new postal system, see Suet. *Aug.* 49 ; Marquardt, i. 418.
[5] Plin. x. 109.

province, an imperial 'constitution' laid down the rule to be followed, and so, in a sense, constituted its *lex provinciae*.[1] A special body was deputed for the hearing of provincial appeals[2]; and the Senate, so far as it had any authority left, was busied almost entirely with appeals from provinces. In exceptional cases the emperor, without superseding the governor, sent a special official to examine the affairs of a province[3]; and, where there was a peculiar need, could appoint a peculiar governor.[4] If there were mistakes in this supreme administration, they arose not from mere laxity and incompetence as under the Republic, but from excessive interference and over-centralisation. New organs were developed on all sides to meet the necessities of Empire. Thus the emperor was assisted by his cabinet; and his secretaries for the conduct of the different branches of the administration became ministers of state.

The provinces which were directly in the emperor's hands appears to have been particularly well governed. The splendid career open to a legate of capacity who was favoured by the emperor, would be endangered if not forfeited by yielding to the mean covetousness which had disgraced the governors of the Republic. A man had more to gain by keeping his hands clean than by fouling them. Staying as they did for a period of years in the province, of which they were often natives, the legates did not regard their period of government as a banishment, as Cicero had regarded it. They became familiar with the needs and peculiarities of their province, and ruled its inhabitants as one of themselves. So much better was

The government of the imperial provinces

---

[1] Plin. x. 71, 72. [2] Suet. *Aug.* 33 ; Marquardt, i. 403.

[3] *Ann.* xiv. 39. Not that this freedman of Nero did or was meant to do any good, but if the system was used once it was probably used often in better circumstances. For an example under Augustus see the mission of Asinius Gallus to investigate a case of murder and riot in Cnidus. Dittenberger, *Syllog. Inscr. graec*, vol. i. 356.

[4] When the cities of Bithynia were in trouble, Trajan sent Pliny there as legate, instead of the usual proconsul.

the condition of the imperial provinces than that of the senatorial ones, that when Achaia and Macedonia begged for relief from their burdens (*onera deprecantes*), their prayer was thought to be sufficiently answered by their transference from the rule of the Senate to that of the emperor.[1] The legates were as a rule men of great capacity, equally at home in the camp and in the business of civil government, and to read a bare list of the commands which many of them held is enough to justify the expression of a modern writer when he calls them 'the glory of the Empire.'[2]

Bad governors.

It is not to be supposed that there were no bad governors under Augustus and his successors. A Licinus, a Varus, and a Lollius are there to undeceive us. But the danger which was now run made such governors the exception instead of the rule. Putting together the accusations of provincial governors mentioned in the Annals and History of Tacitus and in the Letters of Pliny, we get a complete list of twenty-seven[3] governors thus accused; of these

[1] Tac. *Ann.* i. 76 and 80. They were attached to the imperial province of Moesia.

[2] Professor Seeley in his Essays, p. 20; cf. Waddington, *Fasti Asiatiques*, p. 18; Ramsay, *Church in the Roman Empire*, 175. I subjoin a *cursus honorum*, one of hundreds of similar ones, taken from Rénier, *Mélanges*, p. 79: 'T. Caesernio Quinctio Macedoni Quinctiano consuli, sodali Augustali, curatori viae Appiae, praefecto alimentorum, legato legionis Piae fidelis, comiti divi Veri per Orientem, praetori candidato inter cives et peregrinos, tribuno plebis candidato, legato per Africam Mauretaniam, quaestori candidato, tribuno militum legionis trigesimae Ulpiae Victricis, triumviro auro argento aeri flando feriundo, patrono coloniae, decreto decurionum. Servilius . . . amico optimo.'
As a rule, a man's whole life can be traced on these inscriptions, as they commonly begin with the first office he held, and go on in chronological order. In this case the office last held and of highest rank comes first, probably because the man had just been made consul, and his friend wished to flatter him by drawing special attention to the honour.

[3] Twenty-one in the Annals, of which sixteen were condemned, five acquitted. One in the Histories—condemned; five in Pliny, of which three were condemned and two acquitted.

seven were acquitted and twenty condemned. Augustus himself showed great severity to guilty governors—*e.g.*, to Cornelius Gallus, once prefect of Egypt.[1] The case of Licinus is a less favourable one ; but, as has been said, if it shows that in exceptional cases a governor could rob with impunity, it shows that it was at all events impossible to make a profit of the robbery.[2]

The regular court for trying cases *de repetundis* was still in form kept up, and cases might occasionally be referred to it, if the Senate did not wish to try them.[3] But as a rule all such accusations came before the Senate, which had the power to decide them, but no doubt settled each case in accordance with the known wishes of the emperor. The provincials could request the Senate to give them this or that advocate to plead their cause,[4] and in some cases appear to have relied upon the talents of their own orators. Thus in one case the ' most eloquent orators of Asia '[5] pleaded before the Senate, probably in Greek, as the use of that language was specially permitted.[6] Now that the Senate had little else to do, these trials were the chief business that came before it, and it is no wonder that, the Senate being itself largely recruited from the provinces, very special attention was paid to them. Pliny in his letters gives far fuller and more elaborate accounts of these trials than he does of any other matter ; and to judge from his description they must have presented striking and impressive scenes.[7]

Above all, Augustus was the great peace-maker. This is the light in which he is most proud to represent him-

Margin note: Accusations of provincial governors.

Margin note: The Empire secured peace.

---

[1] Suet. *Aug.* 66. For Lollius cf. Vell. ii. 102 ; Licinus, Dio Cass. 54, 21 ; Varus in Syria, ' quam pauper divitem ingressus dives pauperem reliquit,' Vell. ii. 117.

[2] Dio Cass. liv. 21 ; Seneca, *Epp.* 119, § 10.   [3] Pliny, *Ep.* iv. 9.

[4] Pliny, ii. 12, iii. 9 ; Marquardt, i. 416, note 9.

[5] *Ann.* iii. 66.   [6] Marquardt, i. 47.

[7] See esp. Plin. *Ep.* iii. 9.

self[1]: and when on his return from Spain and Gaul the Senate consecrated an altar in the Campus Martius to *Pax Augusta,* they paid him the best and most appropriate of compliments. This is the final justification of the Empire as against the Republic, that it succeeded in this first duty of securing peace. Even under Nero we read, 'never had there been so profound a peace[2];' and it was in this aspect that the Empire most powerfully impressed both Romans and provincials.[3] The fault was that the peace did not last long enough. After all, the Romans ought not to have failed in keeping back the barbarians. Once admitted that the empire was rich enough in money and men, Augustus may have been wrong when he dissuaded any attack upon Germany[4]; for if that country had once been held and civilised, the balance of power would have inclined to the side of the Empire, and not to the side of the Northern races which overwhelmed it. But the fault lay deeper, and was one inseparable from any despotism, however well planned and skilfully administered. Ideally Rome's true aim should have been to prepare the peoples to stand by themselves, to civilise and organise them so as to be fit for freedom. The wholesome tendency was in the direction of independence, the dangerous and fatal tendency was in the direction of a bureaucratic centralisation. It was, however, inevitable that the latter tendency should prevail. The power of

---

[1] *Mon. Anc.,* § 13 (where he records that the temple of Janus was closed for the third time in his reign).

[2] *Ann.* xv. 46.

[3] Strabo, iv. 6, § 9, and passim in Books iii. and iv. ; Tac. *Hist.* iv. 74 ; Pliny, *N. H.* iii. 6 ; Vell. ii. 89 : finita vicesimo anno bella civilia, sepulta externa, revocata pax, sopitus ubique armorum furor, restituta vis legibus, iudiciis auctoritas, senatui maiestas, imperium magistratuum ad pristinum redactum modum. Cf. Ib. 126.

[4] The question is discussed by Mignet, *Introduction de l'Ancienne Germanie dans la société civilisée;* De la Berge, *Trajan,* p. 66 ; Congreve, *Roman Empire of the West,* p. 38. Freeman, *Cont. Rev.,* 1884.

self-government can only be gained by use and practice; and there was no self-government except in the towns. On one side the central government, on the other side the municipia; those were the only centres of political life. ' A Roman province with its municipal life was far above a satrapy, though far below a nation.' [1] That is very true, but municipalities without federation have little power of self-defence, and will fail in the hour of need. The provinces could not have defended themselves without Rome ; for 200 years Rome defended them ; but if a wiser system had been used, if real provincial militias had been maintained, if the provincial councils had been made into real parliaments, and not restricted to their so-called religious duties.; above all, if there had been a regular and organised representation of the provinces in the central government, Rome and her provinces together might have defended themselves for a thousand years instead of two hundred. It is, however, idle to ask what might have been ; and a Roman statesman might complain that we were trying his country by transcendental standards, that the debt of the modern world to Rome is already sufficiently great, and that no other people would have done better in their place. It is impossible for us to be sure how far the policy of Rome was dictated by military necessities. It is very possible that a Roman might have doubted the safety of such a treatment of the provinces. Above all he might have doubted the fitness of the provincials as a whole to be entrusted with self-government and a share of Empire. It is hard, as we see by India, for the conquerors to regard themselves as equal to the conquered ; and though the provincials as a whole were more nearly on a level with the Romans than the Hindoos are with their English rulers, still the Romans felt that it was they who ruled,

[1] Goldwin Smith, *The Greatness of the Romans ; Contemporary Review*, May, 1878, p. 333. See also Ramsay, *The Church in the Roman Empire*, p. 359.

organised and civilised, and that they had proved their capacity, while their subjects had not. The weakness of those who have conquered and ruled with eminent success, is to be sceptical with regard to the fitness of others to do a similar work ; and a Roman governor would probably have been as incredulous if you had spoken to him of a genuine parliament at Lyons or Cordova as an Indian official would be if you suggested a Hindoo parliament at Delhi.

Evils of the un-acknow-ledged character of the early Empire.

The unacknowledged character of the despotism which Augustus created was a more indisputable evil. It retarded the admission of the provincials within the Roman circle; and it prevented a rational settlement of the succession. If Julius really aimed at an hereditary monarchy he was wiser than his successor, whose ultra-Roman pedantry sought to maintain intact all the forms of the constitution after they had lost their vitality. The only excuse for Augustus is that men are often far readier to give up the reality than the name of freedom, and that the disregard of forms is often a greater offence than the disregard of rights. As the work of Augustus consisted to a large extent in a return to the old Roman exclusiveness in politics and religion, he fostered all the ideas which regarded the Romans as a peculiar people, and made it difficult for an emperor to be liberal with the franchise. In the first century, at all events, the prestige of Augustus' example was so great that one of the signs of a 'good' emperor was this obsolete and preposterous *Romanism*.[1] Still more important was the way the succession was settled, or rather unsettled. To leave it in form to the Senate and people as did Augustus, while really confining it to the members of one family, was an arrangement by which neither the advantages of an elective presidency nor of an hereditary monarchy were secured. A nominal consent of the people and a real consent of the

[1] See Freeman's *Essays*, Second Series, p. 321.

army formed a very bad basis for any government.[1]   A
strictly hereditary system is to a certain extent a safeguard
against revolution, and a strictly elective system is a safeguard against being ruled by a Caligula or a Nero. 'We
must not forget that it is to the entirely Roman system
of adoption that we owe the century of the Antonines.'[2]
Perhaps Augustus might have made this system the principle of the succession. Too much depended upon the
character of the individual emperor to make the hereditary
principle a safe one. Some system which would enable the
Senate and emperor together to name the heir, as the
Senate and Nerva together named Trajan, would perhaps
have been the best solution. But it must be remembered
that not only had the wish of the army to be deferred to,
but even when the principle of adoption was tolerably
established, a wise man like Aurelius was blind enough to
let a Commodus succeed him. As there was practically no
check upon the emperor, there was nothing to prevent his
yielding to merely personal feelings in this all-important
matter. The real evil lay in the very nature of the imperial
rule; and the history of the Empire is only another instance
of the shallowness of the dictum which would make a good
and permanent administration independent of forms of
government.[3]

The military character of the Empire becomes prominent Tiberius'
with Tiberius. Julius possibly,[4] and Augustus certainly, reliance
had kept this aspect of it in the background; but Tiberius on the
while pretending to leave everything to the Senate, at once army.
took upon himself the direction of the army,[5] and guarded

---

[1] Duruy, iii. 390, note 3.   [2] Ib. iii. 374.

[3] ' For forms of Government let fools contest,
      Whate'er is best administered is best.'
                                               POPE.

[4] Mommsen scouts the notion of Caesar having sought to establish
a purely military despotism, and maintains that he abhorred it; but
Suet., *Jul.* 26 and 77, hardly squares with the theory.

[5] *Ann.* i. 7.

his person with troops.   The last case of a general being
saluted as Imperator occurs in his reign[1]; and when
Germanicus won his victories across the Rhine, it was not
he, but Tiberius as commander-in-chief, who was so
saluted.   Tiberius was himself a consummate soldier, who
had won his own laurels in a series of difficult and dangerous
campaigns ; and his intimate familiarity with the different
parts of the Empire, derived partly from his long exile at
Rhodes and partly from his campaigns on the Rhine and
Danube, fitted him to become a capable and beneficent
administrator.

Tiberius'
adminis-
tration
of the
provinces,
A.D. 14-37.

Whatever we may think of the life and character of
Tiberius as a whole,[2] there can be no question of the excellence of his government of the provinces.   He had shown
himself a friend of the provinces even before he was
emperor[3]; and his reign did not belie the hopes then raised.
Tacitus himself commends his choice of governors,[4] and his
habit of leaving his governors for exceptionally long periods
in their provinces, though disparaged by Tacitus,[5] was
viewed very differently by the provincials.   ' Tiberius,' says
Josephus,[6] ' permitted those governors who had been sent
out to their governments to stay there a great while out of
regard to the subjects who were under them.'   That is, as
he explains, the temptation to make a rapid fortune by
extortion would be lessened.   The governors were under
the strict control of a man who detested misgovernment
and disorder, and was sure to punish with severity.[7]
Even Tacitus admits his care for the provinces.   ' He was

---

[1] Vell. Pat. ii. 125 ; cf. Tac. *Ann.* iii. 74.

[2] The question was started by Ihne and Duruy ; see Duruy's
History, iii. 409, where he gives a full list of subsequent works ; to
which add Mr. Beesly's Essay, a discussion by Church and Brodribb,
Annals, p. 419, Tarver's *Tiberius the Tyrant* (1902), and Schiller,
Kaiserzeit, 286, note 9.

[3] Suet. *Tib.* 26, 32.   [4] Tac. *Ann.* iv. 6.   [5] Ib. i. 80.

[6] Jos. *Antiq.* xviii. 6; Church and Brodribb, *Annals*, p. 340.

[7] Philo, *In Flacc.*, p. 965 ; Duruy, iii. 489, note 4.

careful not to distress the provinces by new burdens, and to see that in bearing the old they were safe from any rapacity or oppression on the part of governors.'[1] In circumstances of special necessity he showed special liberality. ' Decrees of the Senate were passed at his proposal for relieving the cities of Cibyra and Aegium in Asia and Achaia, which had suffered from earthquakes, by a remission of three years' tribute.'[2] On the occasion of the still more terrible earthquake which destroyed twelve famous cities of Asia, he promised a million sesterces for the relief of the one which had suffered most, Sardis, and remitted its debts to the fisc or the emperor's privy purse for a period of five years. Eleven other towns or states were similarly assisted, and a special commissioner was sent to afford present relief.[3] In all this we see the brightest side of a paternal despotism.

Tiberius had seen too much of war not to be a peacemaker. His solicitude for peace was most genuine and even painful, and Piso's worst crime in his eyes was that he had ' carried war into a province.'[4] At the same time, as an old soldier he knew that sometimes peace can only be secured by energetic war ; and the brigand Tacfarinas could not long commit his depredations with impunity, even in the African country which both Rome and France have found so unfavourable to regular troops. Even the worst evils of his rule were not evils to the provinces. The informers for instance were dangerous to Romans, but to the provinces they provided a means of avoiding much of the trouble and expense of a prosecution. The merciless severity of his punishments was all in their favour ; and while the emperor felt himself hated by those immediately around him, he was all the more ready to give ear to provincial petitions or complaints. His own legates do not

---

[1] *Ann.* iv. 6.   [2] Ib. iv. 13.
[3] Tac. *Ann.* ii. 47 ; cf. Suet. *Tib.* 49 ; Vell. Pat. ii. 126.
[4] *Ann.* ii. 64, iii. 14.

seem to have needed punishment[1]; the proconsuls had terrible examples to warn them against neglect of duty, and if a province needed relief it was given by a simple transference to his direct command.[2]

The revolt in Gaul.   One of the most important events of the period was the revolt in Gault, due, says Tacitus,[3] to the burden of debt, but perhaps still more to the intrigues of two ambitious men. The loyalty of Gaul had been often proved under the early Empire.[4] Roman civilisation had penetrated here with wonderful rapidity. The wealth of Southern Gaul was notorious : 'those millionaires' a speaker in the Senate calls the Aedui.[5] Augustodunum (Autun), so famous a city under the later Empire, was already the centre of culture and civilisation.[6] Here the noble youth received a liberal education, and were taught to be Romans, as Sertorius had taught the Spanish youth at Osca. A generation later we find the works of the younger Pliny in request at Lyons, almost immediately after their publication.[7] The people paid for this perhaps too rapid and immature bloom by the loss of the manlier virtues. We often hear allusions to 'Gallic effeminacy'[8] and to the country's 'wealthy and un-warlike population.'[9] 'As for the Gauls,' says Civilis, 'what are they but the prey of the conqueror?'[10] But their immense material prosperity is too well attested to allow us to take the protestations of Florus quite seriously, and he is inconsistent with himself when he contrasts the vigour of Gaul with the exhaustion of Italy.[11] But no doubt the

---

[1] All the accusations in the first six books of *Annals* are of senatorial governors, except of Capito, a procurator, with whom Tiberius seems to have been more than usually angry.

[2] As Achaia and Macedonia (supr. p. 134).   [3] *Annals*, iii. 40.

[4] Cf. Tac. *Ann*. i. 34, 43, xi. 24.

[5] *Ann*. xi. 23 : divites illos quorum avi proavique exercitus nostros ferro vique ceciderint. Cf. Ib. xi. 18, 24, xiii. 43, 6.

[6] Ib. iii. 43.   [7] *Ep*. x. 11.

[8] Tac. *Germ*. 28.   [9] *Ann*. xi. 18.   [10] *Hist*. iv. 76.

[11] *Ann*. iii. 40: Disserebant de continuatione tributorum, gravitate fenoris, saevitia ac superbia praesidentium.

passage may be taken to prove that the trade of the negotiator was not eradicated by the Empire; and indeed under Nero we hear complaints of the ' boundless usury ' by which Seneca ' exhausted the provinces ' and accumulated his enormous wealth. It is significant however that the word *negotiator* loses in this period its evil meaning, and becomes applied to legitimate merchants. It is in this sense that it is probably used when we are told that London was ' frequented by crowds of negotiatores.'[1] Florus' complaints of the tribute are to a certain extent supported by the more peaceable but not less urgent complaints of Syria and Judaea.[2] The immense sums left by Tiberius in the treasury were perhaps larger than they should have been for the welfare of the provinces.[3]

Caligula, that best of slaves and worst of masters,[4] exemplifies the saying of Tacitus that bad emperors are most fatal to those in their immediate neighbourhood.[5] It was Rome that suffered from his hideous eccentricities of cruelty; and it was on Rome and Italy that he inflicted new burdens of taxation.[6] Of the features of his government of the provinces we know little. Perhaps his most important measure was the one already mentioned, the establishment of a legate in Africa by the side of the proconsul. An oppressive governor of Egypt was punished, the suffrage liberally granted, and rich provincials were raised to equestrian rank. His pretended campaigns against Germany and Britain merely exposed his own insane vanity and incompetence. His pretensions to divinity

Caligula, A.D. 37-41.

---

[1] Tac. *Ann.* xiv. 33 ; Vell. ii. 110.

[2] Ib. ii. 42 ; iii. 40.

[3] Suet. *Calig.* 37. [4] Ib. 10.

[5] ' Saevi proximis ingruunt '; Tac. *Hist.* iv. 74.

[6] He began by remitting the ducentesima rerum venalium (it had been reduced from 1 to ½ per cent. by Tiberius), Suet. *Cal.* 16, but laid on a great number of new taxes afterwards ; Ib. 40. For the Jews see Philo. *Legat. ad Caium ;* for other acts mentioned, id. *in Flacc.* v. p. 969, and Dio. 59, 9.

and determination to thrust his worship on the Jews led to serious disturbances both at Jerusalem and Alexandria.

Claudius,　Far more important as a ruler of the provinces was the A.D. 41-54. despised and perhaps underrated emperor who succeeded him.　Claudius' liberal treatment of the provinces, if in part due to mere placid good-nature, must in part be ascribed to a deliberate and statesmanlike intention.　His governors were kept in excellent control[1]; and by the arrangement that there should always be an interval between two provincial commands, an opportunity was secured for bringing any accusations that might be necessary.[2]　In granting immunity[3] or autonomy[4] to provincial towns he was very liberal; and if in some cases a town secured such privileges for very inadequate reasons, in others the help met a real need.[5]

But it is with regard to the franchise and to the admission of provincials into the Senate that his action is most interesting and important.　If a passage in Seneca[6] is to be taken seriously, he had the widest designs in regard to the bestowal of the franchise.　'He had determined,' Clotho is introduced as saying, 'to see all the Greeks, Gauls, Spaniards, and Britons in the toga.'　He was very severe to those who pretended unlawfully to the possession of the citizenship[7]; as was natural, considering that the payments exacted for it, where it was not either given by the emperor or secured by passing through the stage of the Latin right,[8]

---

[1] Dio, lx. 24, 25 ; Tac. Ann. xii. 22 ; Jos. Ant. xx. 5.

[2] Dio, lx. 25 : ὅπως τε μὴ διακρούοιντο οἱ τοιοῦτοι τοὺς ἐθέλοντάς σφισι δικάζεσθαι οὐδενὶ ἀρχὴν ἐπὶ ἀρχῇ παραχρῆμα ἐδίδου.

[3] Ann. xii. 58 ; Suet. Claud. 25 ; Ann. xii. 60.

[4] E.g., Rhodes ; Ann. xii. 22 ; Jos. Ant. xx.

[5] E.g., Byzantium ; Ann. xii. 63.　This case points to excessive taxation, but the circumstances appear to have been exceptional.

[6] De Morte Claudii, 3.　But see Mommsen in Hermes, xix. 79, who suggests that only Latin rights are denoted.

[7] Suet. Claud. 15 and 25 ; Classical Review, xi. 65.

[8] Plin. Paneg. 35: ' Seu per Latium in civitatem seu beneficio principis venissent.'

must probably as early as this have formed a regular source of income.[1] But he was himself liberal in bestowing it. A decree of his, of the year A.D. 46, on the franchise claimed by the Anauni has been found at Trent. It runs as follows: 'Of the Anauni, Tulliassi, and Sinduni (now "Non," " Dolas," and " Saone," near Trent) I am informed that part has been attributed[2] to the Tridentines; part, however, not. I know that the Roman franchise of these people does not rest on a very sound foundation,[3] but what with long usurpation and what with long commingling with the Tridentines, from whom they could not be separated without injury to that splendid municipium, I allow them to retain the franchise they claim; and am the more induced thereto because some of these people are soldiers in my praetorian guard, others have been centurions, and some have judged in the decuriae[4] at Rome.' Still more interesting is the debate recorded in Tacitus whether the Aedui and other Gauls of Gallia Comata should be allowed access to the Senate, and so become eligible for the Roman magistracies. Claudius himself made an elaborate speech in favour of the proposal, which is not only reported in Tacitus, but was engraved on brazen tablets, one of which by a fortunate chance was discovered at Lyons in the sixteenth century.[5] It is a specimen of those imperial orations which

[1] *Acts* xxii. 28; Suet. *Vesp.* 16, 18; Finlay, i. 45. A passage in Dio Cassius, lx. 17, shows that these payments were introduced at all events as early as Claudius.

[2] The verbs *attribui, contribui* are used indifferently of minor towns or peoples attached to a more important town, which gave them the law, and raised taxes from them, and with which they in process of time, as here, tended to amalgamate. See p. 146. For the inscription see Dessau, i. 206; Mommsen, in *Hermes*, iv. 103; Nissen's *Köln*, p. 150.

[3] 'Non nimium firmam id genus hominum habere civitatis Romanae originem.'

[4] Cf. Orelli, 3805, Judex ex v. Decuriis, and 3877. Augustus made four decuriae, Caligula raised them to five.

[5] In 1528 or 1529. The tablet was broken into two parts, and is

the emperor used either to deliver himself in Senate or to get delivered by his quaestors—*Principis Candidati*.[1] At first they needed a senatus consultum to be law; but this was soon dropped. The Codex Theodosianus formally gives them the force of law, but they had had it in practice long before. There were two kinds of such orations, one a mere outline which the senatus consultum filled up, and the other giving reasons for the law and full heads of it. To this latter class belongs the oration of Claudius. That such orations were commonly engraved on bronze we know from a passage in Pliny[2]; and copies were no doubt procured by or sent to any states or cities which such orations might concern. Of all such orations this of Claudius is the only one in existence. The account of Tacitus[3] shows that the immediate occasion for the Aedui putting in their claim was the fact that Claudius had just ejected a number of members from the Senate, and that there were therefore vacancies to be filled up. It must not be supposed that Claudius gave all Gallia Comata the *jus honorum*, it was only the men of rank and wealth who had previously gained the franchise.[4] The chief men of the Aedui were given it first, after them the notabilities of the rest of Gallia Comata; but it would be an absolute error to suppose that the common people obtained the same privilege. Else how explain the passage of Pliny where, writing after Claudius, he divides Gaul into the regular classes of allied, Latin, and Roman towns? Of those who had the franchise some had either themselves won it or had received it from their fathers —were in fact 'free-born'; others had it as being members of Roman towns—of which latter there were four, Lugdunum, Colonia Agrippina, Colonia Equestris (Nyon), and

Claudius' oration in the Senate.

only a fragment of the whole. See Bruns, 195 ; Dessau, 212. Furneaux, *App.* to Tac. *Ann.* xi., C. I. L. xiii. 1668 and references.

[1] *Quaestores Caesaris* were also *candidati.* Willems, *Le Sénat*, p. 452.
[2] Plin. *Paneg.* 75.   [3] Tac. *Ann.* xi. 23-5.
[4] Tac. xi. 23 ; Suet. *Aug.* 47.

Augusta Rauracorum (Augst near Basle). The worst of it
is that we only know the status of Lyons for certain—it
undoubtedly had full Roman right. It is a mistake to
suppose that Augustus gave all Gaul the franchise, apart
from the *jus' suffragii* or *jus honorum*, for all that Dio,[1] who is
the only authority, says, is that Augustus gave some cities
liberty and the franchise, and took it away from others.
Augustus probably gave the franchise without the vote to
those Gauls who had deserved well of Rome; but there is
no reason for ascribing to him any liberal or comprehensive
measure, which besides would have been contrary to the
whole drift of his policy.[2]

The comparison of the real speech with Tacitus' version
is very curious. Besides transposing and changing the
order, Tacitus has cut out those deviations from the point
and those needless and verbose displays of learning in which
the antiquarian soul of Claudius delighted, and by which
he wearied out even the slavish patience of his Senate.[3]
In the *Annals* the speech is an admirable specimen of simple
and statesmanlike eloquence. Of the character of the real
speech something can be made out from the following
fragments.

In the first column he defends himself against those who
might accuse him of being an innovator. ' Why, our history
is full of innovations!' To prove which profound thesis the
imperial antiquary plunges with great zest into a regular
chronicle, beginning with the early kings : if he went on with

The real speech not given by Tacitus.

---

[1] Dio Cass. liv. 25.

[2] Still see Dio Cass. li. 16. There he is said to have granted the
privilege of entering the Senate to all except the Alexandrians.

[3] For Claudius' defects as an orator, see Dio, lx. 2 ; Suet. *Claud.*
39, 40 ; Seneca, *de Morte Claudii*, 4 ; for his policy in Gaul, Mommsen,
Provinces, i. 99, in *Hermes*, xvi. 485. Pelham (*Classical Review*, ix. 441)
argues that what Claudius did was to give the Gauls admission *inter
quaestorios*, therefore making them eligible to other offices. All citizens
at this time were required to be *laticlavii* before standing for office, and
that depended on the emperor.

the same fulness for the whole history of Rome he would have kept the Senate day and night. It is the oddest, most eccentric, most characteristic production that was ever engraved on bronze; interspersed with such remarks as 'this too is a disputed point among the historians'; or, 'if we follow our own authorities'; or 'if we follow the Etruscan writers,' &c., &c.; and with little parentheses to show his command of Tuscan (nam tusce Mastarna[1] ei nomen erat), or his knowledge of the world. Even here he begins to think he is getting a little lengthy, and asks 'Why now should I mention the discovery of the dictatorship &c.; why the transference of power from the consuls to the decemvirs, &c.; why the partition of the consular power among several, and the so-called military tribunes with consular power, six of whom, and often even eight, were appointed (this last touch is delicious in its inconsequence); why the sharing of office afterwards with the commons, and that not only of the regular magistracies, but even of the priesthood?' Why indeed? A few lines further on the bewildered reader, who imagined he was going to study a speech on giving the *jus honorum* to the Gauls, is relieved by lighting on the word *civitatem*; but this time the bronze plays us false, and the rest of this column of the inscription has perished. Let us turn to the remains of the other column.

It seems to begin by alleging the example of Augustus and Tiberius in favour of his design. This is an interesting sentence: 'It was the wish of my uncle Tiberius that all the flower of the colonies and municipia everywhere, that is, of the men of standing and means (bonorum scilicet virorum et locupletium), should be in this curia.' He goes on: 'What then? Is not an Italian senator preferable to a provincial? When I have begun to justify to you this part of my censorship, I will show you by acts what I think about that matter.[2] But I do not think that even provincials

---

[1] *Rhein. Mus.* liii. 609; *Bulletin Epigraphique de la Gaule*, vol. ii.
[2] 'Quid de ea re sentiam rebus ostendam.'

should be rejected, if only they can adorn the curia. See for how long a time the most beautiful and powerful colony of Vienna has contributed senators to this curia.' He mentions L. Vestinus, a native, and inveighs without naming him against L. Valerius Asiaticus,[1] 'who,' he says, 'was consul before his native colony had received the full privileges of Roman citizenship.'[2] At this point the Senate naturally get impatient and interrupt : ' It is time, Tiberius Caesar Germanicus, that you should reveal to the conscript fathers what your speech is aiming at, for you have already reached the furthest boundaries of Narbonensis.' Whereupon Claudius continues : ' All these noble young men[3] whom I see before me are no more to be ashamed of as senators, than is that noble Persicus, my friend, ashamed to read the name of Allobrogicus among the images of his ancestors. And if you grant this, what further do you require than that I should prove to you by pointing my finger that the country of itself beyond the boundaries of Narbonensis is already sending you senators, since we are not ashamed of having senators from Lugdunum.[4] With trepidation indeed, patres conscripti, I have transgressed the accustomed and familiar provincial limits ; but now without disguise I must plead the cause of Gallia Comata. And if any one objects that these same Gauls waged war for ten years against Divus Julius, let that man put over against that fault the unchanging loyalty of 100 years and an

---

[1] For whom cf. Tac. *Ann.* xi. 1-4 ; Dio, lx. 29. He was of Vienna.

[2] For promotion from the status of Latin to full Roman Colony, see Mommsen and Hirschfeld in C. I. L. xii., p. 218.

[3] *Insignes Juvenes* could hardly mean senators. Perhaps it means equites who had the right of attending the Senate ; in fact, the equites illustres ; cf. *Ann.* xi. 4 ; Dio, lx. 11 ; for *Laticlavii*, see Suet. *Aug.* 38 : liberis senatorum, quo celerius reipublicae assuescerent protinus latum clavum induere et curiae interesse permisit.

[4] *Ex Lugduno.* It is not possible to name any. Perhaps Claudius means *himself* as born at Lyons. Lyons as a full Roman colony would be exempt from the restrictions imposed on the rest of Gallia Comata.

obedience more than tried in many of our dangers. It was they who, when my father Drusus was subjugating Germany, kept a safe and sure peace in his rear, and that, though he had been called to war from the conduct of the census, an operation then new and unfamiliar to the Gauls. And how difficult and perilous to us is this business of the census, although all we require is that our public resources should be known, we have learnt by an experience only too considerable.'[1]

The imperial freedman. I have already mentioned the new power and privileges bestowed by Claudius on the procurators.[2] This was a very questionable policy : still worse were the extravagant powers bestowed on the imperial freedmen. At all times the freedmen were 'a widely diffused body ; from it the city tribes, the various public functionaries, the establishments of the magistrates and priests were for the most part supplied, as well as the cohorts of the city guard; very many too of the knights and several of the senators derived their origin from no other source.'[3] But it was Claudius who made them ministers of state and governors of provices ; and Nero imitated his example. As it was not exceptional ability but merely a turn for subservience, a certain talent for intrigue and an eye for the weak sides of human nature which raised such men as Pallas or Narcissus or Polyclitus to their position, they did not justify the lowness of their origin by any excellence of their administration. They accumulated fabulous wealth ; Pallas could refuse a present of 15,000,000 sesterces without self-denial ; and it was not wealth obtained by good means. Felix, before whom St. Paul appeared, was one of these freedmen, and Tacitus describes him as 'indulging in every kind of bar-

---

[1] The dislike of the census even at Rome is to be gathered from the severity of the penalties upon the *incensi* from the earliest times. See Dionys. iv. 15, v. 75 ; Livy, i. 44 ; Cicero, *pro Caec.* 34 ; Ulp. xi. 11 ; Gai. i. 160 ; Zonaras, vii. 19. The lex Julia Municipalis enforced the duty of making returns. Bruns, p. 103 ; Cic. *Att.* xiii. 33.

[2] Suet. *Claud.* 12, 24 ; supra, p. 125.   [3] *Ann.* xiii. 26-7.

barity and lust,' and as 'exercising the power of a king in the spirit of a slave.'[1]

No less than five provinces were added to the empire in this reign. Claudius was no soldier himself, but he chose his generals well. Besides the two new provinces in Africa,[2] Thrace, which had long been held in semi-subjection, was put under a procurator[3]; Lycia, in which there had been some disorders, was added to Pamphylia[4]: and Southern Britain was conquered and made into an imperial province under a consular legate. *Accessions of territory under Claudius.*

Another noteworthy feature of this reign is the determined position of hostility taken by Claudius against the Druids. As their religion had a political significance[5] the Romans never regarded them with tolerant indifference, as they did other creeds. Augustus had incorporated Hesus and their other deities in the Roman Pantheon, but the Druids would not come forward and accept the priesthoods under Roman direction and control. Claudius persecuted them in Gaul, and perhaps his expedition to Britain was caused by the desire to uproot the last stronghold of their preponderant influence.[6] In another part of the Empire, a famine in Greece serves to point out that country as still the least prosperous part of the Roman dominions.[7] On the Rhine the establishment of the Colonia Agrippinensis marks the birth of the city which is still famous as Cologne.[8] *Claudius and the Druids.*

---

[1] *Hist.* v. 9 ; Henzen, 5404. The use of freedmen ceased after the organisation of an equestrian civil service by Hadrian. See Mommsen in *Hermes,* xxxiv. 151 (1899).

[2] Mauretania Tingitana, Mauretania Caesariensis.

[3] There is a good summary of the relations of Rome and Thrace in Church and Brodribb, p. 411. See also Mommsen, *Provinces,* i. 201 ; *Eph. Epigr.* ii. 250 ; Kalopothakes, *de Thracia prov.* (Leips., 1893).

[4] Dio, lx. 17 : Τοὺς δὲ Λυκίους στασιάσαντας ὥστε καὶ 'Ρωμαίους τινὰς ἀποκτεῖναι ἐδουλώσατο, καὶ ἐς τὸν τῆς Παμφυλίας νομὸν ἐσέγραψεν. Suet. *Claud.* 25.

[5] Suet. *Claud.* 25.   [6] Duruy, iii. 526.

[7] Duruy, iii. 537, note 2, and his authorities.   [8] *Ann.* xii. 32.

Nero,
A.D. 54-68.

Nero, who was only a boy when he became emperor, started with excellent professions. He 'was for relieving the allies'; he started a wild scheme of abolishing all indirect taxes, and along with them the publicani [1]; and Josephus testifies to the justice of his decisions.[2] He issued an edict to prohibit any provincial governor from exhibiting shows of gladiators or other such entertainments, as it was found by experience that this was only a form of bribery.[3] But the intoxication of power was too much for that vain head and cruel heart; and the rest of his rule was not in harmony with the fair promise of its beginning. After the great fire of Rome he sent some of his freedmen on an excursion to get what they could out of the provinces. Acratus in particular distinguished himself by the forcible robbery of statues and pictures; and when Barea Soranus, who governed Asia like a Scaurus, did not punish the people of Pergamos for their violent resistance to the freedman's impudent depredations, he incurred the bitter enmity of his master.[4] Nero openly told his governors that he expected them to plunder for him [5]; and the revolt of Britain was due in part to the burden of taxes, and partly to the 'boundless usury of the money-lenders.' [6] The circumstances of this revolt, in particular the treatment of Boudicca and her daughters, show what the rule of the provinces could still be under a bad emperor.

General prosperity of the provinces.

But if a newly-conquered province could still be thus treated, it is impossible to mistake the general growth in prosperity and influence of the provinces as a whole. It would be easy to ascribe too much importance to the gift of freedom which the well-flattered emperor made to the province of Achaia.[7] The immunity from

---

[1] Ib. xiii. 50.   [2] Josephus, *Antiq.* xx. 8, § 11.
[3] Tac. *Ann.* xiii. 31.   [4] Ib. xvi. 23.   [5] Suet. *Nero*, 32.
[6] Tac. *Ann.* xiv. 32, xiii. 42.
[7] Suet. *Nero*, 24. The speech at Corinth in which the emperor announced the concession, as well as the reply of the Greeks, are pre-

taxation which generally went with this gift of freedom
was a positive boon enough, but it was revoked by
Vespasian; and if Pliny tells a friend of his who was
appointed to the province that he was 'sent to a society
of men who breathe the spirit of true manhood and
liberty,' [1] it is to be feared that he is only indulging his
natural love of phrases. The gift of the Latin rights to
the people of the Maritime Alps [2] was one much better
worth having. These rights implied all the privileges of
the Roman franchise except the jus suffragii and perhaps
the provocatio; and moreover opened a regular access
to the full franchise, as all magistrates of Latin towns
became ipso facto Roman citizens. [3] 'It likewise enjoys
the rights of the Latin towns, so that in Nemausus you
meet with Roman citizens who have obtained the honours
of the aedile and quaestorship,' says Strabo of the present
town of Nismes. [4] The extension of these rights to the
provincials began when Pompey's father, Pompeius Strabo,
gave them to the Transpadanes. [5] Caesar had a plan for
extending them to the whole of Sicily, and Augustus was
apparently more liberal with this minor privilege than
with the full franchise. It is easily intelligible that when
a town had once gained as much as this, it had good
hopes of gaining the full privilege. [6] Such concessions as

served in an inscription discovered in 1888; cf. *Bull. Corr. Hellén.* 12,
510; *Philol. Woch.*, 1889, pp. 106-7; Henderson, *Life and Principate of
Nero*, p. 390, where a translation is given.

[1] Plin. *Ep.* viii. 24.   [2] *Ann.* xv. 32.

[3] Cic. *ad Att.* v. 11; Merivale, ii. 100. The scourging of the magistrate at Comum is declared by Cicero to be an abuse of the law, even
if he were not a magistrate but only a 'Latin.' It is a curious fact
that a 'Latin' who built a ship for the corn traffic gained the franchise,
or ius Quiritium, the technical term for the civitas conferred on a
'Latin.' See Willems, *Droit Public*, p. 374, note 9. Suet. *Claud.* 19.

[4] Strabo, iv. 1, § 12. See also § 21 of the *Lex Salpensana*.

[5] Strabo, v. 1, 6.

[6] I have not mentioned two distinctions which are yet of importance
—(1) between Latin Coloniarii and Latin Juniani, the former in-

these show in which direction the stream was going ; and there are other indications of the rapid gain of the provincial upon the merely Roman element. Many of the provincial governors were themselves provincials ; and all the governors seem to have been really controlled by the wishes of the people they had to rule. No wonder men of the old school, like Paetus Thrasea, complained of 'the new insolence of provincials,' and that votes of thanks to ex-governors were forbidden by senatorial decree, when a rich provincial could boast his power to decide whether or no a governor should receive such a vote, and when the governors were seen going about at the latter part of their time 'seeking votes like candidates.'[1] That the inflexible and tyrannous Roman governor should be turned into a complaisant popularity hunter was a change indeed. The wealth of the provinces is sufficiently shown by such facts as that, when Laodicea was overthrown by an earthquake, the inhabitants without any relief from Rome rebuilt the town by their own resources[2]; and that on the occasion of the great fire at Rome Lyons alone offered a subscription of four million sesterces. Southern Gaul was in fact more prosperous in this than in any period of its history. There was an immense marine trade, an active internal navigation, and the towns reached a great size and were inhabited by a dense population.[3]

---

habitants of Latin towns outside Italy, the latter a particular class of freedmen who were given Latin rights by a Lex Junia Norbana (A.D. 19) ; and (2) Latium Majus and Minus, the former being when the decuriones and the magistrates got Roman franchise, the latter when only the magistrates got it (Gaius, i. 96).

[1] *Ann.* xv. 20, 21 ; cf. Plin. *Pan.* 70, which shows that such votes were used for elections at Rome. Pliny, *Ep.* vi. 13, illustrates the freedom of language used by the Bithynians before the Senate.

[2] Tac. *Ann.* xiv. 27.

[3] See some interesting remarks in Lentheric, *Les Villes mortes du Golfe de Lyon*, pp. 232, 401, 433, 441. Vell. Pat. ii. 39, where the author seems to say that Gaul pays almost as much to the treasury as the whole of the rest of the empire.

Nero was not one of those who much extended the boun- Acces- daries of the Empire. The Alpes Cottiae which had been sions of territory under the nominal rule of a client prince were made into a under province, and put under a procurator.[1] This may have Nero. still further strengthened and secured the communication between Italy and Gaul, but could otherwise have been of little consequence. More interesting is the addition of the Greek city of Tyra to the province of Moesia, an event which occurred in this reign.[2] In this part of the world the policy of Rome was one of beneficent encroachment. The few Greek towns which showed like bright centres of civilisation amidst the clouds of barbarism could hardly hold their own unaided, and the services rendered by Rome were of the most real and precious kind.

The fearful year of civil war which followed the death of The three pretenders, A.D. 68-69. Nero could not of necessity be of much consequence for the provincial administration. It is noticeable, however, that Italy suffered very much more than the provinces[3]; the sack of Cremona[4] recalls the worst horrors of Corinth or Magdeburg. The time was gone by when it was Asia or Greece that was the battle-field and the prey of the con- queror, and the turn of Italy was now come. It is impos- sible to say which of the three pretenders would have made the best emperor. All three had distinguished themselves as provincial governors.[5] Galba was too old and too narrow in his views (he was very chary of giving the franchise[6]) to become a great emperor ; but he was cer- tainly an honest man. Vitellius was profusely extravagant

---

[1] Suet. *Nero*, 18.

[2] Henzen, 6429 ; Marquardt, i. 150. For an interesting letter of Severus and Caracalla to the people of Tyra in answer to a claim of immunity they had set up, see Bruns, p. 230.

[3] Tac. *Hist*. ii. 56, 87, iii. 49.   [4] *Hist*. iii. 33.

[5] Galba in Africa and Tarraconensis ; Suet. *Galba*, 7, 9 ; Tac. *Hist*. i. 50. Otho in Lusitania ; Suet. *Otho*, 3 ; Tac. *Hist*. i. 13. Vitellius in Africa, Suet. *Vit*. 5.

[6] Suet. *Galba*, 14.

in bestowing such privileges as remissions of tribute, immunity, the Latin rights, and the privileges of treaties[1]; but there seems to have been no settled plan in this, any more than in other parts of his conduct after his head had been turned by the prospect of Empire. Perhaps Otho, notwithstanding his profligate youth, showed the most promise of the three. His bestowal of the franchise on the Lingones may possibly indicate that he would have been a liberal emperor.[2] When Vespasian became emperor he succeeded to all the difficulties bequeathed by the civil war. He himself declared that there was need of 4,000 million sesterces to make the State solvent; and if he found any such deficit as that, it is hardly wonderful that he was a hard master in regard to the taxation. The tribute of all the provinces was increased, of some doubled; and he is even accused of deliberately appointing rapacious procurators, in order to squeeze them afterwards.[3] The same absolute necessity of getting money was the motive for an act which must have been in the highest degree invidious and ungracious. He deprived of their freedom Achaia, Lycia, Rhodes, Byzantium, and Samos[4]: that is, he obliged them to pay taxes as before. His general administration, however, was much better than some of his previous acts would have led men to expect.[5] He was an enormous worker,[6] and animated with the best intentions. There can be no doubt that he did much to secure a stable

Vespasian,
A.D. 69-79.

---

[1] Tac. *Hist.* iii. 55.

[2] Tac. *Hist.* i. 78, but there is a doubt whether a Spanish people is not meant, and anyhow, the magistrates of the Gallic Lingones had received the franchise before (*Ann.* xi. 23). They had also taken the side of Vitellius, and if Otho did grant them this it must have been a hasty bid for their favour, which would hardly count as deliberate policy.

[3] Suet. *Vesp.* 16 for all the statements in the text.

[4] Suet. *Vesp.* 8.

[5] Cf. *Hist.* ii. 84. As to his governorship of Africa, Suet. *Vesp.* 4, and Tac. *Hist.* ii. 97, are in absolute contradiction.

[6] Suet. *Vesp.* 21 ; Plin. *Ep.* iii. 5.

administration, which Domitian did not overturn, and which was strengthened and consolidated by the Antonines. An interesting feature of his rule was his bestowal of the Latin rights upon the whole of Spain[1]; while the most important event of the reign was the siege and capture of Jerusalem.

Titus (A.D. 79-81) did not live long enough to fulfil the promise of his first years of empire; and though we are tolerably acquainted with the life of Domitian, our knowledge refers rather to his cruelties in Rome than to his administration of the provinces. We know, however, that in the first part of his reign, at all events, he was very severe to his governors, and that they never ruled better than when under him.[2] He did some important work across the Rhine in repressing the Chatti; his campaigns on the Danube were without permanent result, yet are interesting as anticipating the advent of a more vigorous conqueror. 'There may be great men even under bad emperors[3];' and Agricola in Britain carried the Roman arms north of the Cheviots, and secured the whole country to the Clyde and Forth by a mixture of clemency and force. The policy which his father Vespasian had commenced in Spain was carried out in detail under Domitian's rule. It is to this date that the existing laws of the municipia of Salpensa and Malaga belong, and that of the colony of Urso was redrafted. It is very probable that all the cities of Spain after they had received the Latin rights from Vespasian had been ordered to make public their municipal law.[4]

Domitian, A.D. 81-96.

[1] Plin. N. H. iii. 4, fin.
[2] Suet. Dom. 8: 'Provinciarum praesidibus coercendis tantum curae adhibuit ut neque modestiores umquam neque justiores ex-stiterint.'
[3] Tac. Agr. 42.
[4] That the law of Salpensa was published under his rule is plain from §§ 24, 5, 6, and § 29 of Malacitana. And as the title of Germanicus is not given, they must have been published between 81 and

The most important act of Nerva's brief reign (A.D. 96-98) was the choice of his successor. Trajan was a good administrator as well as a consummate soldier, and no choice could have been more fortunate. With him begins the long line of warrior emperors, who spent most of their time upon the frontiers. He added four new provinces to the Empire,[1] and in one case at all events his departure from the policy of Augustus proved a signal success. Though perhaps a little too exclusive in his views as to the claims of Italy over those of the provinces, he yet showed a genuine solicitude for all parts of his Empire. His campaigns had given him a great experience of the most different provinces[2]; and the modest scale of his journeys was a great contrast to the barbaric progresses of Domitian.[3] There were bad governors in his reign— the African Classicus[4] plundered Spain, and the Spaniard Marius plundered Africa[5]—but Marius was banished, and Classicus either died too soon for punishment or anticipated his sentence by suicide. Trajan's correspondence with Pliny shows at any rate the unwearied and constant application to details which marks a successful administrator. Nor is the charge of over-interference, often brought against him, well founded. The circumstances under which Pliny was sent to Bithynia as legate instead of the ordinary proconsul were wholly exceptional, and we have no right to argue from his conduct in this case to his conduct in other provinces.[6]   The cities of Bithynia had fallen into

---

84 ; cf. C. I. L. ii. 1945, where the magistrates of Aluro (Alora) thank Domitian for having attained the franchise through their duumvirate. The law of Urso is of a much earlier date, but the character of the writing shows it to have been formally published at that time. The text of these laws in Bruns, 142-157.

[1] Dacia, Armenia, Arabia, Mesopotamia.

[2] Plin. *Pan.* 15.   [3] Ib. 20.   [4] Plin. *Ep.* iii. 9.

[5] Ib., *Ep.* ii. 11 ; Juv. i. 45. The Spaniards made a grim joke on the maltreatment of themselves and Africa by an African and a Spaniard respectively. (Both the injured provinces were senatorial.)

[6] This is well stated by De la Berge, p. 120.

financial difficulties, due partly to mismanagement, partly perhaps to such dishonesty on the part of their magistrates as that which Cicero mentions in Cilicia under the Republic[1]; and Pliny was sent there for the express purpose of inquiring into their municipal affairs, and, if possible, putting them upon a satisfactory footing.[2] He was welcomed with gratitude; and even an allied town, though in right free from any interference of the governor, was glad to submit its affairs to his examination. It is very natural, therefore, that in these novel and untried circumstances the governor should refer more largely than usual to the supreme decision of the emperor; and the sense and tact with which Trajan answers Pliny's sometimes rather unnecessary questions excites our admiration. It is noteworthy, for instance, that he refuses to sanction any rough-and-ready measure of general application to all the cities of the province, but insists on a particular examination of each case by itself.[3] His jealousy of all associations, though it seems to us excessive,[4] was probably dictated by a consideration of the welfare of the towns themselves as much as by the desire for an untroubled administration. His strictness in giving leave to private persons to travel by the public post[5] must certainly have been welcome to the provincials. But the great work of Trajan's reign was the conquest of Dacia. 'The Dacian descending from the banded Danube'[6] had long been an object of some fear to the Romans. 'A people which can never be trusted' is Tacitus' description of them[7]; and

[1] A law of Trajan (*Dig.* xlviii. 13, 4, 57) made such thefts peculatus.
[2] Plin. *Ep.* x. 41.   [3] Ib., *Ep.* x. 14.
[4] Ib., *Ep.* x. 43, 94, 97. Caesar abolished all guilds except the most ancient. See Suet. *Jul.* 42; *Aug.* 32; C. I. L. vi. 2193.
[5] Ib., *Ep.* x. 14, 121. For Trajan and the postal system, see Merivale, viii. 53; De la Berge, 122; Hudemann, *Gesch. des röm. Postwesens während der Kaiserzeit*, 1878, p. 19.
[6] 'Conjurato descendens Dacus ab Istro'; Virgil, *Geo.* ii. 497; cf. Horace, *Od.* iii. 6, 13.
[7] *Hist.* iii. 46.

when they had consolidated themselves into a nation under a powerful chief, they showed themselves really formidable. Domitian won very little glory from his campaign against them, and is said to have paid them a regular tribute.[1] Trajan's two campaigns ended not so much in the conquest of the people as in their annihilation or expulsion; and their place was taken by immigrants from all parts of the Empire.[2] The Romanisation of the province was extraordinarily rapid and permanent. There was only one town in the country when Trajan conquered it—the royal residence, Sarmizegathusa. He established four colonies— Apulum, Napoca, Dierna, and another Ulpia Trajana at the old capital; and Dacia is one of the provinces in which the growth of the town system is most obvious and most interesting. To this day the language of the Roumanians testifies to their origin. The country still remains an integral part of the Latin world, though isolated from the rest, and profoundly modified by its after history. ' The two names which are still the most popular in all the valley of the Lower Danube are those of Trajan the victorious organiser and Justinian the great constructor.'[3] Trajan's dispossession of the prince of Armenia and substitution of a legate was not a measure of much consequence. It was abandoned by Hadrian, who also gave up his conquests beyond the Tigris, on the principle on which Augustus had abstained from taking Armenia. Trajan's new province of Arabia was a more important and more permanent acquisition; and Roman civilisation seems to have made considerable strides in this quarter. The two most important towns were Bostra and Petra, of which the former appears to

---

[1] Dio Cass. lxvii. 6 ; Merivale, viii. 26 ; De la Berge, 37.

[2] Eutrop. viii. 6: Ex toto orbe Romano infinitas eo copias hominum transtulerat ad agros et urbes colendas; De la Berge, 59.   For Galatians at Napoca, see Marquardt, i. 155.

[3] Desjardins, *Les Antonins d'après l'épigraphie*, p. 654.

have received special benefits from Trajan, and the latter from Hadrian.[1]

Hadrian has been called 'the first emperor who really cared for the provinces.'[2] Perhaps this is unjust to Trajan; but the praise which it implies is well deserved. Hadrian had the most intimate familiarity with all his dominions. 'No emperor traversed so many countries at such a rate.' To read the sketch of his life by Spartianus is like watching a panorama which carries you from one end of the world to the other. After he had returned from the East to Rome on the death of Trajan, his first journey was to Gaul and Germany, where he made himself remarkable by the strictness of his discipline. Then he crossed to Britain and built the wall known by his name. Returning to Gaul he built a splendid basilica at Nemausus (Nismes), crossed the Pyrenees, and remained the winter at Tarraco. His next journey was to the Archipelago, Asia, and in particular Achaia, in which province he especially favoured Athens— being himself so fond of Greek learning as to be nicknamed *Graeculus*—and conferred many benefits upon it. The next resting-place was Sicily; whence he crossed to Africa, and did much to improve the condition of the African provinces. Thence he returned to Rome, but hardly halting there made his way again eastwards, passing through Athens to dedicate the temple he had commenced on his previous visit, and Asia. Passing through Syria, where the insolence of Antioch earned the people his hearty aversion, as it did

(margin: Hadrian, A.D. 117-138.)

---

[1] Marquardt, i. 275.

[2] Freeman's *Essays*, Second Series, p. 334. I have said something about this already, but must add a speech of Trajan to Neratius Priscus, whom he intended to make his successor (see Roby's *Digest*, p. clviii) : 'Commendo tibi provincias, si quid mihi fatale contigerit' (Spart. *Hadr.* 4, 8). I seem to detect in these words a full consciousness of his responsibilities, and none of that merely Roman sentiment which has been ascribed to him. There is a good account of the various activities of Hadrian, and the literary movements of his time in Gregorovius, *The Emperor Hadrian*, Engl. tr. by Robinson (1898).

afterwards that of the gentle M. Aurelius, and through Trajan's new province of Arabia, he came to Egypt, thus completing the circle of the Roman provinces.

Hadrian's adminis- tration. The immense knowledge thus acquired was made available for the purposes of an excellent administration. Notwith- standing his liberal remissions of taxation,[1] he yet introduced so excellent and economical a management of the exchequer,[2] that the great expenses of his buildings in the provinces[3] do not seem to have exceeded his means. Bad governors were severely punished, and in particular the procurators, who seem to have done their best all through the Empire to act the part of the publicani they had supplanted, were kept in check by a strong hand. He imitated Trajan in keeping his freedmen in their due subordinate position ; discouraged informers, and showed an almost excessive complaisance to the Roman Senate. He was liberal in his bestowal of the Latin rights[4] ; and one of the best measures of his reign was to ameliorate the wretched lot of the slaves.[5] His establishment of the four consular judges in Italy[6] to try more serious cases in four different districts, shows the commencement of the tendency to treat Italy much like a province[7] ; for the evidence goes to prove that these magistrates were not merely judges, but discharged general executive functions as well.[8]

Hadrian's foreign policy. As already mentioned Hadrian gave up Armenia and Mesopotamia, and thought, according to Dio, of giving up Dacia. His was a peaceful reign, and the military measures

[1] Spartian, 6, 7, 21.   [2] Ib. 20.
[3] ' In omnibus paene urbibus et aliquid aedificavit et ludos edidit '; Spartian, 19. Several towns were called after him simply Hadriano- polis, in token of gratitude, as he did not like honorary inscriptions.
[4] Ib. 21. O. Hirschfeld, *Lat. Recht.* 12, note 3.
[5] Ib. 18.   [6] Ib. 22 ; Capitol. *Antonin.* 2.
[7] Already under Trajan Pliny, *Ep.* iii. 7, calls Campania a ' province.
[8] There is a list of these juridici drawn up by Mommsen in Lach- mann's *Gromatici Veteres*, ii. 192. They were revived by M. Aurelius, and were beneficial in relieving the mass of business in the courts of the capital.

which he took were generally those of self-defence. Besides his wall in Britain, he completed the line of fortifications begun by Domitian to protect the *Agri Decumates* on the North from the German tribes. This triangular piece of land needed special defence, as it was the only place where it was possible for the barbarians to press into the Empire without crossing either the Rhine or Danube; and the soldier-like Probus refortified the *limes* of Hadrian by again driving a wall from stream to stream. The country had its name in all probability from the payment of a tithe by the inhabitants to Rome, and Roman civilisation seems to have held its own there for at least two centuries.[1]

The successor whom Hadrian had chosen, M. Antoninus Pius, imitated and perhaps even exceeded his solicitude for the provinces. He, however, preferred to rule the Empire from what was still its centre—Rome. ' With such diligence did he rule the subject peoples that he cared for all men and all things as his own. All the provinces flourished under him.'[2] Such is the express testimony of his biographer, and this though the disasters of the time were numerous.[3] As a means to this end he kept good governors long in their provinces, some for seven or even nine years. The procurators were kept in order, as they had been by Hadrian. The municipal towns were assisted with money to commence new buildings or restore old; the decay of the municipia, mainly owing to the bad state of their finances, is a melancholy change of which the traces are beginning to appear. In foreign policy an interesting feature is the support given to the Greek cities of the Euxine against the barbarous Scythians. Olbiopolis was so effectually succoured that the tribe which had attacked it were forced to give hostages

Marginal note: Administration of Antoninus, A.D. 138-161.

---

[1] By 369, at all events, the Rhine was again the boundary; Marquardt, i. 125. E. Huebner, *Der röm. Grenzwall in Germanien;* Vopiscus, *Probi vita*, 13, 14; Amm. Marcell. xxviii. 2, 1.

[2] Capitol. 7.

[3] Famine, earthquakes in Rhodes and Asia; fires in Rome, Narbo, Antioch, and Carthage; Capitol. 9.

for their good behaviour. The time of peace was utilized for completing the *limes* against the Germans and that against the Caledonians. The revolt of Egypt at the beginning of the reign was no doubt due to the unruly turbulence of the Alexandrians, who were the first to urge their governor to rebel against the ruling emperor; and if they could not seduce him from his loyalty, would still revolt on their own account. The fact that all Gaul had received the franchise by the end of this reign[1] shows how rapidly the Empire was tending to uniformity; and the decree of Tergeste (Trieste) throws an interesting light upon the interior of a municipality during the period.[2]

M. Aurelius, A.D. 161-180.   With the accession of M. Aurelius we first find that partition of powers between more than one emperor, which was to be made the basis of the imperial system by Diocletian.[3] Lucius Verus, however, does not seem to have contributed anything to the dignity and welfare of the Empire, and his sudden death in A.D. 169 relieved M. Aurelius from a compromising associate. M. Aurelius was a good ruler of the provinces,[4] liberal to the municipia, and ready to give exemptions from taxation in case of need.[5] If his lot had been cast in times of peace he would probably have thrown his energies into the details of the administration, and done something more to merit his popularity with the provincials.[6] But the hard necessities of his time kept the man who, above all men, would have loved a life of peace and quiet study, engaged in arduous

[1] Mowat, *Une inscription inédite de Tours*, p. 28.

[2] Henzen, 7168, C. I. L. v., p. 53. Tergeste was a Roman colony in the tenth region of Italy, to which the tribe of Catali had been 'attributed' by Augustus. In this decree a statue is set up to a citizen Fabius Severus, who had obtained from the emperor Antoninus the concession that such Catali as held magistracies at Tergeste should become full citizens, and members of the local Curia.

[3] Capit. 7. All inscriptions, consequently, in which Augg. instead of Aug. occurs are at all events not earlier than A.D. 161.

[4] Capit. 17.   [5] Ib. 23.

[6] Ib. 26 : ' Orientalibus provinciis carissimus fuit.'

and unceasing warfare against ever-gathering masses of the barbarians. A great internal movement seems to ¡have begun among the trans-Rhenane and trans-Danubian peoples in this period. The northern races were pressed down southwards by still fiercer nations in their rear, and being thus compelled to become invaders they attacked all who refused to give them a refuge.[1] M. Aurelius appears to have led the Roman armies with constancy and ability, and was greatly beloved by his men. According to his historian, his conquests were considerable enough to allow him to think of making a new province or provinces out of the land of his principal enemies, the Marcomanni, Hermunduri, Quadi, and Sarmatae ; and he would have carried out his idea had it not been for his too early death.[2] However this may be, he certainly inflicted some severe defeats upon the barbarians, and was able to transplant a number of them to Roman territory, thus employing the system of *Coloni*, which is so important a feature of the Empire under Diocletian.[3] But the beginning of the end had come. It was not only on the Rhine and Danube that the Roman Peace was rudely interrupted. The Moors devastated parts of Spain, and though Aurelius' legates fought against them with success, yet the depopulation of the country had to be met by an infusion of Italian blood.[4] There were disturbances also among the Sequani in Gaul,[5] and in Egypt.[6] Aurelius' necessities were so pressing, and

---

[1] Capit. 14.

[2] Ib. 24, 27. An inscription of honour to him was set up by the Senate and people as 'omnes omnium ante se maximorum imperatorum glorias supergressus, bellicosissimis gentibus deletis aut subactis' (Dessau, 374).

[3] Ib. 24 ; Schiller in *Philologische Wochenschrift*, xii. 344.

[4] Capit. 21 and 11 : 'exhaustis Hispaniis.' The cause is not mentioned, but is probably the one stated in the text. Perhaps the plague, too, had its share. Spain had apparently been prosperous under Trajan ; De la Berge, p. 125. For the invasion of the Moors, see Boissière, p. 289 ; Hübner, in *Hermes*, i. 124.

[5] Capit. 22.　　　　　　　　　[6] Ib. 21.

the ravages of the plague [1] had been so fearful, that he was obliged to make soldiers of slaves and of the brigands of Dalmatia, and to hire German mercenaries to help him to destroy the Germans.[2] From this time forward the Imperial rule became strictly military in character ; emperors were chosen exclusively for their qualities as soldiers ; and reforms were dictated solely by military necessities.

Summary of the period.   These two first centuries of the Empire were for some countries the flower of their history. Asia Minor was rich and populous,[3] and studded with innumerable cities. The immense sums which these cities voluntarily spent upon their aqueducts, amphitheatres, and other public works, were perhaps excessive and extravagant, but attest a grandeur of conception and a superb indifference to economy which could only have sprung from a great material prosperity. The same facts appear in Syria. There were 100,000 Christians alone in Antioch in the fourth century. Jerusalem had a population of 600,000. Egypt was inhabited by seven and a half millions of people, besides

---

[1] A vivid account of this plague, said to have been brought back by soldiers from Mesopotamia, is contained in Capitolinus and Ammianus. It extended over Italy and all the West, destroying half the population (Eutrop. viii. 12), and immense numbers of soldiers. Superstition and persecution were rife, and the defence of the frontier from this time perceptibly weakens (A.D. 167).

[2] Capit. 21.

[3] Cf. what Pliny says of the province of Bithynia, which was certainly not one of the most prosperous of the peninsula ; Plin. *Ep.* x. 50. Nicomedia, which Diocletian sought to make a rival of Rome, was in the third century very populous, with circus, arsenal, basilicae, mint, palaces, etc. Pergamum had a population of 120,000. Caesarea, in Cappadocia, of 400,000. For the Troad see *Quarterly Review*, January, 1884, p. 172. The facts about the theatres, etc., are interesting. The theatre at Syracuse seated over 30,000 ; the second century amphitheatre at Tarraco a like number ; the amphitheatre at Arles, 25,000, and the theatre 16,000 ; ditto at Nismes ; Stephan, *Das Verkehrsleben in Alterthum*, p. 24. For Ancyra, the capital of Galatia, see Perrot, *De Galatia*, p. 76 et seq. For some interesting figures of the population of Spain, see Pliny, *N. H.* iii. 4, sub fin. ; also Jung, *Fasti der Provinz Dacien*, 18, 42, § 3.

300,000 settled in Alexandria.[1] Strabo and Pliny give similar testimony as to Spain and Gaul[2]; and Africa in particular enjoyed a prosperity which has never fallen to its lot before or since.[3] The Danubian provinces were equally well off, and the towns both more numerous and more important than they are at present, while those that are still the most considerable, for instance Widdin, Sistova, Nicopolis,[4] and, farther south, Adrianople, are all Roman foundations.

I have already spoken of the fundamental defects which made it impossible for the rule of Rome to be permanent. And it should also be mentioned that the taxation, though lightened as far as possible under the rule of the many capable and well-meaning rulers of this period, still pressed heavily upon the people.[5] The frequent remissions and exemptions granted in special cases show this clearly enough, and the day was coming when all such means of relief would be done away. Then when the barbarians were thundering at the frontiers, and the tax-gatherers demanding the means for an administration which ruled but did not protect, the provinces were all the more wretched from the contrast with the former brilliance of their prosperity. Rome had undertaken an impossible task, that of ruling an immense Empire without federation and without a representative system, where the only sources of power were the supreme central government and the

Fundamental defects of the Roman rule.

---

[1] Marquardt, ii. 117, and his authorities. For Alexandria, in particular, Marquardt, i. 297, 304. Strabo calls it τὸ μέγιστον ἐμπόριον τῆς οἰκουμένης.

[2] For Gaul, see esp. Plin. N. H. iii. 5, init.

[3] Marquardt, i. 403 ; Boissier, L'Afrique Romaine, passim.

[4] Pick's Antike Münzen Daciens und Moesiens (1898), p. 328.

[5] Cf. the case of the little island of Gyarus, whose scanty population of fishermen had to pay more taxation than they could afford, Strabo x. 5, § 3. For Syria, see Tac. Ann. ii. 42, provinciae Syria atque Judaea, fessae oneribus, deminutionem tributi orabant (A.D. 17) ; cf. ib. i. 76 for Greece.

army.   It would be puerile, however, to blame her for not
having grasped and applied ideas which were foreign to
antiquity, and which have only been worked out by the
slow experience of centuries.   We should rather wonder at
what was achieved by 'the weary Titan,' as we see her

> 'Staggering on to her goal
> Bearing on shoulders immense
> Atlantean, the load
> Well-nigh not to be borne
> Of the too vast orb of her fate.'

CHAPTER V.

The Period of the Later Empire (180-306).

THE period from the Antonines to the accession of Constantine is the least known of any period in the history of the Empire; and is yet of vast importance for our subject. The praises of a rhetorician[1] and the invectives of a sworn opponent[2] are the chief materials for the history of an emperor whose reforms effected a revolution in the whole system of administration. It is in a sense fortunate that the emperors between M. Aurelius and Diocletian effected so little, even in the best cases, but a successful resistance to the barbarians on the frontiers. At all events it makes us the less regret that the materials for their history are so scanty. It would be tedious and superfluous to collect every scattered notice of each emperor that flits across the theatre and is gone. I will only attempt to give some account of the chief administrative changes, especially those effected by Diocletian, and of the material condition of the provinces.

The Edict by which Caracalla in the year A.D. 215 bestowed the Roman franchise upon all provincials must not be regarded as a measure peculiarly honourable to its author. Dio[3] distinctly informs us that Caracalla's reasons *Bestowal of the franchise on all provincials.*

---

[1] Eumenius. [2] [Lactantius] *de mort. Pers.*
[3] Dio, lxxvii. 9. See Mommsen, in *Hermes*, xvi. 474 : *Staatsr.* iii. 570, 623, 643, 699. Coulanges, *Cité Antique*, 470 ; Muirhead, *Roman Law*, 304. Schiller, *Kaiserzeit*, i. 750. Maine, *Ancient Law*, 144, 145 ; Krüger, *Geschichte der Quellen und Litt. des röm. Rechts*, 118 ; Seeck, *Geschichte des Untergangs der antiken Welt.*

were purely financial.   Under the existing system the land-
tax was paid by the provincials and the legacy-duty by the
Roman citizens in Italy, who were exempt from the former
impost.   By giving the Roman franchise to all the provincials, Caracalla made them pay the *vicesima hereditatium*
as well as and over and above the tribute.   Thus the provincials had to bear a double burden, while Italy, though it paid
the legacy-duty, was still left exempt from the heavier tax.
Nor is it easy to say what definite privileges, except perhaps
in securing the right of appeal,[1] the provincials obtained by
this concession.   It is a melancholy feature in the history
of the Empire that the needed reforms come too late to be
of use, and that when they do take place, they imply new
burdens rather than new privileges.

Italy itself becomes a province.   But the exceptional position of Italy was one that could
not long continue.   Now that Italy no longer gave her
blood to defend the provinces, her privileged position was a
monstrous and indefensible injustice.   I have already remarked how the ideas of an absolute difference between
Italy and the provinces had been fading in the course of the
last century ; and it needed scarcely two generations after
Caracalla before all difference between her and the provinces
had ceased to exist.   The country itself became a province,[2]
or rather a group of provinces, and the land-tax was imposed on it as upon any other part of the Empire.   Hence-

---

[1] The right of all citizens to appeal to the emperor is believed to
have been established by a Lex Julia of Augustus, and probably was
intended to apply to the sentence of governors outside free states.
Various modifications were introduced, and by the end of the second
century most governors had the *Jus gladii* over the lower classes (*humi-
liores*), the *honestiores* continuing to possess the right of appeal to Rome.
Even free cities gradually surrendered jurisdiction in more serious cases
to the governor.

[2] So under M. Aurelius in a letter of Fronto, bk. ii. epist. 11, to a
juridicus of North Italy, we find him applying the term *provincia* to his
friend's authority.   See this point discussed by Zumpt, *Comm. Epig.*
ii. 48.   The *juridici* were practically much the same as provincial
governors.

forth we regularly find Italians designated as provincials, and Etruria and Campania as provinces.[1]

The predecessor of Caracalla had marked the advent of a new race to the direction of the Empire. There had been a succession of Spanish emperors ; now it was the turn of another country, and Septimius Severus was the first African emperor ; the next, and in some ways greatest series of all, was that of the Illyrian emperors. Severus was naturally a friend to his native country ; he gave three of its cities— Carthage, Utica, Leptis—the *jus Italicum*, or exemption from the land-tax ; and executed many works of permanent utility. He it was also who created the province of Numidia, and established in it as a regular governor the legate who had previously held that anomalous and invidious position by the side of the proconsul, which we have already endeavoured to describe. He broke up the great military commands, as in Britain and Syria, that no ambitious general might get the throne as he had himself done by being at the head of three legions,[2] and established a legionary force in Italy.

Septimius Severus, A.D. 193- 211.

The many short-lived emperors after Caracalla spent their reigns contending against the barbarians ; and it is seldom possible to ascribe to this or that emperor definite administrative changes. It appears, however, that the separation of civil and military functions, which is commonly ascribed to Diocletian, must have been the work of some earlier emperor. An inscription of the time of Carinus (A.D. 281 circa) proves that the governor of Numidia at that time did not call himself legate, but simply by the civil title of *praeses*, and was not of higher than equestrian rank.[3]

The separation of civil and military functions.

---

[1] Cf. C. I. L. x. 858 ; Henzen, p. 386.

[2] *Rheines. Mus.* xlv. 208, cf. Ceuleneer ' Essai sur la vie et le règne de Septime Sevère.'

[3] ' Viro perfectissimo, praesidi provinciae Numidiae.' Now, *perfectissimo* is a title which could never have been used loosely, and always implied equestrian, just as *clarissimus* implied senatorial rank. *Praeses* was the title for any governor, and had been usurped by the pro-

Another inscription of the year A.D. 261 testifies to the existence at that date of a legate of Numidia. So in the twenty years between A.D. 261 and 281 the change must have occurred. Now it would be absurd to ascribe any such change to the indolent and incompetent Gallienus, who let Gaul sever itself from the Empire because he would not take the trouble to protect it ; and if we glance through the list of the other transitory rulers of the period, there is but one man who conceivably might have done it. That man

Aurelian, A.D. 270-275.

is Aurelian, the same who established the new office of *corrector* in Italy ; and it is very probable that we are to ascribe to him these new *praesides*, and also the creation of the new office of the *dux limitis Africae*, a military commander who about this period appears in Africa by the side of the *praeses*. Putting the facts together, it comes out plainly that the governor was no longer allowed to hold civil and military powers in his single hand, but that with lesser dignity and inferior rank he was assigned the jurisdiction and other civil duties, while a new officer took the command

Gallienus, A.D. 253-268.

of the troops. We may connect with all this the changes effected by Gallienus, who forbade senators to leave Italy, and so precluded them from all provincial command. The emperors were jealous of their provincial governors, and were already casting about for means to diminish their authority. Under the existing system a successful provincial governor was sure some day or other to rebel against his superior, and we cannot wonder if the emperor regarded self-preservation as the first law of nature. In any case, whether Aurelian commenced this work or not, it was carried out and perfected by Diocletian.

The barbarians.

During all this third century the barbarian invasions

curators who governed provinces, as the only title open to them. But no legate would have called himself simply *praeses* from choice ; cf. Boissière, p. 309 ; Hirschfeld, in *Philol. Woch.* ix. 1159. Suet. *Aug.* 23, uses it as a general title for any sort of governor. It is never used of a municipal official.

were ever becoming more formidable. The Alemanni pressed into Italy at its north-eastern corner, where the approach was comparatively easy, and reached Ravenna ; the Goths spread over Greece and devastated the western coast of Asia Minor ; while on the Rhine and Danube the Suevi, Alemanni, Marcomanni, Carpi, and many other tribes maintained an unceasing struggle with the defenders of the frontier.[1] In such a state of things an emperor had to do two things : to protect the frontiers, and to secure himself against the pretenders whom their military ability or their popularity with the soldiers were ever bringing to the front. It is not surprising therefore that already before Diocletian became emperor we see signs of change and transition. ' One is compelled to recognise in the whole of this third century an epoch of transition, and even of anarchy, but also of gradual elaboration of the new adminis-trative system—a system which at first confused, and only with difficulty disengaging itself from the traditions of the past, did not reach its official development and definite con-secration till the long reigns of Diocletian and Constantine.'[2]

With the deposition of Gallienus and the election of Claudius, A.D. 268, comes the beginning of a better time. Claudius won the name of Gothicus by defeating the Goths in a tremendous battle at Naissus ; and his successor Aurelian (270-5) was a man of still greater vigour and capacity. His murder after five years' successful rule was not only a misfortune, it showed clearly that at all costs the tyranny of the soldiers must be done away. There was no

The period from Claudius to Dio-cletian, A.D. 268-284.

---

[1] A.D. 240, the Franks in Gaul and soon afterwards in N.E. Spain, from which they made piratical attacks on the African coast ; A.D. 256, the Alemanni before Ravenna ; A.D. 258, Temple of Diana of Ephesus burnt by the Goths, who had previously burnt Trapezus and Nicomedia, and plundered Greece ; A.D. 260, rise of the Persian monarchy under Shapur, defeat of the Roman army, and capture of the Emperor Valerian. The Persians had shaken off the Parthian yoke in A.D. 226, and for four centuries remained the principal enemy of the empire on the east.

[2] Desjardins, quoted by Boissière, p. 312.

hope for the Empire if, after a capable man had been raised to the throne, and was giving promise of a great reign, it should then be in the power of a brutal and capricious soldiery to rid themselves of him with impunity. Any system which taught the soldiers to know their place would be a benefit to the Empire. That this was more or less clearly felt by the good and capable men of rank in the army itself is shown by the meeting of the generals at Milan, and their decision to leave the choice of an emperor to the Senate. This looks very much as if, weary of a mere military despotism, they wished to found something in the nature of a constitutional monarchy. But the solution of the problem did not lie here ; and Tacitus, the gentle old man whom after eight months' delay the Senate at length appointed, was murdered by his troops before the year was over. This time the choice again reverted to the army, and Probus was elected (A.D. 276). During the years 275 and 276, encouraged probably by the brief interregnum, during which there was no emperor, the Franks had made a fearful inroad into Gaul and burnt seventy towns. Probus at once marched against them, inflicted a terrible defeat, and followed the fugitives across the Rhine. He resumed the *Agri Decumates* which had been given up by Caracalla, and built a still more powerful wall than that of Hadrian, to protect the country. On his murder in 282 he was succeeded by the Illyrian Carus. Carus sought to establish the hereditary principle, and when he died fighting against the Persians, his two sons, Carinus and Numerianus, shared the throne between them. Numerianus was a respectable man of letters, but no soldier. He was probably murdered by his uncle Arrius Aper, and on his death the officers chose Diocles, an Illyrian who had fought his way from the lowest to the highest station, to succeed him as emperor (A.D. 284). They probably little knew how momentous a step they were taking, for this Illyrian was the great emperor afterwards known as Diocletian (A.D. 284-305).

Diocletian spent the first years of his reign partly in a campaign against Carinus, whose murder by one of his own tribunes left him undisputed emperor ; partly in driving back the Germans across the Danube from Pannonia. In 286 he took the memorable step of dividing the Empire with Maximian, assigning to him the Western, while he himself retained the Eastern provinces. The reasons for this measure were mainly, no doubt, military. Several distant parts of the frontier had to be protected at once. Part he could guard himself ; but part could not but be committed to another general. The powers that general must have were too great for a subordinate ; and it seemed therefore best and safest to give him at once a share in the throne. There was a close friendship between Diocletian and Maximian ; both were Illyrians, and had been brothers-in-arms for many years. The measure was greatly facilitated by the sterling good sense of the rough soldier, who, always recognising the moral superiority of the older emperor, willingly carried out orders and consented to measures which sometimes perhaps he did not understand, or even actively disliked.

Maximian found much work ready to his hand. The state of Gaul demanded all the energies that could be brought to bear upon it. From Gallienus to Aurelian (A.D. 260-272) Gaul was sundered from the Empire, and governed by emperors of its own (Lollianus, Victorinus, and others), who resided at Trèves, and protected the country against the barbarians. They seem to have discharged this paramount duty with some success,[1] but there was a good deal of *internal* disturbance under them, as was natural. Aurelian conquered the last of these emperors, Tetricus ; but scarcely was the land quieted internally, than the Germans

---

[1] Treb. Pollio, *Trig. Tyr.* 5, says of them : ' Quos omnes datos divinitus credo, ne quum illa pestis (Gallienus) inauditae luxuriae impediretur malis, possidendi Romanum solum Germanis daretur facultas.'

began invading it from without. In the interregnum between Aurelian and Tacitus these inroads were so far-reaching that the whole country seemed lost ; and scarcely had Probus driven out the barbarians when two generals —Proculus and Bonosus—raised the standard of revolt at Cologne. They were soon put down, but the Germans broke in again on Probus' death ; the *Agri Decumates* were again lost ; and at the same period unfortunate Gaul was visited by the Bagaudae.[1] The insurrections of these Bagaudae are to be compared to those of the Jacquerie in France in the fourteenth century ; and an account of the causes which led to them will throw a good deal of light on the condition of the provinces.

The peasantry. The state of the peasantry was miserable in the extreme in the last centuries of the Empire. In Italy an eighth part of the rich Campania was untilled and desolate ; and similar causes produced in the provinces similar results. ' Latifundia perdidere Italiam, iam vero et provincias,' says Pliny already towards the end of the first century.[2] Roman citizens often held large estates in the provinces, Agrippa for instance in Sicily,[3] Rubellius Plautus in Asia[4]; the emperors in particular had domain-lands in almost every province.[5] Plantations in Sicily, mines in Spain, cattle-pastures in Dalmatia, to give a few out of a long list, were all owned by Roman citizens, and all worked by multitudes of slaves.[6] In Africa, according to Pliny, six proprietors owned half the country.

---

[1] Preuss, p. 29.

[2] Pliny, *N. H.* xviii., § 35 ; Juv. xiv. 140 ; Finlay, i. 54, 89.

[3] Horace, *Epist.* i. 12, 1 : ' Fructibus Agrippae Siculis quos colligis, Icci.' He owned also the Thracian Chersonese, which he left to Augustus, and which therefore was always Imperial domain-land when Thrace became a province (Dio Cass. liv. 29) ; and Atticus had estates on the mainland opposite Corcyra.

[4] *Ann.* xiv. 22.

[5] E.g., Nero in Spain ; Plut. *Galba*, 5. The *procuratores rei privatae*, though, strictly speaking, only the emperor's bailiffs and appointed to look after these properties, were yet important officials.

[6] Stephan, *Das Verkehrsleben in Alterthum*, p. 25.

With this increase of great estates the small proprietors could no longer maintain the fruitless struggle, and, as a class, wholly disappeared. Some, no doubt, became soldiers; others crowded into the already overflowing towns; while others voluntarily resigned their freedom, attached themselves to the land of some rich proprietor, and became his villeins, or *coloni*. But this was not the chief means by which this class was formed and increased. When Savigny wrote his famous essay[1] on the *Coloni* in 1828, he asked: How did this class of coloni rise? a man might be born a colonus, and indeed a common name for the class as a whole was *originarii*; but how did the first and original coloni come into existence? After pointing out the evidence which proves that in some cases free men became coloni by their own act, he goes on to state that a constitution of the Codex Theodosianus (A.D. 409), discovered shortly before he wrote, throws a new light on the matter. This constitution gives public notice that any landowner may apply to the praefectus praetorio for labourers from the newly-conquered Scyrians (in the present Moravia); which labourers are to be used not as slaves, but as coloni. 'Thus we have a very remarkable example, indeed the only known example, clearly pointing out the manner in which bodies of coloni on a large scale originated. The emperors might have sold the barbarians who had fallen into their hands, as slaves, but preferred (without doubt from politico-economical grounds) giving them away as coloni. Now one might conjecture that the whole class sprang up originally after the same manner, so that this single instance should be only a repetition of similar previous ones.' His final conclusion is that the class might no doubt have originated in this manner, but that on the other hand it might not, and that it is better not to be

Extinction of small proprietors.

Formation of the class of coloni.

---

[1] Translated in the Philological Museum, ii. 117-145. For further light upon the *coloni* see Maine's *Ancient Law*, chap. vii.; Fustel de Coulanges' *Collected Essays* (1885); Mommsen, in *Hermes*, xv., p. 410; Seebohm, *English Village Communities*, 269; Willems, *Droit Publ.*, 617; Pelham, in his collected essays.

dogmatic on the point. These transplantations of population and this peculiar tenure begin at an early date.
Augustus settled the Triumpilini, an Alpine tribe, in Italy,[1]
and after him it became the regular practice, after having
inflicted a defeat on a barbarian tribe, to transport them
to some place far away from the frontiers and settle
them on the land with the status of coloni. M. Aurelius
made great use of this system. ' He settled an infinite
number of men from the different barbarian peoples, on
Roman soil,' says his biographer[2] ; and succeeding emperors
pursued the same policy. After a successful war these
serfs were given, as is indicated by the passage of the Codex
Theodosianus, to landed proprietors without payment ; and
in this way not only was the class of free peasants diminished
or altogether destroyed, but—a happier result—the slave
system was directly attacked.

Distinc-   The coloni themselves were not slaves. The codes
tion
between directly distinguish them from slaves, in several imperial
the coloni constitutions they are called *ingenui*, and in the second
and
slaves. century were still tenants, paying their rent in money and
able to leave their holdings on the expiration of their lease.[3]
They could contract a legal marriage, and could hold
property. It is true that a colonus had to pay his master
(patronus) a certain sum of money for permission to marry,[4]
and that though he could hold he could not alienate property.[5]
But a slave could contract no marriage at all in the eye of

[1] ' Venalis cum agris suis populus ' is the expression of Pliny, *N. H.*
iii. 20.

[2] Capit. 24 ; cf. Suet. *Aug.* 21, where we find Augustus settling
Germans in Gaul ; Eutropius, vii. 9 ; Dio Cass. lxxi. 11 ; Kuhn, i. 260 ;
Marquardt, ii. 234. Such settlements are recorded besides of the
Piceni (Strabo, 5, 4, 13), of the Ligurian Apuani (Livy, 40, 38), of
Galatae in Dacia (Henzen, 7202), of various peoples in Moesia (Schiller,
Kaiserz. 355), of Germans in Gaul by Tiberius (Suet. *Tib.* 9).

[3] Savigny, *Phil. Mus.* ii. 122.

[4] Ib. 130. The sum was not to exceed a *solidus.*

[5] Ib. 132, Cod. v. tit. xi.

the law, and could not reclaim his property if deprived of it. On the other hand, the coloni were like slaves in that they were liable to personal punishment.[1] What their exact position was is shown by a passage in the Codex where they are called *servi terrae*, 'slaves of the soil.'[2] A colonus was indissolubly attached to the land, and could not get quit of the tie, even by enlisting as a soldier. The proprietor could sell him with the estate, but had no power whatever of selling him without it; and if he sold the estate he was compelled to sell the coloni along with it. The coloni paid the proprietor a yearly rent for their land, generally in kind. The rent was settled by custom, and the proprietor had no power to raise it above what had been usual.[3]

The position of these villeins came to be a very miserable one, the harsher system having apparently grown up among the barbarian prisoners whom emperors of the third century transplanted to estates within the provinces. Besides the rent payable to his patron for his bit of land, the colonus had to pay not only the poll-tax, which was levied on all who did not pay the land-tax, but also a tax on his corn, or cheese, or cattle, or anything else which he might sell at the market in the neighbouring town.[4] Then there were the extraordinary exactions, which could not be foreseen or calculated upon, and which caused endless misery. What was still worse, coloni had no protection against the arbitrary cruelties of their patron, who could scourge or imprison them, and at all times make their lives hateful to them by unending labours. The patron was responsible for the poll-tax of his coloni, and we may be very sure that he exacted the last farthing from them. Finally, as the corporation system spread in the fourth century, the coloni, now bound to the soil, were liable for a very large share of

Miseries of the coloni.

---

[1] Cod. tit. ix. ; Savigny, 123.   [2] Ib. 124.

[3] For these statements, see Savigny's *Essay* and Willems, *Droit. Publ.*

[4] Preuss, 26.

the taxes, and in many cases sank into slaves or fled to the barbarians.

The Bagaudae.

Under Diocletian these coloni in Gaul combined together, were joined by the remaining free peasants, whose lot was not less wretched than their own, and, forming into numerous bands, spread themselves over the country to pillage and destroy. They were called Bagaudae, from a Celtic word meaning a mob or riotous assembly,[1] and under this name recur often in the course of the next century both in Gaul and Spain. Their power rapidly increased; some towns were so wretched that they opened their gates willingly to them; and in the year 285 they set up two emperors of their own. Their head-quarters were in Northern Gaul, and their chief stronghold was built on a tongue of land at the juncture of the Marne and Seine.[2]

The state of Gaul.

When Maximian was made emperor the first task entrusted to him was the reduction of these Bagaudae. This was quickly and easily accomplished; but the causes of the revolt were not removed. A good deal, however, was done both now and later by Constantius to remedy the depopulation of the country. Maximian planted large bodies of conquered barbarians in the parts which had been desolated by the Bagaudae; and when Constantius conquered the Franks who had settled, and absorbed the Batavi, on the Rhone mouth, he planted such numbers of them over Northern Gaul, particularly in the districts of Amiens and Troyes, that all that part of the country must have been thoroughly Germanised. Attempts were also made, particularly by Constantius, to improve the material condition of the country. A good deal in particular was done for the gallant city of Augustodunum, which after having been captured by the usurper Tetricus, and given up to massacre and sack, had then suffered from the Bagaudae and the

---

[1] Preuss, 30 ; Jung. *Recht. L.*, 79 note ; Gibbon, ch. xiii. Salvian *de Gubern. Dei* v. 6.

[2] Preuss, 31.

Franks.[1] But the whole country had suffered from many years of neglect, when men had neither the power nor the will to attend to anything but the protection of their lives and property against the barbarians. The water-courses were not looked after, and whole districts had sunk back into moor and morass ; others had become desert, and were inhabited only by wild beasts.[2]

No sooner had Maximian crushed the Bagaudae, than he had to repel the swarms of the Burgundians, Alemanni, Heruli, and Chaviones, who had forced the frontier and poured into Gaul. In the next two years (287 and 88) he not only defeated them in Gaul, but drove them across the Rhine and made an inroad into Germany. Meanwhile the new confederacy of the Franks, whose devastations in Gaul some years before have been already mentioned, had formed a permanent settlement at the mouth of the Rhine, there learnt sea-faring from the Saxon races with which they had allied themselves, and became the pirates of the Channel. Carausius, whom Maximian sent against them, turned traitor, seized Britain on his own account, and took Franks and Saxons into his pay. The sea campaign which Maximian conducted against him was a failure, and it was agreed that he should be recognised in his empire of Britain. Here, four years afterwards, he was murdered by his lieutenant Allectus, who sought to take his place ; but Constantius won back the province to the Empire by a single battle in which the murderer fell. Perhaps Britain did not gain by the exchange.[3] Carausius had ruled it well, its commerce had flourished beyond all former precedent, and for the first time in its history the island had learnt to regard itself as mistress of the seas.

---

[1] Preuss, 59-65, gives a very interesting account of the fortunes of Augustodunum.

[2] Eumenius, *Schol. Rest.* 18 *Grat. Act.* 6-7 ; Preuss, 63.

[3] The rhetorician Eumenius has no doubt as to the benefits of the change. See *Paneg. Const.* 18 ; *Schol. Rest.* 18.

Diocletian in the East.   Meanwhile Diocletian was busy in the East. In the summer of A.D. 286 he was at Tiberias in Palestine. The Persian king Dahram II. sent an embassy and asked for a treaty, being then at war with a rebellious brother, and so not venturing in any way to provoke Rome. This state of things among the Persians permitted the Romans to recover their client-kingdom of Armenia. Tiridates, who had been brought up at Rome and was nevertheless a gallant soldier, was restored to his hereditary kingdom, and his subjects received him with enthusiasm. After this fortunate settlement of the East Diocletian straightway

Military ability of Diocletian.   returned to Europe, drove the barbarians out of Pannonia and Rhaetia, secured the frontier of both provinces, and then had an interview with Maximian. Probably at this interview it was settled that they should assume the surnames respectively of *Jovius* and *Herculius*, designations which well characterised their mutual relations, and which were at once seized upon by the Rhetoricians. A great deal had been accomplished, but a great deal still remained to do. It was fortunate that just at this period the task of Diocletian was greatly facilitated by dissensions among the barbarians themselves. ' The Goths destroy the Burgundians. The Alemanni take up arms for the conquered. The Thervingii, another branch of the Goths, also rush to arms, with the help of the Taifali, against the Vandals and the Gepidae.'[1] Rome had no wars with the Goths from this date till A.D. 323. This state of things left Diocletian free to direct his energies eastwards. In the year 290 we find him again in Syria. After defeating and capturing many of the Saracens who were making inroads on Roman territory, he straightway returned to Pannonia. ' Scarcely had Syria beheld him, when now Pannonia welcomed him.'[2] At the beginning of the following year he met Maximian

---

[1] Mamert. *Geneth. Maxim.* 17 ; Preuss, 46.

[2] ' Illum modo Syria viderat, jam Pannonia susceperat ;' Mamert. ibid., 4.

in a famous interview at Milan. Rome was carefully avoided, and the senatorial deputation sent to greet the arrival of the emperors on Italian ground learnt nothing of the purport of their interview.

It was probably at this meeting that the further partition of power was arranged which was made public in 293. The necessity of new wars for the security of the frontier, and the impossibility of Diocletian's leaving the East to conduct them, led to the nomination of the two Caesars, Constantius and Galerius. Galerius was a Dacian, born not far from Sophia, and had been a cowherd, whence he was nicknamed Armentarius. He was an ardent persecutor of the Christians, and a man of rough and even brutal character. Constantius was an Illyrian of good birth, and in every way a distinguished personage, yet modest and kindly. Gaul was well off under his rule. On March 1, 293, both were solemnly proclaimed as Caesar,—Galerius at Nicomedia, Constantius at Milan. Galerius married Diocletian's daughter Valeria; Constantius, Maximian's step-daughter Theodora. Young Constantine, Constantius' son, was summoned to the East, and there learnt the art of war under Diocletian and Galerius. *Further partition of power.* *The two Caesars.*

To Constantius was assigned the task of recovering Britain. He accomplished this, as already mentioned, with celerity and success; and on his return to Gaul did his best to restore its former prosperity. It is a symptom of the advance of Britain and decay of Gaul in this period that when he recrossed the Channel he brought with him a number of British artisans and architects to help him to rebuild the towns of Gaul. The Franks were so badly beaten as not to reappear as invaders till the reign of Constantine ; and a murderous defeat was inflicted on the Alemanni. *Constantius recovers Britain.*

Maximian, besides the general control of the Western provinces, had Italy, Spain, and Africa committed to his special charge. His fixed residence was Milan, but we find *Maximian in the West.*

him at one time at Aquileia, at another on the Rhine, at another in Africa. When in 297 the Moors made a formidable inroad into Roman Africa, it was he who defeated them, captured a number of them, and settled the prisoners in other provinces.

Galerius on the Danube.

From 293 to 296 Galerius was on the Danubian frontier. His enemies were the Jazyges, and more particularly the Carpi. The latter tribe he attacked and annihilated, with the exception of those whom he settled as coloni in Dacia. The Carpi do not reappear in history.

Diocletian in Egypt, A.D. 297.

Egypt.

Above all, Diocletian had an arduous task before him in the reduction of Egypt. Though well and kindly treated, the Egyptians had always been insolent to their rulers, and ready to rebel. They were at this time a stiff-necked and obstinate race, not fit for freedom, and yet refusing to obey, and needing the lesson which Diocletian was not slow to give it. For ten years Egypt had been severed from the Empire and ruled by the usurper L. Elpidius Achilleus, a native of the country. When after a long siege Diocletian took Alexandria he punished it with terrible severity. He had determined to stop the spirit of rebellion once for all, and he set to work in the spirit of a Strafford. He also reorganised the administration, getting rid of Augustus' arrangements, and dividing the country into three provinces, Aegyptus Jovia, Aegyptus Herculia, and Thebais. While

War with Persia, A.D. 297-98.

Diocletian was in Egypt the Persian king Narses seized the favourable opportunity of invading Armenia, drove out Tiridates, and occupied the country. Diocletian entrusted the war to Galerius, who, in A.D. 297, rashly attacking without waiting for Diocletian to come up, was defeated with great loss ; and he and Tiridates only just secured their own escape. The reception he met with from Diocletian at Antioch was not such as to encourage him to a repetition of rash experiments. In the following year, however, he retrieved his character by the crushing defeat he inflicted on the Persians. The capture of Narses' wife and children was still more decisive even than the victory. Narses was willing to accept any terms to recover them, and after some preliminaries, peace was finally signed on the following terms : — 1. The Tigris was made the boundary ; and thus all Mesopotamia became Roman. 2. Rome relinquished her claim to lands on the north-east of the Tigris, the modern country of Northern Kurdistan. 3. Tiridates was reinstated, and compensated for the loss of the above-mentioned lands by a considerable share of Persian territory. 4. The Iberian kings (who were of importance as holding the passes of the Caucasus) were to be dependent on Rome instead of on Persia.

Tiridates died, after a long reign, king of Armenia. No Persian war occurs again till Julian. Then the defeat of the Romans, A.D. 363, gave back all that Rome had gained by this treaty.

Peace had now been everywhere secured. The legions were no longer to be feared, for even if they wanted to mutiny, no general would dare to lead them against four different emperors. It was no mere hypocrisy if Diocletian was called 'restorer of the world,' or 'parent of the golden age.' With nothing to fear either from the army or the barbarians, he could now devote himself to the work of organisation. The first great change was the division of the supremacy among four rulers. Before this there had been two emperors simultaneously—M. Aurelius and Verus ; and many emperors had named their sons Caesar or Augustus, so as to secure a peaceable succession. Similarly the army and Senate had elected two Gordians, and had put Maximus and Balbinus on the throne together. But the success of these two last cases had not been such as to encourage imitation. In 286 Maximian was undoubtedly given Gaul, Britain, Spain, probably also Italy and Africa ; while Diocletian retained the rest of the Empire from the East to Rhaetia. All troops in the West were under Maximian's supreme command ; victories were ascribed to his auspices ; and he had

Interval of peace.

power of life and death over all his military subordinates. He had also the supreme civil power; he administered his own treasury in his own provinces; supervised justice, and issued rescripts. In 293 the Empire was divided over again. Diocletian had the East, with Egypt and Libya to the borders of Numidia, Asia Minor and the islands. Galerius had Thrace, Pannonia and Moesia, including East and West Illyricum, Macedonia, Greece, and Crete. Maximian had Rhaetia, Italy, Africa, and Spain. Constantius Gaul,

Relation of the Caesars to the Augusti.

the Germanies, and Britain. It is not easy to make out the exact relation between the Caesars and the Augusti.[1] But when circumstances require it, the Augustus appears with troops in the Caesar's provinces and takes the command in chief. In 296 we find Maximian on the Rhine, in 293 and 94 Diocletian at Sirmium; or, on the other hand, the Augustus invited the Caesar into his own province. But we never find Galerius in the West nor Constantius in the East. There are no constitutions or rescripts in the name of the Caesars alone. Most of the coins and inscrip-

Pre-eminence of Diocletian.

tions bear the names of all the four rulers. But the supreme legislative power lay with the Augusti, or in point of fact with Diocletian.[2] The Augustus sent the census officials into his Caesar's provinces, and also controlled the official appointments. It is a proof of Diocletian's pre-eminent position that he did not hesitate on occasion to send orders to the governors of Maximian's provinces; for instance, to those of Spain and Africa. On the other hand, each of the four had large separate powers; made war and peace on his own account; and exercised supreme jurisdiction. The

---

[1] Professor Bury, note 18 to Gibbon, ch. xiii. The Caesars had no legislative powers, no control over the imperial revenue, nor consistorium; nor had they the right of appointing the officials in their dominions. Their military powers were dependent on the Augusti, to whom all their victories were ascribed. They wore the purple, but not the diadem.

[2] Preuss, 89; Mommsen, *Über die Zeitfolge der Verordnungen Diocletians* (*Abh. der Akad. der Wiss. zu Berlin*, 1860, p. 419).

general edict against the Christians was not carried out in Constantius' provinces, and those provinces did not suffer from the taxation as much as the rest.

Diocletian was not satisfied with quartering the world. He further subdivided the provinces, making them much smaller and more numerous, and established a new civil official, the *Vicarius*, between the Caesars and the provincial governors. The whole Empire was divided into twelve dioceses, the smallest of which—Britain—consisted of four provinces, the largest—Oriens—of sixteen. Lactantius describes this subdivision as follows: ' The provinces also were cut into fragments. Many governors and more officials settled upon each single district, almost upon each single city.' [1] Individual governors, besides being deprived of military power, had such a small territory under them that the danger of revolt was reduced to a minimum. The 101 provinces thus formed were under different governors of different rank. There was a *proconsul* in Africa Zeugitana, and probably in Asia, Achaia, and Baetica. Then came the *consulares* with rank of clarissimi. Then the *correctores*, some of whom had rank of clarissimi, others only of perfectissimi. Lastly, the *praesides* with the rank of perfectissimi. This title of praeses supplanted the old title of procurator.[2] The title of legate, if it had not ceased already, does not at all events occur after this reign.

Important also as well as permanent was Diocletian's appointment of a vicarius to each diocese. These officials

Subdivisions of the provinces.

The vicarii.

---

[1] Lact. *de Morte Pers.* 7 : ' Provinciae quoque in frusta concisae, multi praesides et plura officia singulis regionibus ac paene jam civitatibus incubare, item rationales multi et vicarii praefectorum.' *Rationalis* is in this period used where *procurator* had been used ; cf. Lampridius, *Alex. Sev.* 45, 'procuratores, id est rationales'; Marquardt, ii. 298; Perrot, *Galatia*, p. 65. The importance of this subdivision is in the increased centralisation—the power of the court was increased, that of officials at a distance diminished. Ramsay, in *Expositor*, January, 1896, p. 53.

[2] Preuss, 99.

had the rank of *spectabiles*, and the consulars, correctores, and praesides were their subordinates. What proconsuls there were had the same rank of spectabilis, and received orders direct from the emperor. Whether the vicarius of Oriens was already at this period called comes Orientis and had a vicarius Aegypti under him is unknown.[1]

Undis-guised absolutism of Diocletian. This system of titles and hierarchy of ranks, though commonly ascribed to Constantine, is a characteristic feature of Diocletian's arrangements. He was the first emperor who is regularly and formally called *dominus ;* his titles were sacer and sacratissmus. He was greeted not by the customary embrace, as between equals, but by bending the knee as to a superior being. He dressed in silk and jewels, and ceremonial difficulties were made about audience. It would be absurd to ascribe all this to personal vanity. Such weaknesses were not part of the man's character, and on such a supposition his voluntary abdication and the simplicity of his after-life would not be easy to explain. It was part of his policy to surround the throne with an atmosphere of mystery. He wished the emperor to be neither citizen nor soldier, but equally above or remote from both. The last relics of the old Republican constitution vanished away. Diocletian paid no attention whatever to the Senate, and only once visited Rome during his reign. He resided at Sirmium or Antioch, or most often at Nicomedia ; and Maximian at Milan. The Romans did

Discontent of Rome. not like this, and there were conspiracies of senators and praetorians, which Maximian put down ruthlessly.[2] The praetorians were reduced in number and replaced by three Illyrian legions of whose absolute loyalty there could be no question. The praetorians still existed as a sort of police force in Rome till 312, when Constantine abolished them for ever.

---

[1] Preuss, 100.   See du Lessert's *Vicaires et Comtes d'Afrique.*   Civil authority belonged to the Vicarius, military to the Comes.

[2] [Lact.] *de Morte,* 8 ; Preuss, 106.

Besides these great and far-reaching changes, there were a number of reforms effected by Diocletian in the different branches of the administration.

In A.D. 294 a law of Diocletian made a great change in the judicial process. The old system had been to try cases by means of a magistrate and a body of judices. The judices were now abolished, and the governors directed to decide cases summarily by themselves. Thus the *cognitio* or summary process, which had been the exception, became the universal rule.

The formulary system replaced by cognitio.

The process of levelling, the progress towards uniformity, had only gradually accomplished itself in the last three centuries. There were still privileges and exemptions. Thus Italian land differed from provincial land, and there were different sorts of status for persons, according as a man was a Roman or a subject. Italy was free from the land-tax, as also were the towns outside Italy which possessed the Italian right. Such an exemption for Italy was impossible when it formed a diocese along with Spain and Africa; and Diocletian reimposed upon Italy the land-tax which it had not paid since 167 B.C.[1] Lactantius has inveighed against a measure which was really just and necessary. The privileged position of Italy had been just when she paid for it with her blood; but now that she did not supply the army, it was unjust. The contemporaries of Constantine look back to the reign of Diocletian as a period when the taxation was moderate and bearable : it was only in the generation after him that it reached a ruinous pitch. Another change of Diocletian's was to take the poll-tax off the towns. Previously it had been paid by every one who did not pay the land-tax, i.e., by the small artisans and workmen in the towns, by the coloni, and by women and children everywhere. The consequence was that by this change the tax pressed harder on the coloni ; and if the modern historian of Diocle-

The land-tax imposed on Italy.

The poll-tax taken off the towns.

---

[1] Preuss, 110 ; Bücher, *die Diokletianische Taxordnung* in *Zeitschrift für Staatswissenschaft,* vol. 1.

tian maintains that this was not so, he must maintain that
of the two alternatives—either that the treasury got less
than before, or that those who still paid, paid more than
before—the former is the more probable.

The
coinage.
A great deal was accomplished for the coinage, which had
been getting lighter and baser ever since Nero. The government purposely issued bad money or plated bronze, and
under Gallienus the silver coinage was in reality nothing
but plain pewter. Then it refused to take its own coins in
payment of the taxes. Aurelian tried to introduce reforms,
and quelled a mutiny of the monetarii which was apparently
excited by his efforts, but died too soon to accomplish anything. Diocletian made the silver pure again. The gold
had not been debased :—' The public taxes and the tribute
of the provinces were generally exacted in gold. It was
therefore the interest of the governors to maintain the
purity of the gold coinage '[1]:—but it had been terribly
lightened ; a state of things due to the fact that the government exacted the payment of the taxes by weight, but paid
its own debts by tale. Diocletian fixed it at a weight which
was maintained by a law of Constantine, and remained in
force till the fall of the Byzantine Empire. Copper money
had ceased to be coined. Diocletian coined two sorts—a
larger coin, called *follis*, and a smaller, perhaps called
denarius. Many of these coins were made at Alexandria.
In the fourth century there were regular mints in the West
at Siscia, Aquileia, Rome, Lugdunum, Arelate, Treviri, and
for the first part of the century at Tarraco ; Diocletian is
The *Edic-*
tum de pre-
tiis rerum
venalium.
also said to have started one at Nicomedia. These measures,
though necessary and in the long run beneficial, probably
helped to bring about the frightful rise in prices, which
resulted in the *Edictum de pretiis rerum venalium*. There was
also a failure of harvest throughout the East, and speculation
had ruined the merchants. The prices of necessaries rose
eightfold, and the soldiers could not live on their pay.

[1] Finlay, i. 49.

Whereupon Diocletian issued an edict, great part of which has been found,[1] to fix a maximum price for all necessaries. To sell at higher prices was punishable with death. The natural consequence was that the need only increased; a number of bloody punishments had no effect; and the edict had to be dropped.

To get rid of the fictitious republican forms which were the legacy of Augustus, and of the tyranny of the army, was the main idea of Diocletian. He established the absolute monarchy undisguised. His subdivisions of the provinces were mainly evoked by the desire to secure the throne against possible usurpers; and though no doubt, from his point of view, necessary and justifiable, the bureaucracy thus established was not a benefit to the provinces. The increase of the official class was so enormous that the receivers of the public money seemed to be more numerous than the payers of it. *Rectorum numerum terris pereuntibus augent.*[2] The excessive centralisation thus established finally broke up the genuine municipal constitutions. The man who would have been previously content with a position as duumvir would now compete for some petty post under government. Under Constantine the municipal offices were of importance only for purposes of taxation, and an unfortunate decurio was bound to his office just as the colonus was bound to his bit of land; persons of humble station were forced into the local senates, the property qualification lessened, and old grants of immunity cancelled. Perhaps no other alternative was open to Diocletian. It was neces-

Diocletian's object.

Great increase of centralisation.

---

[1] In Caria, 1709; another part in Egypt, 1807; fragments in Carystos, Megara, and Lebadea in 1860. Published by Mommsen, 1851; Waddington, 1864; by Blümer, 1897 (*Der Maximaltarif des D.*), C. I. L. iii. 801, cf. F. F. Abbott, *The Common People of Ancient Rome*, 145 sq. Another fragment has since been discovered, see *Bull. d'Epigraphie*, v. 147.

[2] Claudian *in Eutrop.* ii. 586; Marquardt, i. 423; Perrot's *Galatia*, 65. For the growth and importance of the financial committees of the local senates called *Decemprimi*, cf. Reid, *Municipalities*, 487-8.

sary that in some way the government should be made
strong and permanent. The day had gone by for doing
this by any means but an immense increase of centralisation.
The great number of new wheels in the machine at all
events enabled it to work smoothly, and prevented it being
so easily stopped or damaged. But a machine the government was, and not an organism ; a dead thing working with
a kind of fatal regularity, and with no healthy principle of
life or growth. It was the weakness of Diocletian's intellect
to think that everything could be accomplished by administrative machinery. He never reckoned enough on human
wills and human hearts other than his own. It is characteristic of him that he should have tried to crush the new
religion by an organised persecution, and should have failed
to see the elements of superior strength and vitality which
it possessed. Constantine saw what he did not see, that
merely as a matter of policy it was better to make terms
with the new power than to seek to crush it. In the same
spirit he attempted to fix prices by a series of cast-iron
regulations, without seeking to remove the causes of the
evil ; and though he crushed the Bagaudae he did not
alleviate the miseries which had made them possible. But
he was a man whose lot was cast in evil days, and perhaps
he did all that was possible for any genius but the highest.
He secured an interval of peace, and he relegated the army
to its proper place. These were real benefits, and we
must not blame him too severely if he failed to remove
the roots of evils which had been growing for a hundred
years.

The system of partition of power breaks down. All the evidence goes to prove that Diocletian considered
his system of partition of power as one that should be
permanent, and the model for succeeding reigns. He meant
Galerius and Constantius to be the new Augusti, and had
made Maximian promise to resign in their favour at the
same time as he did himself (305). But he ought to have
seen that the circumstances which had made the system

work well in his hands were quite exceptional. His own undisputed superiority and the loyalty of the other three to him were the main causes of its success ; and was it to be expected that those necessary conditions should recur ? Supposing the case of two emperors on the throne of equal age and equal claims, who were not bound together by those ties of loyalty and affection which bound Maximian and the Caesars to himself. It might have been foreseen that there would be a struggle. Here, as in some other parts of his policy, Diocletian did not reckon with human nature. Nor with respect to the accession did he even maintain a consistent and intelligible policy. When he and Maximian abdicated in 305, the two Caesars, Galerius and Constantius, naturally became the new Augusti. The only question was who should be the new Caesars. The logical and consistent arrangement would have been that each emperor should choose a Caesar. In this case of course Constantius would have chosen his son Constantine, a man (for he was now thirty years old) who had given ample proofs of capacity, and who had a right to be dissatisfied if passed over. But Diocletian made the great mistake of thinking that his own Caesar, Galerius, was competent to play the same pre-eminent part that he himself had played. Diocletian had no doubt originally decided the choice of both Caesars, and that was natural enough. But it was not by any means equally natural that Galerius should appoint a Caesar for Constantius as well as for himself ; and when Diocletian consented to such an arrangement he was responsible for the wars which followed. On Constantius' death the soldiers, with whom both father and son were popular, called Constantine to a share of Empire. After six years of divided rule, the battle of the Milvian bridge (312) left him and Licinius joint emperors ; and eleven years later the great battle of Adrianople left him the sole and the first Christian emperor.

CHAPTER VI.

The System of Taxation.

Section I. *The taxes in the period of the Republic.*

Ager publicus in Italy.

When in the year 167 B.C. the tribute was taken off Italy, the expenses of administration and public works were undisguisedly supported by the taxation of the provinces. There was still a good deal of public land in Italy, particularly in Campania,[1] and the customs duties were a regular source of income; but by the end of the Republic all public land in Italy had vanished, and the customs duties were in abeyance, at all events for a period of fifteen[2] years. Before examining the chief taxes of the provinces it will be necessary to take a brief view of the numerous varieties of tenure subsisting in them. Speaking generally, it may be said that free and allied towns paid no taxes; that Roman colonies and municipia did pay taxes, and were so far in a worse position than Roman colonies or municipia in Italy; that Latin towns paid; and that, lastly, the remainder of the provincials formed the great body of tax-payers, and were currently designated as stipendiarii. With these facts in mind it is possible to understand the Lex Agraria of 111,[3] which, along with the *Verrines*, is our main authority for the provincial taxation under the Republic.

[1] Cic. *de Leg. Agr.* i. 2. Cicero professes to attach great importance to the revenue from this land ; *de Leg. Agr.* ii. 29. Cf. *Phil.* ii. 39.

[2] Cic. *ad Att.* ii. 16, for their abolition by a lex Caecilia (62 B.C.) ; Dio Cass. xxxvii 51 ; Suet. *Jul.* 43, for their re-establishment by Caesar.

[3] C. I. L. i. 200 ; Bruns, p. 73.

194

In this law three different tenures of land are mentioned. Land might be either *Ager privatus ex jure Quiritium*, or *Ager privatus ex jure peregrino*, or *Ager publicus populi Romani*. The first tenure was that of the colonists settled in Africa by C. Gracchus, to whom, after that reformer's laws had been abrogated and a curse laid upon the site of Carthage, the land was assigned over again, not as to members of a colony, but *viritim*.[1] The second tenure was that of the seven cities —Utica, Thapsus, Hadrumetum, Leptis Minor, and three others—which aided Rome in the Third Punic War, and of the 2,200 deserters who joined the Romans under Himilco Phameas. This land was the absolute property of the towns, which were no doubt *immunes* as well as *liberae*,[2] and therefore paid no vectigal, and could not be touched by the tax-gatherer. The third tenure is the one which is important for our present purpose. This land was that which had either belonged to obstinate enemies like Carthage, or had been the domains of former kings. All the land of a conquered country became in theory Roman, but practically only that part was kept which came under one of these two categories. That, however, the *stipendiariae civitates* in any province were much more numerous either than the Roman colonies or municipia, or than the free and allied towns, might be expected, and is proved by abundant evidence.[3] But I must not give the impression that all *Ager publicus* was necessarily tributary. It was further subdivisible into the following classes, all of which are mentioned in the Lex Agraria of 111 : Firstly, *Ager privatus vectigalisque*, that is to say, land

---

[1] To have a claim to this land, however, each of these original colonists had to give in his name to the commissioners in order to be confirmed in the possession of his share ; and it is to this *professio* that the first portion of the law refers. If a man's land had been sold *pro publico* at Rome, an equivalent amount was to be restored to him.

[2] *Hist. bell. Afr.* 7, pervenit ad oppidum Leptim *liberam civitatem et immunem*.

[3] Pliny, *N. H.* iii. 3, for instance. The Roman colonies and municipia, however, also paid taxes, unless specially privileged by the *ius Italicum*.

sold by the praetor or quaestor at Rome, and alienable or bequeathable by the buyer. It paid a vectigal, but the amount was a nominal one, and only imposed to show that the State still asserted its property in the land. We find land of this kind opposed to and distinguished from land really *vectigalis* by the gromatic writers. It approached very nearly in fact to being private property. As reasons for the creation of this class of land may be suggested that for an assignation of land a law was necessary, while for a sale a senatus consultum sufficed ; and that it was a regular method of paying the interest due to the creditors of the State, to hand them over land under the fiction of a sale. Secondly, *Ager stipendiarius*.[1] This land, like the *Ager publicus* in Italy, was simply let out, and the Romans could resume it at any time. It consisted of the old land restored to the old inhabitants under a tax ; and included by far the largest portion of the provincial land.[2] Thirdly, *Ager publicus populi Romani a censoribus locari solitus*.[3] In the case of Africa, this was the land of Carthage or other cities conquered by force of arms, excepting of course land actually within the walls of Carthage, or given to colonists, or sold, or granted to allies, or reserved for public uses, or let out to stipendiarii. Though in fact these numerous exceptions embraced by far the greatest portion of the land, still a part was left which was let out by the censors at Rome. The tenants were probably in the main the original inhabitants, who now had their own lands let to them again, but revocable at pleasure. It was a mere life-tenancy, and there is no word in the law of the tenants being able to sell or bequeath. This land paid both *decumae* and *scriptura*, but there are indications that the author

---

[1] Cf. Cic. *in Verrem*, iii. 6.

[2] ' Land in the provinces belonged to the State, its occupants having strictly no more than a right of usufruct or possession (Gaius, ii. §§ 7, 21, 27) ; yet the tenure was popularly spoken of as *dominium*, and protected by what was called a vindication.' Muirhead, *Roman Law*, pp. 250-1.

[3] Cic. *in Verrem*, iii. 39, v. 13 ; Marquardt, ii. 175.

of the law was thinking more of pasture than of corn-land.[1] It is specially provided that the occupier should not pay more to the publicani than had been arranged to be paid by the law of the last censors of 145 B.C.[2] So these tenants were better off than an ordinary tenant, in that they could not have their rent raised on them. Fourthly, the roads, *viae publicae*, were and remained the property of the Roman people.[3]

The taxes, therefore, really lay on the second and third of these divisions; principally, of course, on the second. In strictness this *Ager stipendiarius* was the property of the Roman people, who, however, permitted its usufruct to the old inhabitants on payment of a rent. It had been the rule for the Romans to compel a conquered enemy, such as Carthage or Macedonia, to pay an indemnity for a term of years, allowing them to raise the money as they pleased, so long as they did raise it. Now what may be called a permanent indemnity was laid on each province, and the way it was to be raised was settled by the Romans themselves on the first organisation of a province. The chief tax is a direct one, and may be of two kinds, either levied on the soil, and generally a tithe of the produce—*decumae*; or a definite sum has to be paid (irrespective of the amount of produce), levied partly on land and partly on personal property, and called *stipendium*.[4]

Ager stipendiarius.

Tithes were paid by Sicily and Sardinia; and, from the Gracchi to Julius Caesar, by Asia. There was no stipendium in these provinces as long as the tithes existed. In

Decumae

---

[1] § 86 of the Law.   [2] Ib. § 85.

[3] In the particular case of Africa there still remain two classes of land: (1) *Ager publicus populi Romani ubi oppidum Carthago quondam fuit* —i.e., the land cursed by Scipio, which it was forbidden to cultivate; (2) *Agri publici regibus civitatibusve sociis permissi.* There are two mentions of this kind of land in the inscription—that given to Massinissa's children, § 81; and that assigned to Utica (and no doubt other towns as well) by the commission of Ten created by the Lex Livia.

[4] Marquardt, ii. 178.

Sicily the Romans maintained the arrangements of the Lex Hieronica, by which the husbandmen in each community had every year to state the amount of their acres and of their seed sown, and then the decuma of a whole district was offered in Syracuse to any one who could undertake it. The man who offered the largest number of bushels got it, and he had to send to Rome the amount of bushels he offered. If it was an exceptionally good harvest, he would gain ; if bad, lose. We find the towns themselves in Sicily bidding for their own decumae.[1] Besides the ordinary tithes there was also the special *frumentum imperatum*, which, perhaps, only fell on towns exempt from ordinary burdens.

Decumae implied publicani. These taxes would in all probability not have exceeded the ability to pay, if it had not been for the illegal exactions of the publicani. But it has always been found that a system of tithes puts the cultivator at the mercy of the tax-gatherer ; and the reform effected by Caesar when he changed the tithes of Asia, and probably also of Sicily, into a *stipendium* was necessary and beneficent.[2]

The stipendium : We know of the existence of a regular stipendium or tributum in Sardinia, Spain, Gaul, Macedonia, Illyria, Achaia, Syria, Cyrene, Africa, and Egypt, and may take it for granted of the rest. Caesar fixed that of the three Gauls at forty million sesterces, Aemilius Paullus that of Macedonia at 100 talents.[3] In discussing this tax, about

---

[1] Cic. *in Verr.* ii. 42.

[2] In Asia see Dio Cass. xlii. 6. For Sicily we have no direct information of the change ; it is inferred from the fact that Varro (*de Re Rust.* ii. prol.) does not enumerate it among the wheat-paying countries. As he wrote in 36 B.C. the change could hardly have been later than Julius Caesar. Cicero, *ad Att.* xiv. 12, mentions Caesar's benefactions to Sicily, and Pliny in his enumeration of towns makes no mention of the *civitates decumanae*, which under the Republic included half the Sicilian communities.

[3] Cicero mentions this tax in the most definite way. *In Verr.* iii. 6, 12 : 'Caeteris impositum vectigal est certum, quod stipendiarium dicitur, ut Hispanis et plerisque Poenorum, quasi victoriae praemium ac poena belli.'

which there is much difference of opinion, the great thing is to bear in mind the conservatism of the Romans in regard to existing arrangements, and to be prepared therefore for differences in taxation in the different countries, not expecting a unity of organisation which did not exist.

The stipendium might be paid in money or kind. It was money in Macedonia and the three Gauls; silphium in Cyrene; wax in the case of a tribe of Pontus, and hides among the Frisii.[1] Both land and persons paid stipendium; sub-but to suppose that there were always the two normal forms divisible of tributum soli and tributum capitis is not in accordance into the with the facts. At any rate the main part of the stipen- tributum dium came from the land : though here again it cannot be soli, supposed that immediately a province was established a regular tributum soli was set on foot. For this would need a regular survey, which only existed, before the Romans did it themselves, in the one case of Egypt ; or at all events a communal census, which only existed in Greek towns. Where there was neither one nor the other all that could be done was to impose about the same amount of taxation as the previous government. This was the course pursued by Aemilius Paullus in Macedonia.[2]

As for the tributum capitis (φόρος σωμάτων), we cannot and tribu-suppose that so rude an expedient as a mere poll-tax was tum intended by it ; though that may have been used now and capitis. then in special cases, and is mentioned in Africa, Cilicia, Asia, Tenos, Britain. We may look upon such a poll-tax as a temporary expedient, employed for instance just after a devastating war, when any ordinary tax on property would be impracticable.[3] What the tributum capitis really meant was any personal tax, and under it were included *taxes on trades*, for instance on pedlars, shopkeepers, prostitutes, etc., or *income-tax*, paid by the richer classes (οἱ τὰ χρήματα

---

[1] Marquardt, ii. 186, notes 11 and 12.
[2] Ib. ii. 188. Paullus says *half* what had been paid before, Liv. xlv. 29.
[3] Marquardt, ii. 192.

ἔχοντες), while the poor only paid a poll-tax. This idea is confirmed by the word ἐπικεφάλαιον being used for a tax on trades.[1] So we find Appian[2] talking of the severity of the φόρος τῶν σωμάτων laid upon the Jews. This could hardly have been a mere poll-tax.[3]

We gather, therefore, that the stipendium cannot be described as a regular tributum soli and a regular tributum capitis, but that the stipendium was as far as possible adapted to the pre-existing state of finance in the country. Supposing the ordinary stipendium was not enough, the income-tax came in as an extraordinary measure to supply the deficiency. It was essentially a supplement.

The portoria.
The chief source of our information as to the *portoria* or customs duties refers to the period of the Empire, but there is evidence enough to make it probable that besides the duties paid on goods crossing the frontier, for instance from Germany into Gaul, or from the far East into Syria, there were also duties levied in each province within the Roman dominions in this period. Italy, for instance, had its own custom-houses, which no goods could pass without a payment of 5 per cent.[4] Nor was this all, for each free town had a right to levy its own dues. It is to these octroi duties that a disputed passage of Cicero, where he mentions the *portorium circumvectionis*, probably refers.[5] One of the advantages of being a Roman citizen in the provinces was that Romans were specially exempted from paying these local dues.

Besides these ordinary legitimate taxes there were also

---

[1] Arist. *Oec.* ii. 1, 3 ; Cic. *ad Att.* v. 16, 2. [2] Appian, *Syr.* 50.
[3] Marquardt, ii. 185. These personal taxes were generally farmed out to publicani. Cicero speaks of the venditio tributorum ; see *ad Fam.* iii. 8, 5 ; *ad Att.* v. 16, 2.
[4] Cic. *in Verr.* ii. 72 and 75.
[5] Cic. *ad Att.* ii. 16, § 4. The point in dispute referred to was whether goods that had been landed at a port in Asia and then re-shipped and taken to another port in the same province, were liable to pay portoria a second time. Cicero gave a legal opinion against the second payment.

such special imposts as that of the ship-money exacted Ship-
from the cities of Sicily and Asia to pay for their defence money.
against the pirates. This was imposed by a senatus consultum in the year of Cicero's consulship, and occasioned
frequent complaints.[1] It is specially noteworthy that the
free or allied towns which were exempt from the ordinary
taxes were not exempt from the payment of ship-money.[2]

The mines, quarries, and salt-works did not all belong to Mines,
the State in this period. The most important ones, how- etc.
ever, did ; and were farmed out by the censors to publicani.
Whether it was the mine itself which was thus farmed, or
only the payments from the mine, is a point which is still
disputed.[3]

During the Republican period the only legal source of Financial
authority for this branch of the administration was the administration
Senate. With its sanction the censors farmed out the in this
domain lands, the indirect taxes, and the public buildings. period.
The treasury was looked after by the two city quaestors,
with a numerous body of clerks for receiving and paying
money and for keeping accounts. As the senators were
forbidden by law to take part in any such business as that
of farming the taxes, it fell to the equites, who, by their
gains, constituted a class of capitalists. The word publicanus is used in a general sense for anyone who accepts
a contract from the State, but more properly and narrowly
for one who farms a vectigal.[4] Whether the Roman system

[1] Cic. pro Flacco, 12 and 14.

[2] Cic. in Verr. v., § 49. Other references for this ship-money are—
for that of Asia, in Verr. i., § 89, iv., § 150 ; for that of Sicily, in Verr. v.,
§§ 43 and 24.

[3] Marquardt, ii. 240, maintains the former; Dietrich, p. 26 et seq.,
the latter view. The bronze tablet of Aljustrel, which is probably to
be ascribed to the latter part of the first century A.D., and which was
found in Portugal in 1876, only mentions a conductor vectigalis throughout. Whence we should gather that only the sums paid for the
privilege of working were farmed. See Flach's edition of the bronze,
p. 12 ; Jung, Lat. Recht, 46.

[4] So Dig. xxxix. 4, 12, § 3 : ' Publicani autem dicuntur qui publica
vectigalia habent conducta.' See Marquardt, ii. 289.

of farming the taxes is to be traced, as Hübner thinks, to a Carthaginian, or, as Dietrich thinks, to a Greek influence, no one can say ; but we may suppose that it naturally originated with the first enlargements of taxable territory. The conveniences of the system, and the difficulties of the direct system caused by the short duration of the Republican magistracies, would be reasons in its favour ; while the great objections to it which might be raised in the interest of the payers were probably not foreseen. The publicanus binds himself to pay a definite yearly sum. So if the real results of the tax exceed the sum to which he binds himself, he gains ; loses if they are less. In this way the State was spared expense[1]; but the provinces suffered for its convenience. As the taxes of a whole province were often all farmed together, for instance decumae, scriptura, and portoria, societies had to be formed to take them (societates publicanorum), the members of which received more or less according to the amount subscribed. Such societies of publicani are first mentioned in the twenty-third book of Livy, but go back to an earlier date, at least for buildings ; and probably the taxes were farmed from the first in the same way as the buildings. It would be erroneous, however, to suppose that the farming of a tax by a single person was expressly forbidden by law ; under the Empire we certainly find a single publicanus in the case of small transactions. But a single person might die before the contract was carried out, and the inconveniences of that, if nothing else, would bring these societies into existence.[2] The manceps of the society[3] offered for the taxes at the

[1] The State lost by it, for much less than the whole tax found its way into the treasury, while the people continually paid more than was required for the administration. The treasury got its money *sooner*, but paid practically a high rate of interest for the advance.

[2] I have made much use of Dietrich's Essay (*Beiträge zur Kenntniss des röm. Staatspächtersystems*, 1877) in this discussion.

[3] ' Mancipes sunt publicanorum principes ;' Pseudo-Asconius, *ad Div.*, p. 113, or p. 290 ; Cic. *in Verr.* iii. 71.

auction, made the contract with the censors, and gave the securities. The contract lasted a lustrum, regularly five years under the Empire, and began on March 15. The business manager of the society at Rome was called *magister societatis*, was appointed for a year, kept the accounts, and carried on the necessary correspondence ; in the provinces there was a *pro magistro*, with a numerous class of officials, who were actually employed in tax-gathering. The manager had also his own tabellarii for correspondence, and slaves for accounts and other routine work. There were different kinds of publicani according as they farmed decumae, scriptura, or portorium. The first stood highest. Their arrangement was not to take over the actual tenth, but to contract before the harvest, calculating on the seed sown and on the average crop.[1]

SECTION II. *The taxes under the Early Empire.*

The land-tax still remained the chief source of income under the Early Empire ; and the survey and census of Augustus, already mentioned, made a rational and just apportionment of it possible. For the purposes of the census a survey was necessary, which should not only distinguish land by its legal title into private property, communal property, and State property, but also by its produce, so as to make a fair impost possible. These differences of produce constituted seven different classes of land—ploughland, with the number of acres and average produce for a ten-year period ; vineyards, with the number of barrels of wine produced ; olive orchards, with the number of acres and trees ; pastures, with the same arrangements as those used for ploughland ; forests, fisheries, and salt-works.[2]

The land-tax.

---

[1] For the status of these *societates*, see vol. iii. of Gierke, *Staats- und Korporationslehre des Alterthums und des Mittelalters*, trans. by Maitland (1901).

[2] Marquardt, ii. 215.

The annona.　　Besides this regular land-tax, but probably not raised in the same districts, there was the *annona*, or payment in kind, originating no doubt in the *frumentum in cellam* for the support of the governor and his staff, of the Republican period. In the great majority of provinces it was called *annona militaris*, and applied to the maintenance of the officers, soldiers, and officials in the province. Egypt and Africa were exceptional in having to supply not only the *annona militaris*, but also the much more considerable *annona civica*. Egypt fed Rome for four months in the year,[1] and therefore supplied an amount of corn which, estimated in money, would amount to about 2,500 talents.[2]

Income-tax.　　We hear of a poll-tax in this period, levied on trades. Merchants paid on ships,[3] slaves, horses, mules, oxen, asses, in fact on their whole movable property; and the whole artisan and shopkeeper class, hosiers, weavers, furriers, goldsmiths, and others also came under the operation of this tax.[4] In so far as a class of coloni existed in this period they paid a poll-tax ; but their contribution to the revenue by no means attained the importance that it did under the Later Empire.

Ager publicus in the provinces.　　The domain lands in the provinces became of considerable importance under the Empire.[5] With the censorship the system of letting them by the censors (*censoria locatio*) came to an end ; and the emperor took over the administration of the domains. Vespasian had them resurveyed, and all cultivated domain land *in Italy* sold or given away. When the provinces were divided into Senatorial and Imperial, the

---

[1] Josephus, *B. J.* ii. 16, § 4.

[2] Marquardt, ii. 226, and his authorities, Milne, *Hist. of Egypt*, for the method of levying and exporting this corn.

[3] Tac. *Ann.* xiii. 51.　　　　　　　　　　　[4] Marquardt, ii. 230.

[5] For the domain lands, see Loria, *Economic Foundations of Society*, p. 238 (1899) ; Mommsen, in *Hermes*, for 1880 ; Ramsay, *Cities and Bishoprics of Phrygia*, vol. i., pp. 10, 103, 131, 256, 260, 283; Karlowa, *Die Finanzielle Stellung des Princeps ;* Pelham, *Essay on the Colonate ; Rev. Archéolog.* x. 290 (for 1887).

domains were also divided, and the vectigalia of those in the Senatorial provinces were paid into the aerarium, and those in the Imperial provinces into the fiscus. This lasted however only to Vespasian ; after whom all domains were under the emperor, and were called *loca fiscalia*.

Different from these lands were the private properties of the emperor in Italy and the provinces. Augustus and his successors owned all the royal domains in Egypt, and the revenues were part of the patrimonium[1]; the Thracian Chersonese was left by Agrippa to Augustus, and was owned by the emperors up to Trajan. These lands were not always acquired in the most honourable manner. Tiberius, Caligula, and Vespasian took possession of the property of condemned persons, and in Christian times emperors ' conveyed ' the private property of Pagan temples.[2] To manage such property the emperor had his bailiffs, like any other proprietor. These procurators were at first the emperor's freedmen, and must be distinguished from the regular procurators of the provinces, who were of equestrian rank. The technical name for all such imperial property was *patrimonium Caesaris*. Whether they belonged to the fiscus or the patrimonium, these lands are divisible into the three classes of arable land, pasture, and mines.[3]

Corn-land which was the private property of the emperor was looked after by his own slaves. The fiscal lands were farmed out, and the money got in by procurators. During some time these contracts were for the regular five-year period ; but later on we find hereditary farmers of the taxes, called *conductores domus nostrae*.[4]

Private property of the emperor in the provinces.

Administration of such lands.

[1] From C. I. L. vi. 701 it seems that some change was made as to the status of Egypt in 10 B.C., and some rearrangement as to the revenues may have followed ; perhaps the balance of revenue was paid into the fiscus.

[2] Marquardt, ii. 249.   [3] Ib. i. 414, ii. 249.

[4] See Cod. Theod., x. 26 ; Ramsay, *Studies in the Eastern Provinces*, p. 305 sq. ; Pelham, *Colonate* in *Essays on Roman History*, 1911 ; Kornemann, in *Philol. Woch.* xvii. ; *Decretum Commodi de Saltu Burunitano*,

The scripturarii ceased under the early Empire ; but public pasture still existed, and was farmed by the procurators of the fiscus. From these pascua the emperor derived an income.[1]

Mines.

Mines had mainly belonged to private persons under the Republic. Under the Empire the most important were taken over by the emperor, part for the fiscus, part for the patrimonium.[2] This was not only the case in Imperial provinces as, with the gold mines in Dalmatia and Dacia,

Administration of mines.

silver mines in Pannonia and Dalmatia, lead and tin in Britain, iron in Noricum, Pannonia, Lugdunensis, but also in the Senatorial provinces, as, for instance, with the copper mines in Cyprus and Baetica.[3] Quarries were withdrawn from private industry. Herodes Atticus owned those in Pentelicus ; but most, and the most famous, both in Italy and the provinces, belonged to the patrimonium. Each mine was superintended by a slave, later by a procurator ; but there was no procurator for the whole number of them ; and each mine or aggregation of neighbouring mines paid directly to the procurator patrimonii. Each procurator of a mine had under him a director of works, an inspector, and an engineer. That is if he managed the mine itself ; but there are cases of his farming it out to a speculator or to a society of publicani. In either case he had to look after the accounts, and for this purpose had several clerks—four can be named—under him. The labourers were either slaves, or hired workmen, or soldiers,[4] or convicts.[5] Such convict

---

Bruns, p. 258. In some cases lands attached to a native temple passed to the emperor, the tenants, who had previously been charged with the maintenance of the worship becoming a college united in the cult of the emperor, and governed by an imperial official exempt from the ordinary provincial administration. Cf. Ramsay's example in Pisidia.

[1] Marquardt, ii. 251.

[2] Cf. Suet. *Tib.* 49 : 'Plurimis etiam civitatibus et privatis veteres immunitates et jus metallorum ac vectigalium ademta.'

[3] Marquardt, ii. 253.   [4] Tac. *Ann.* xi. 20.

[5] 'Proxima morti poena metalli coercitio,' *Dig.* xlviii. 19, 28.

mines are mentioned in Palestine, Cilicia, Cyprus, the
Lebanon ; and after the conquest of Jerusalem part of the
captured Jews were sent to work in the mines of Egypt.[1]

One of the new taxes which the emperors introduced was The
the legacy-duty. In the year A.D. 6 Augustus made the legacy-
duty.
people of Italy pay their share of the State burdens, not by
imposing a tribute, but by a vicesima hereditatium, or tax
of five per cent. on legacies, only payable by Roman citizens
in Italy. Near relations did not pay, nor usually legacies
under 100,000 sesterces.[2] It was thus essentially a tax on
the rich ; and brought in large sums. Caracalla gave the
Roman franchise to all provincials for the purpose of making
everybody pay this tax, so that in future the wretched provincials had to pay the vicesima as well as the tribute.
Till Caracalla did this it is probable that Romans in the
provinces, paying as they did tributum, did not also pay the
vicesima ; for the original idea of the vicesima was that it
should be paid by those who did not pay tributum, and so
put Italy upon a level with the provinces.[3]

Of the indirect taxes the most important were the *portoria* The
or customs duties. Under the Empire there was a thorough-
portoria.
going customs system on the frontiers. Some wares, especially iron, were absolutely forbidden to be exported ; and
all imported wares paid duty. Besides this there were
special taxation provinces which were organised by themselves, and formed a smaller whole within the larger whole
of the Empire. Sicily was such a unit ; so were the Spanish
provinces, Gallia Narbonensis, and the three Gauls. All
imports paid two and a half per cent. on crossing into the
three Gauls—quadragesima Galliarum—and we can point

---

[1] Josephus, *Bell. Jud.* vi. 9, 2.

[2] The condition was that the whole amount received should not
exceed that sum. It was raised by Caracalla to 10 per cent., reduced
by Macrinus to 5 per cent., and later abolished (cf. Dio C. 77, 9 ;
78, 12 ; *Philol. Wochenschrift*, v. 573).

[3] Marquardt, ii. 261.

out at least five custom-houses on their frontier—at Conflans, St. Maurice, Zurich, Coblenz, Statio Maiensis between Chur and Bregenz. Metz and Cologne are less certain. Britain, even before it was a province, had to pay dues on its exports into Gaul.[1] Moesia, with the Ripa Thracia, Pannonia, Dalmatia, Noricum, were all administered as a taxation unit, according to Appian; and the portorium Illyricum mentioned in inscriptions[2] may be supposed to have been dues levied on all goods crossing their frontier; so that, once this paid, goods could circulate freely through all this country without let or hindrance. Owing however to the fact that only one custom-house can be pointed out with certainty along this line of frontier, while several seem to be within it, Marquardt inclines to the belief that besides the general outer boundary for the whole, each of these districts also levied its own dues, or rather had its own dues levied for it. The portorium Illyricum was farmed, but the contractors for it had imperial procurators set over them. Asia had a quadragesima of its own; and Bithynia, Paphlagonia, and Pontus had one between them. Both were farmed, but here also were imperial procurators.

These taxes were very important in the case of Egypt. Most of the articles of Roman luxury came from the East through Syria or Egypt. Pliny[3] puts the yearly value of Indian goods imported through Egypt at fifty-five million sesterces; and that of pearls by the same road at 100 million sesterces. Alexandria was the chief entrepôt for these goods, but in all harbours of the Red Sea duties of twenty-five per cent. were levied on the landing of all Indian or Arabian imports. For Ethiopian goods duty was raised at Syene[4];

---

[1] Strabo, iv. 5, § 3. These dues seem to have been accepted in lieu of the tribute imposed by Julius Caesar, which was paid for a time (Diodor. v. 21); probably there was a custom-house somewhere on the Gallic coast at which dues on both exports to and imports from Britain were levied at this period.

[2] C. I. L. iii. 752; Marquardt, ii. 264, note 6.

[3] Pliny, *N. H.* vi. 101.   [4] Marquardt, ii. 266.

at Schedia near Alexandria an export duty was also levied, and in fact at all the mouths of the Nile.

The portorium was levied in the form of a percentage on the value of the goods. But this percentage differed ; for instance, it was five per cent. in Sicily, two per cent. in Spain, two and a half in the Gauls, Asia, Bithynia, and the Illyrian provinces. In the fourth century it seems to have risen everywhere to twelve and a half per cent.[1] In other provinces there was a regular tariff for different wares, for instance, in Africa ; and under Commodus we find such a tariff for Eastern goods.[2] Besides the portoria there were the following indirect taxes. *Centesima rerum venalium,* imposed by Augustus after the civil wars.[3] Tiberius reduced it A.D. 17 to ducentesima (half per cent.). Caligula remitted it altogether, as we know from two authorities,[4] who, however, disagree in the amount of it—Dio calling it ἑκατοστή, and Suetonius ducentesima.[5] But the tax appears again and lasted the whole Empire through. We have no distinct testimony whether this tax was applied to provinces as well, but from Suetonius' phrase ' *Italiae* remisit,' Marquardt infers that it was. On the principle of the *vicesima hereditatium* we might infer that, after having been first applied only to Italy, it came to be applied also to the provinces ; the only objection to both arguments being that this is hardly likely to have happened so easily with the centesima, when it did not happen till Caracalla with the vicesima.[6]

Another indirect tax was that of the four per cent. on all

Portoria varied in amount.

Other indirect taxes.

---

[1] Cod. Just. iv. 61, 7, of the year 366 : ' Quin octavas more solito constitutas omne hominum genus quod commerciis voluerit interesse dependat.'

[2] Marquardt, ii. 268.

[3] Tac. *Ann.* i. 78 : ' Centesimam rerum venalium, post civilia bella institutam,' perhaps in imitation of the Egyptian τέλος ὠνῆς.

[4] Dio Cass. lix. 9 ; Suet. *Calig.* 16.   [5] Marquardt, ii. 269, note 8.

[6] Marquardt mentions one of the Spanish inscriptions, which reads as follows, ' proc(uratori) Aug. prov(inciae) Baet(icae) ad ducem ' ; and says that the last two words may very likely mean ad ducentesimam. See C. I. L. ii. 2029 ; Marquardt, ii. 269, note 8.

The quinta et vicesima venalium mancipiorum. purchases of slaves (*quinta et vicesima venalium mancipiorum*) instituted by Augustus in A.D. 7. Tacitus says that it was taken off the buyers and put on the sellers, *i.e.*, on the Asiatic slave-dealers; but that it came to the same thing in the end, as the tax was added on to the price. There was a bureau to look after this tax.[1]

Among the extraordinary sources of income, the most important are the confiscated property of condemned persons (*bona damnatorum*), the lapsed legacies or *caduca*, and the so-called *aurum coronarium*.

Bona damnatorum. Any capital punishment (in which term exile was of course included) was followed by such confiscation. The property fell to the aerarium, a system which lasted at all events to the end of Tiberius' reign; for Sejanus' property was so applied.[2] But cases also occur of the emperor's appropriating the money, and this became the accepted practice, so that these moneys fell regularly to the fiscus, and we find a *procurator ad bona damnatorum*. Besides unclaimed property (*bona vacantia*) certain rights to *caduca* were introduced by

Caduca. the Lex Julia et Papia Poppaea (A.D. 9). Properly the term means money left by will, but for some reason unclaimed; but the law made it impossible for bachelors between certain ages to receive legacies from testators not related within the sixth degree, and so there were many of these *caduca* under the Empire. If not claimed by relations within the third degree such moneys fell to the aerarium, after Caracalla to the fiscus. Augustus failed to induce people to marry; but his law, though frequently evaded, brought in something to the treasury.

Aurum coronarium. The ' coronary gold ' was originally a gold crown offered to a victorious general by provincials and allies to grace his triumph. But already under the Republic it was really a

---

[1] Tac. *Ann.* xiii. 31 ; Dio Cass. lv. 31. A tax on the sale of slaves under 20 had been levied by Cato in 184 B.C., the property of the owner being disproportionately assessed by the censors (Liv. 39, 44).

[2] Tac. *Ann.* vi. 2.

compulsory payment to the governor.[1] Under Augustus we
first find *Italian* towns regularly giving him aureae coronae,[2]
but on a previous occasion he had received an *aurum coronarium* from Italy.[3] Later on Augustus would only receive
this from the provinces. In the later Empire it was paid
exclusively by the decuriones. That this 'benevolence'
was something considerable is proved by the sum mentioned
in the Monumentum Ancyranum—35,000 lbs. of gold. It
appears to have been regularly offered on the accession or
adoption of a new emperor, both by Italy and the provinces;
and Hadrian[4] and M. Antoninus[5] are mentioned as having
done themselves credit by remitting a portion of it.

It is impossible to say what a year's total revenue was at
any period. We do not possess the necessary materials.
In some provinces the expenses of administration absorbed
all the revenues from it; for instance, Mesopotamia and
Britain.[6] Marquardt calculates the vectigalia in the time of
Cicero at 200 million sesterces. And the following figures
are known. The treasuries at the deaths of Tiberius and
Antoninus Pius contained 2,900 million sesterces. 'Nero
had squandered in presents 2,200 million sesterces.'[7] Vitellius
wasted 900 million sesterces in the course of a few months.[8]
Under Hadrian the stipendium of Asia was 28 million
sesterces. Gaul paid 40 million sesterces immediately after
its conquest; and under Constantine, Savigny thinks it paid
360 million sesterces. Sixteen years' arrears of that province before Hadrian amounted to 900 million sesterces.[9]

[marginal note:] Sum total of the revenue.

---

[1] Cic. *in Pison.* 37 ; *de Leg. Agr.* ii. 22 ; Dio Cass. xlix. 42. See
edict of Alexand. Severus in Egyptian papyri remitting its payment
in Italy and the whole Empire, *Philol. Wochenschrift*, 21, 781. See also
Welcken, *Ostraka*, i. 295.

[2] Dio Cass. xlviii. 4.   [3] Ib. xlii. 50.
[4] Spartian, *Hadr.* 5.   [5] Capitol. *M. Anton.* 4.
[6] Cicero, *pro Leg. Man.*, § 14, says that this was often the case with
all the provinces except Asia, and even there war, or fear of war, might
ruin trade, and consequently the revenue.

[7] Tac. *Hist.* i. 20.   [8] Ib. ii. 95.   [9] Marquardt, ii. 288.

According to Augustus' arrangements the whole field of finance administration was subdivided as follows :—

The aerarium. 1. The *aerarium Saturni* had been the single treasury under the Republic. With the division of the provinces into imperial and senatorial, the *aerarium* became the senatorial treasury, into which, besides its previous sources of revenue, the taxes of the senatorial provinces were paid. The Senate had nominally full power over this,[1] but really it came under the emperor.[2] The supervision was transferred by Augustus from the quaestors to special prefects, at first chosen by the Senate, then by lot from the praetors or expraetors ; Claudius restored the quaestors, who were found too young and inexperienced. From Nero's time prefects of praetorian rank were nominated by the emperor. Also we find the emperor appointing extraordinary commissions to regulate the aerarium and to limit its outgoings. At the beginning of the Empire the aerarium was empty owing to the civil wars, and we find Augustus[3] and Nero's guardians[4] lending to it. Generally speaking, the endeavour of the emperor was to draw all the more important revenues to the fiscus. This happened, for instance, with the revenues of the domains, with the income from aqueducts, with the *bona damnatorum*, and the *caduca*. By the time of Severus the distinction between senatorial and imperial provinces seems to have ceased; and all provinces paid into the fiscus. So the aerarium, which we find in existence as late as the beginning of the third century,[5] became the treasury merely of the municipality of Rome, the Senate then practically taking the place of a town council.

[1] Suet. *Tib.* 30 ; Tac. *Ann.* ii. 37.

[2] See Dio Cass. liii. 16 ; λόγῳ μὲν γὰρ τὰ δημόσια ἀπὸ τῶν ἐκείνου ἀπεκέκριτο, ἔργῳ δὲ καὶ ταῦτα πρὸς τὴν γνώμην αὐτοῦ ἀνηλίσκετο : also lv. 22. Cf. Tac. *Ann.* vi. 2 : ' Et bona Sejani ablata aerario ut in fiscum cogerentur, *tanquam referret*,' and ib. xiii. 29 for the changes in the appointment of controllers; also Suet. *Aug.* 36.

[3] *Mon. Anc.* § 17.   [4] Tac. *Ann.* xiii. 31 (A.D. 58).

[5] Marquardt, ii. 295, note 3.

2. The fiscus dates from Augustus.[1]   It was exclusively The
under the emperor.[2]   In Greek the fiscus is called τὸ fiscus.
βασιλικόν, the aerarium τὸ δημόσιον.[3]   The chief expenses of
the fiscus were—the support of the army, fleet, and war-
material ; the payment of officials ; the supplying of Rome
with corn ; the cost of military roads ; the post, and public
buildings.   The chief revenues were derived from the
imperial provinces, for which there were *procuratores*, the
chief procurator in each province being a knight, the subordinate ones imperial freedmen.   Also the fiscus asserted
itself in the senatorial provinces ; and we find there also
procuratores.   Such officials looked after domain lands,
bona damnatorum, and *caduca ;* also superintended the different
payments in kind, and personal services demanded for the
imperial magazines, for military support, equipments and
transport, and for buildings.[4]   Whether the fiscus also
claimed its share of the regular stipendium and portoria of
a senatorial province is unknown.[5]   Anyhow the emperors
disposed of these taxes as they pleased, as is clear from the
case of Hadrian, who allowed Herodes Atticus—the ' corrector civitatium Asiae '—to build an aqueduct at Troas,
and assigned him three millions from the tribute for the
purpose.   But it cost seven millions, and the procuratores

[1] It seems that the word ' fiscus,' for the separate treasury of the
Emperor, was probably not used till the time of Claudius, though
Suet. uses it of an earlier period (*Aug.* 40, 101).   It was used for local
treasuries, specially in Sicily, long before.   Cicero, *Verr.* 1 Act, § 22 ;
ii., §§ 197, 183 ; Asconius in 1 Act, § 22.   Dio Cass. lvi. 36, says that
the Emperors practically controlled both treasuries.   Yet the distinction
was in fact observed, though possibly not with rigour.

[2] ' Res enim fiscales quasi propriae et privatae principis sunt; '
Ulpian, *Dig.* xliii. 8, 2, § 4.

[3] Dio Cass. lxxi. 32.

[4] Marquardt, ii. 296.

[5] Mommsen, *Staatsrecht*, ii. 937, note 2, conjectures that it did from
the following passage of Tac. *Ann.* ii. 47 : ' (Sardianis) quantum
aerario aut fisco pendebant in quinquennium remisit,' but it is possible
that senatorial dues were remitted in virtue of a special decree pro-
moted by Tiberius.

complained that the whole revenues of the province were employed on a single building. So we find a fiscus in every province, for instance, ' fiscus Gallicus provinciae Lugdunensis '; 'fiscus Asiaticus.'[1] The fiscus in Rome is called simply fiscus without any such epithet, and its administration is called *summa res rationum*. The chief official was originally an imperial freedman, with the title of *a rationibus*. This post was one of great influence. Pallas occupied it under Claudius and Nero,[2] Claudius Etruscus under Domitian.[3] He was also called procurator a rationibus, procurator summarum rationum; and, after Hadrian, was commonly a knight (later known as *rationalis*) who had been procurator of several provinces before attaining this dignity, and who was afterwards advanced to the praefectura annonae or *ab epistulis*.

The patrimonium Caesaris. 3. The Patrimonium Caesaris also dates from Augustus. A numerous body of officials was wanted for its administration, both in Rome and the provinces. They were the slaves and freedmen of the emperor ; and were called *procuratores patrimonii*. The emperor controlled and directed them, and there was no one among them with a position anything like that of the *procurator fisci*. The emperor having the fiscus as well as this patrimonium at his absolute disposition, a question always arose at the death of every emperor what property he had a right to bequeath, and what part naturally descended to the State and to his successor. The domain lands and revenues of Egypt belonged to the patrimonium, and one of its highest officials was the ἰδιόλογος (which was the name of the king's steward under the Ptolemies), who as *procurator rei privatae* received such moneys as the *caduca*, which in other provinces belonged to the fiscus or aerarium. It was understood that such *res privata* as Egypt passed on to the next emperor. So we want a new distinction, and we

---

[1] But these *fisci* of the provinces are to be distinguished from the *fiscus* of the Emperor.   See Furneaux on Tac. *Ann.*, vol. ii., p. 28.

[2] Suet. *Claud.* 28.   [3] See Statius, *Silv.* iii. 3.

get it in that between patrimonium and *res familiaris ;* the first being the emperor's official income—just as the Chancellor of the Exchequer with us is given £5,000 a year for being Chancellor of the Exchequer—and the latter his private means. Severus first clearly assigned them to different procuratores ; and afterwards the procurator rei privatae became a very important personage, more so than the procurator patrimonii, and on a level with the procurator of the fiscus.

4. The *Aerarium Militare* was the treasury out of which the pensions to veterans were paid. Originally established by Augustus and endowed with 170 million sesterces,[1] it was kept up out of the proceeds of the two taxes—*vicesima hereditatium* and *centesima rerum venalium*—which were regularly devoted to it. Also money came in to it now and then from extra-ordinary sources; for instance, the goods of the banished Agrippa Postumus.[2] Augustus put the fund under three men of praetorian rank, chosen by lot, and serving for three years. In Dio's time they were named by the emperor,[3] each with the title praefectus aerarii militaris. Their office lasted till the third century.[4]

The system of farming the taxes continued under the Empire, but was controlled and modified. The *decumani,* who under the Republic had formed the first and most influential class among the publicani, came to an end. But other taxes were still farmed,[5] and during the whole

---

[1] *Mon. Anc.,* § 17 ; Tac. *Ann.* i. 78 ; Suet. *Aug.* 49 ; Dio, lv. 25.

[2] Dio, lv. 32.

[3] Ib. lv. 26. The vicesima legatorum seems also to have gone to this account, as well as voluntary contributions from States and princes, Dio Cass. lv. 25.

[4] Tac. *Ann.* v. 8 ; Marquardt, iii. 302.

[5] Cf. Tac. *Ann.* iv. 6 : ' At frumenta et pecuniae vectigales, cetera publicorum fructuum societatibus equitum Romanorum agitabantur.' See the important chapter, Tac. *Ann.* xiii. 50, where Nero thinks of abolishing all indirect taxes—a good passage for the use of the term vectigalia. Noticeable phrases are—' immodestiam publicanorum,' ' vectigalium societates,' ' publicanorum cupidines,'

Empire we find the system employed both by the State and by the municipalities.[1]   After the disuse of the censorship the locators were generally imperial procurators.   In Africa we find procuratores quattuor publicorum Africae side by side with conductores quattuor publicorum Africae.[2] The two tributes were no longer farmed by publicani, but raised directly, in senatorial provinces by the quaestor and his subordinates, in imperial by the procurator of the province and his subordinates.   There was a *tabularium* (a sort of audit office) in each province, where the survey-documents and census-lists were kept; also in each province a *fiscus provinciae*, from which the governor paid the troops and officials in the province, and sent the surplus to Rome.[3] For all private revenues, which did not come in to this fiscus provinciae, there was in each province a special imperial procurator, with a central bureau for them all in Rome.

Minor branches of the adminis-tration.   Besides these main branches of finance administration there were a number of minor ones, about which indeed we are more completely informed (by inscriptions) than about the more important.   For instance, we find a *procurator a caducis*,[4] officials for aqueducts, public buildings, etc., for the *cura annonae*, and for the coinage.[5]   With every separate detachment of troops there was a *fiscus castrensis*, a *procurator castrensis*, and a commissariat official, *a copiis militaribus*. The *patrimonium* and the *res privata Caesaris* also employed numerous procurators, to look after the emperor's private properties and receive the legacies left to him.   We find them employed also for such matters as games, libraries, picture-galleries, and the like.[6]

---

[1] See the *Lex Malacitana*.

[2] See Henzen, 6648, 6650, quoted by Marquardt, ii. 303, note 2.

[3] Dio Cass. lvii. 10.

[4] C. I. L. iii. 1622.

[5] E.g., 'Procurator monetae' at Tarraco ; C. I. L. ii. 4206.   Also 'officinatores monetae.'   See Orelli, 3226, 3227, 1090 ; Marquardt, ii. 304, note 3.

[6] Orelli, 2417.

There were also regular administration-districts for getting in the *vicesima hereditatium* and *vicesima manumissionum*, or *libertatis*. Thus, there was one for Pamphylia, Lycia, Phrygia, Galatia, and the Cyclades[1]; another for the two Pontus', Bithynia, and Paphlagonia [2]; another for Baetica and Lusitania; another for Hispania Citerior; another for Gallia Lugdunensis, Belgica, and the two Germanies; while in Italy there was one for Lucania, Apulia, and Calabria; and another for Umbria, Tuscia, Picenum, and Campania.[3]

SECTION III.   *The taxation of the Later Empire.*

As Caracalla had given the civitas to all the provincials, so Diocletian completed the levelling process, and imposed the tribute upon Italy.   Diocletian divided the eastern part of the Empire into *juga*—that is, really existing divisions with definite boundaries, varying from five acres to sixty, but all alike of one and the same value.   For instance, the five acres might be five acres of vineyard; the sixty would be sixty acres of indifferent corn-land, and their money value would be the same.   It has been a question about these juga whether they really existed or were only abstractions, ideal divisions for the convenience of reckoning. Savigny thought the latter.   But a codex of A.D. 501 of the Eastern Empire proves the contrary [4]; and we also learn from this codex that a re-survey of the Empire took place under Diocletian for the purpose of this division into juga.[5] From these materials a *catastrum* was drawn up, giving in each district the number of juga, and the sum due from them.   The decuriones in the capital of the district distributed this total among the landowners, and paid over the receipts, for which they were responsible.   Some of the

The division into juga.

---

[1] Henzen, 6940.   [2] Ib.

[3] See Marquardt, ii. 305, note 5, where the authorities are given.

[4] The Codex is in the British Museum, published (1862) in Land's *Symbolae Syriacae*.

[5] Marquardt, ii. 220.   Catastrum = capitastrum.

lists which had to be kept have been found, and generally
contain the name of the owner, the name of the property, its
position, and the amount of tax payable for it in denarii.
In case of a remission of taxation either the number of juga
was reduced, or the amount payable by each province. So
in the case of the Aedui, Constantine reduced the number
of juga from 32,000 to 25,000.[1] It is not to be supposed
that there was the same arrangement of these juga in all
provinces alike. In Africa the jugum is called *centuria*, and
consists of 200 acres. In Italy there is a larger unit called
millena, whose larger size is easily explained by the existence
of latifundia.[2]

The coloni, who have been already discussed, were the
chief payers of the poll-tax after Diocletian had taken this
In-
creasing
burden of
taxation.
tax off the towns.[3] The portoria were growing heavier
during this period, till they reached the frightful rate of
12½ per cent. in the fourth century. The new imposition
of the legacy-duty on all provincials was bad enough ; but
it was the land-tax after all which was the crushing burden.
It was this which made slaves of the municipal magistrates
(*decuriones*), and which made the hard-tasked victims of the
terribly perfect machine of administration await the
barbarians rather with hope than with despair.[4]

[1] Eumenius *Gratiarum Actio*, ii. et seq. ; Marquardt, ii. 222 ; and for
the latter case, Lampridius, *Vita Alex. Sev.* xxxix. 6 ; Ammianus, xvi.,
§ 14.   Sidonius Apoll. *Carm.* 13, 19 :
> ' Geryones nos esse puta monstrumque tributum :
> Hic capita, ut vivam, tu mihi tolle tria.'

[2] Marquardt, ii. 224.

[3] The landlord paid the tax (which, though levied by capitation, was
a land-tax), but extracted it from his *coloni*, who were therefore prevented by the State from running away from their holdings.   Coulanges, *Récherches*, pp. 81, 91.

[4] Ib., with Schiller's Review in *Philol. Wochenschrift*, xii.

CHAPTER VII.

Towns in the Provinces.

SECTION I. *Towns the basis of the administration.*
Increase of towns under Rome.

THE use which Rome made of the towns in carrying out Use of the
towns for
her administrative system has already been mentioned, and adminis-
may be looked on as an inheritance from Hellenic civilisa- trative
purposes.
tion. When Cicero is mentioning the taxes of Asia, he
speaks of them as the 'tribute of the cities' (*tributa civi-*
tatum).[1] The towns formed the administrative means of
raising the taxes. Each town comprehended a district of
'tributary lands' (*fundi tributarii*), the names of which and
of their occupiers were deposited with the town magistrates,
as for instance in Sicily.[2] When there were no towns we
find *homines stipendiarii* instead of *civitates stipendiariae*, and
in such cases the State itself had to look after the lists, and
direct all that machinery of administration, which elsewhere
was taken off its hands by the towns. Even under the
Empire the tribute of a province was paid by a certain
number of towns ; and when we hear of remissions of taxes,
it is to towns that the remissions are given. In all towns
of Greek constitution a census already existed, and it is

---

[1] Cic. *ad Qu. Fr.* i. 1, 8. The following will be found useful on
this subject : E. Kuhn, *Die stadtische und bürgerliche Verfassung des
Römischen Reichs bis auf die Zeiten Justinians*, 2 vols. (Leipzig) ; Hirschfeld, *Gall. Studien*, vol. i. p. 300 et seq. ; H. Nissen, *Ital. Landeskunde*,
vol. ii. (Berl. 1902) ; Liebenam, *Städteverwaltung im röm. Kaiserreiche*
(1900).

[2] Cic. *in Verr.* iii., § 120.

tolerably certain that the Romans introduced it wherever it did not, partly in order to introduce a timocratic constitution, partly to secure a fair apportionment of the taxes. Censors are expressly mentioned in Sicily and Bithynia, and no doubt existed everywhere.[1]   It was at the towns also that justice was administered. Fifty-five populi, according to Pliny, had justice administered to them at Caesar Augusta in Spain, and sixty-five at Carthago Nova,[2] though this does not mean that such peoples were necessarily subordinated to their assize-town for financial purposes.

Could the towns act together ? A question naturally arises how far these towns had any capacity of united action. The general impression we get from a survey of the facts is that the opportunities of united action were limited and occasional, and that within any province the governor on the one side, and the municipal magistrates on the other, constituted the only two sources of power. But this impression is not exact, and a more particular examination of the *concilia* or provincial parliaments will correct it.

The provincial parliaments. These parliaments, which are mentioned by Tacitus,[3] were either older than the province itself, or were established under the first emperors, or, in the case of countries which did not till a late date become provinces, were at once introduced. The Romans at first dissolved all such assemblies, for instance in Greece, Sicily, and Macedonia ; but afterwards permitted them to exist mainly for religious objects. These religious objects concealed a political object, for these parliaments formed a centre for the worship of the emperor. The high-priest of this worship (ἀρχιερεύς, or *sacerdos* or *flamen provinciae*) was, apart from Roman officials, the most important personage in the province. He was elected by the

---

[1] Marquardt, ii. 180 and 81.

[2] Plin. *N. H.* iii., §§ 24, 5. Though the Roman Empire rested on a system of town-states, there were exceptions to the rule, as in Egypt, and the more backward parts of Asia Minor.

[3] Tac. *Ann.* xv. 22. See Hardy's *Provincial Concilia* in *Studies in Roman History* (1906), p. 236 sqq.

deputies[1] of a certain number of the most important towns, and, like them, held his office for a year. He was elected from those who had either discharged all municipal offices in their town, or were of equestrian rank. He was exempt from taxation, and if a mission was sent from the province to the emperor he conducted it. The parliament met yearly, and after having taken part in the religious festival, re-assembled as a secular body. After settling any points connected with the temple, passing the accounts, and deciding any proposal as to statues or other honours which might be brought before it, it chose the high-priest for the next year. Then either a vote of thanks was voted to the outgoing governor, or, more important, a complaint was drawn up against him, and forwarded by special mission to the Senate or emperor.[2] This could be done without asking the governor's consent; and the emperor's reply was sent direct to the parliament. Thus we find Hadrian writing to the Council of Baetica, Antoninus Pius to that of Asia.[3] We may probably regard this as a regular means whereby the provinces exercised a control upon their governors, and as an element in the improvement of their condition.[4]

[1] These deputies were the members of the provincial concilium. For flamen provinciae as another title for the high-priest, see C. I. L. ii. 160, 4248.

[2] Cf. the phrases in Pliny, *Ep.* vii. 6, ' decreto concilii,' ' decreto provinciae,' in reference to an accusation brought against a governor.

[3] Marquardt, i. 371, note 5 ; Harnack, *Das Edict des Antonin. Pius,* p. 38; Fougères, *de Communi Lyciorum* (1898) ; *Philol. Wochenschrift,* xix. 74 ; Monceaux, *de Communi Asiae* (1885) ; Szanto, *Das griechische Bürgerrecht* (1892).

[4] Most of the statements in the text are from Marquardt, i. 365-377, and from the same writer's important essay on the subject in the Ephemeris Epigraphica, i. p. 200 sqq. Mommsen, *Schweiz in römischer Zeit.,* p. 8, discusses the famous parliament of the sixty-four Gallic states at Lugdunum, which is mentioned by Strabo. But he speaks ironically of the right of complaint, as if it were almost always negatived by a complaisant majority. The passages from Tacitus and Pliny, already referred to, hardly perhaps bear out this pessimistic view. See also Guiraud, *les Assemblées Provinciales dans l'Empire Romain.*

Increase of towns under Rome.

But though in endeavouring to form a conception of the internal affairs of a province it is necessary to assign a certain part to these parliaments, it still remains true that the single towns were of far greater importance when isolated than when thus combined. When the Romans had to organise the provinces they used towns wherever they could ; and in countries of Greek or Phoenician civilisation, in Greece proper, Sicily, Western and Southern Asia Minor and Carthaginian Africa, they found towns with definite territory ready to hand. Where they did not find them in these parts of the world they would make a village into a town, or compose a town out of several neighbouring villages. Thus Orcistus in Phrygia was made into a town,[1] and Aperlae, Simena, Apollonia, and Isinda in Lycia were made into one community with one Senate, and forming one δῆμος. The other provinces when conquered by Rome were in different stages of the development, through which the Greek and Phoenician countries had long passed. Thus when Romans appeared in Spain the system of *pagi* or cantons, as opposed to the system of towns, was widespread (except in Baetica, where earlier civilisations had left strong traces). In the statistics compiled by Agrippa and used by Pliny,[2] we find 293 peoples enumerated in Hispania Tarraconensis, of which 179 dwelt in towns, while 114 had no town. We may be sure that this list shows an immense advance upon the number of real towns as opposed to mere strongholds, which existed before the commencement of the Roman rule. A century later Ptolemy, writing under Antoninus Pius, shows us the rapid extension of the town system within that period, for he enumerates in the same province 248 towns, and only twenty-seven of these townless communities. So in Gaul there were before the Romans

---

[1] Marquardt, i. 17; Mommsen in *Hermes*, xxii. 309.

[2] Plin. *N. H.* iii. 4. For the large number of towns said to have been destroyed by Tib. Gracchus in Spain, see Livy, xl. 49; Strabo, iii. 4, 13. They were probably little more than robber strongholds.

entered the country no real towns, with the exception perhaps of a few which were neither Greek nor Roman in Narbonensis.[1] When Cæsar conquered Gaul, the country was divided among a number of tribes, each containing several *pagi*. It was out of these that Augustus organised sixty-four states,[2] each with a capital of its own, though in Gaul more than elsewhere the administration remained tribal. Yet from these capitals arose some of the principal towns of France, for instance Amiens and Nantes. Lugdunum was the capital of all sixty-four states, and the centre of all administration, imperial and municipal.[3] In the Transpadane districts the first care of the Romans was to found towns, to which they made the Gallic tribes subject. By the Lex Pompeia of 89 B.c. the peoples of the Eastern Alps were put under Tridentum, Verona, Brixia, Cremona, and Mediolanum, and the authorities of such towns had important duties connected with these populations, as the levying of soldiers, the quartering of troops, the responsibility for envoys, the maintenance of the roads, and the exaction of the taxes.[4] Glancing through the other provinces, we see that in Pannonia important towns like Nauportus (Ober Laibach) and Pettovia (Pettau) were of Roman origin.[5] In Dalmatia towns must originally have been very scarce, as even under Rome the circuits (conventus) were made up not of towns, but of *decuriae*. Important towns like Scardona were established by the Romans, and there were five Roman colonies in the country.[6] In Moesia the

---

[1] E.g., Illiberris, Narbo, Nemausus, Baeterrae; cf. Lentheric, *Les Villes Mortes*, etc., pp. 306, 390; Kuhn, ii. 407-25.

[2] Tac. *Ann.* iii. 44; Strabo, iv. 192; Marquardt, *Ephem. Epig.* i, p. 203.

[3] Haverfield deduces from the Gallic Inscriptions (C. I. L., vol. xiii.) that the administration was plainly tribal, not municipal; Lugdunum being the only town north of the Cevennes in which Italian city life was known. *Classical Rev.* xiii. 327; Mommsen, *Provinces*, vol. i., pp. 87-93.

[4] Marquardt, i. 14.   [5] Ib. 139.   [6] Ib. 146.

towns, such as Novae (Sistova), Odessus (Varna), Istros, Tomi (Tomisvar), are either of Greek or Roman origin; and in Dacia, as already mentioned, a number of flourishing cities were planted by the Roman conquerors.[1] The same policy was followed in Thrace, where the Romans founded many towns,[2] and in those provinces of Asia Minor, such as Bithynia or Galatia, which were not already covered with cities of Hellenic origin. Pompey founded eleven towns in Pontus, and twelve in Bithynia; other places were villages. In the course of time the number of towns considerably increased.[3] Galatia, inhabited by a brave and semi-barbarous people which did not yield to Rome without a struggle, was late in adopting the town-system, but when it was adopted there it was a great success.[4] The number of towns in Cappadocia was originally two. This was much augmented by the Romans, and from the Christian sources of the sixth century we gather that the Roman garrisons and stations on the military roads had gradually risen into towns, which were the seats of Christian bishoprics.[5] In Syria the town-system was begun by the Seleucidæ and completed by the Romans, with aid from the Jewish kings, to whom were due such towns as Caesarea and Samaria.[6] In Africa the towns played a great part in civilising and Romanising the country. Of one tribe, which was yet untouched by Roman influence (the Musulamii), Tacitus informs us that they had ' none of the civilisation of cities.'[7] But partly by means of direct colonisation, and partly by means of the gradual growth of towns from the villages of veterans, the ' civilisation of cities ' was fully applied to the country, and with the happiest results. In Pliny's time there were in Africa thirty free towns, fifteen municipia, and six colonies[8]; and modern

---

[1] Marquardt, i. 155.   [2] Ib. 159.   [3] Ib. 199.

[4] Perrot, De Galatia Provincia Romana, p. 83.

[5] Marquardt, i. 216; Appian (Mithr. 117) says that a tablet borne in Pompey's triumph credited him with the foundation of eight cities in Cappadocia, others in Cilicia, Coele Syria, and Palestine.

[6] Marquardt, 270.   [7] Tac. Ann. ii. 52.   [8] Marquardt, i. 317.

travellers notice with astonishment the ruins of what must have been flourishing cities far beyond the present limits of Algerian civilisation.[1]

The development of this town-system must in the majority of the cases have been gradual; it was not often that it was imposed full blown upon a country, as it was in the case of Dacia; and it is interesting to watch, where we can, the gradual growth of the garrison into the village, and the village into the town. The most natural way in which a town grew up of itself in a Roman province was from the buildings adjoining a Roman camp,[2] and of course still more readily from the camp itself.[3] Even in the case of a temporary camp the settlers pitched their tents just outside the rampart[4]; and where the camp was permanent, as in Syria or Africa or on the Rhine or Danube frontier, these fortuitous aggregations of merchants and camp-followers soon grew into something like a town. The *castra stativa* of the legions in the majority of cases gave birth to towns, some of which never had any name but that of the legion to which they owed their origin.[5] ' This inscription '[6] (of

Gradual growth of a town.

---

[1] Playfair, *Travels in the Footsteps of Bruce*, p. 69 and passim. Strabo, i. 4, 9, uses ἀστείους of certain barbarians who were civilised.

[2] Cf. Tac. *Hist.* iv. 22.

[3] As Lambaesis in Africa ; cf. Dio C. 36, 48, for Nicopolis in Cappadocia, where Pompey's veterans and wounded soldiers were joined by voluntary settlers from the surrounding country. Sometimes a camp was set up near a native settlement, the two communities gradually amalgamating.

[4] Caesar, *B. G.* vi. 37.

[5] E.g., Leon and Caerleon as mentioned supra. A list of camp-towns is given by Jung in *Hist. Zeit.* xxxi. 28. See id., *Fasten der Provinz Dacien*, 166-173 ; Schulten, ' *Das territorium Legionis* ' in *Hermes*, xxix. 481.

[6] The inscription is as follows : ' Pro salute imperatoris Caesaris Trajani Hadriani Augusti, Gaio Valerio Pudente veterano legionis quintae Macedonicae et Marco Ulpio Leontio magistris Canabensium et Tuccio Aelio aedilibus, dono dederunt veterani et cives Romani consistentes ad Canabas legionis Quintae Macedonicae.' See Mommsen, in C. I. L. iii., p. 999.

Troesmis in Lower Moesia) 'shows us how these towns came into existence. Sutlers and merchants came to settle in the neighbourhood of the camp, and these built huts, *canabae*, the aggregate of which soon formed a village. When this village had attained sufficient importance to have an administration of its own—a *res publica*—it was given, along with the title of *vicus*, the administration of a *vicus* ; that is, one consisting of two *magistri*, two aediles, and a council composed of *vicani* or decurions.'[1] Another inscription mentioning these canabae has been found at Argentoratum (Strasburg), three more at Apulum (Karlsburg) in Dacia,[2] and others elsewhere. We may suppose that the first canaba grew out of the legion known as VIII. Augusta, which was stationed at Argentoratum, and the latter from that known as XIII. Gemina, which was stationed in Dacia, and the name of which occurs on two of the inscriptions of Apulum. In one of the latter we find the phrase ' Kanabensium legionis XIII. Geminae,' and we may suppose that, strictly speaking, *Canabae* or *Canabenses* was never a complete title by itself, but needed the addition of the name of the legion to become intelligible. Where, however, everyone knew the name and number of the legion,

---

[1] Rénier, *Inscriptions de Troesmis*, in the Revue Archéologique, xii. 414.

[2] (1) ' Fortunae Augustae sacrum et genio Canabensium L. Silius Maximus veteranus legionis I. adjutricis piae fidelis, magistras (sic) primus in Canaba dedicavit et Silvia Januaria et Silius Firminus ' (No. 433 in Ackner and Müller). (2) ' Libero patri et Liberae Claudius Atteius Celer, veteranus legionis xiii. Geminae Gordianae (Severianae?) decurio Canabensium cum suis votum libens solvit. Locus datus decreto decurionum ' (No. 358). (3) ' Pro salute Augusti Matri deum magnae sanctum Titus Flavius Longinus veteranus ex decurione alae II. Pannoniorum, decurio coloniae Dacicae, decurio municipii Napocae, decurio Kanabensium legionis xiii. Geminae, et Claudia Candida conjunx et Flavius Longinus, Clementina, Marcellina filii ex imperio pecunia sua fecerunt. Locus datus decreto decurionum ' (No. 387). Cannaba occurs twice in the *Itin. Anton.* (pp. 189, 191, ed. Wesseling), in both cases on a Syrian road.

they might very naturally be omitted on the inscription, as it was not worth while spending time and labour to add them.[1]

However it originated, a town always included a considerable surrounding district; and in many cases the smaller towns were not themselves independent units, but were included in the territory of a larger city. Nismes and Marseilles had a great number of these smaller towns thus 'attributed' to them. Marseilles had at one time authority over Nice and Antibes, among others ; and Nismes over no less than twenty-four smaller towns, each of which possessed the Latin right like herself.[2] In Italy itself the *regio Herculanensium* or *pagus Herculaneus* (it is called by both names)[3] was included in Naples; and Baiae stood in the same relation of subordination to Cumae.[4] Andes came under Mantua, the powerful colony of Vienna (Vienne) in Gaul included all the country of the Allobroges.[5] There were 293 states dependent on others in Tarraconensis.[6] In almost all provincial municipia and colonies there was no doubt a portion of the surrounding population thus attributed; the *contributi* are mentioned for instance in the Lex Ursonitana, and we learn from that law that they shared the military duties of the full citizen.[7] I shall have something to add upon this subject later. At present the ground has perhaps been sufficiently cleared to allow of an examination of the

Relation of a town to the surrounding district.

---

[1] For the Canabae, see Mommsen in *Hermes*, vii. ; Desjardins, iii. 407 ; *Philol. Wochenschrift*, xiii. 993, 994.

[2] Plin. *N. H.* iii. 4 ; Strabo, iv. 1. 12 ; Appian, *B. C.* ii. 26 ; Zumpt, *Decr. Terg.*, p. 10. For Marseilles, Caesar, *B. C.* i. 35 ; *Staatsrecht*, iii. 765.

[3] Orelli, 3801 and 3795.

[4] Orelli, 2263. The official acting at Baiae calls himself *pro magistro* in his inscription ; cf. Zumpt, *Comm. Epig.* ii. 54.

[5] Hirschfeld in C. I. L. xii. 217 ; Merel, *Genève et Vienne.*

[6] Plin. *N. H.* iii. 4.

[7] § 103 of the law.

different classes of provincial towns,—the non-Roman towns (including the free and federate states), the colonies, and the municipia.[1]

SECTION II.   The non-Roman Towns.

Three classes of non-Roman towns.

In the enumeration which Pliny gives of the 175 towns of Baetica he enumerates nine colonies, eight municipia, twenty-nine Latin towns, six free towns, three federate, and 120 tributary (stipendiariae).[2]   In the list which he gives of the towns of Tarraconensis the numbers are different, but the proportions are precisely similar.[3]   It appears therefore, and this is what might have been anticipated, that the unprivileged towns were far more numerous than those provincial towns which under the name of free or federate possessed autonomy and immunity, in addition to those composed of citizens with either the full Roman or the Latin franchise.   Unfortunately it is of this larger class that least is known.   We possess a large amount of evidence as to the internal arrangements of a Roman colony or municipium, and something is known of the constitutions of the more important free or federate towns; but of the great mass of the 'stipendiariae civitates' our information is exceedingly scanty.   It will be better therefore to set out what is definitely known of the free and federate states before proceeding to the discussion of the other far more numerous class of non-Roman towns.

1. Both the federate towns and those which were called simply 'free' might, if desirable, be grouped under the one head of 'free towns.'   But it is convenient to separate them in practice, because though all federate towns were free,

---

[1] The Roman town system was not carried out fully in certain provinces, as in Africa, where the latifundia caused authority to be exercised by great landowners, in the Rhaetian Alps, and in mining districts in Spain, as Vipasca.   *Eph. Epigr.* iii. 187.

[2] Pliny, *N. H.* iii. 3.

[3] Ib. iii. 4.

not all free towns were federate.   The federate towns were those which had made a definite treaty with Rome, sworn to on both sides, and carved on brazen tablets, of which one was kept in each contracting city.   Their position was the most favourable of all provincial towns, and as Rome acquired a position of absolute predominance, no more were made.[1]   But there were one or two in almost every province. **Federate towns.**   There were three in Sicily ; one in Tarraconensis; three in Baetica ; one, Marseilles, in Narbonensis, besides whole peoples—the Remi, Aedui, Carnuti, Vocontii, and Lingones —in *Gallia Comata*.   Athens, Rhodes and Tyre were federate towns, and four can be pointed out in Asia Minor. Cicero mentions it as an exceptional thing and as a stigma on Sardinia, that in all that island there was no town which was 'free and united by friendship with the Roman people.'[2]

It is difficult to make out the precise relation of these towns to Rome.   In every case the treaty—though varying in other respects—expressly forbade an independent foreign policy.   It was open to such a town to adopt the civil law of Rome or not, as it pleased; but it had no choice about ratifying or declining to ratify matters concerning the Empire, the wars, the safety or the victories of Rome.[3] All of these towns were exempt from the ordinary taxes[4] and from the jurisdiction of the provincial governor ; and all had the right if they pleased of using their own laws. Even Romans living in a federate town pleaded before its

---

[1] For distinction of foederati and liberi, see *Staatsr*. iii. 657.

[2] Cic. *pro Scauro*, § 44.   For the whole subject, see Zumpt, *Studia Romana*, p. 315 ; Marquardt, i. 348.   For the position of Athens, see Pausan. i. 36 ; Cic. *in Pis*. 16 ; Livy, *Ep*. 81 ; Appian, *Mithr*. 38.

[3] Cf. Cic. *pro Balbo*, 8, and E. G. Hardy, *Pliny's Letters to Trajan*, No. 92 (on Amisus in Bithynia).   They had the right of coinage, of receiving exiles, and only lost their privileges for open rebellion or grave sedition.   Thus Trajan, though opposing clubs in general, was obliged to allow their continuance at Amisus.

[4] See Cic. *in Verr*. ii. 69, iii. 40, iv. 9 for illustrations of this immunity ; also *de Off*. iii. 22.

courts in civil cases.[1]   But, these common features apart, there were the greatest varieties in the position secured to the different federate towns by their treaties with Rome. Such treaties were regularly divided into favourable (aequa) and unfavourable (iniqua).[2] An instance of an *iniquum foedus* is that made with the Helvetians and other barbarous peoples, in which it was expressly stipulated that no one of them should ever become a citizen of Rome.[3] The treaty of Heraclea on the other hand was so exceptionally favourable that its citizens were very doubtful whether they should accept the offer of the privileges of Roman citizenship.[4] In Sicily the treaties made with Messana and Tauromenium differed in the important respect that the people of Messana were bound to furnish a vessel at their own expense, while from this burden the Tauromenians were expressly excused.[5]

Interference in the internal affairs of these towns.

Though in all cases the foedus laid down the exemption of such towns from the interference of the governor,[6] and though they had a legal right to maintain any sort of political constitution they might think fit, we do as a matter of fact find them interfered with, and we may be sure that means were pretty generally taken to bring their constitutions up to the usual timocratic level.   The answer which Pompey gave to the people of Messana when, on the ground of their treaty, they claimed exemption from his jurisdiction, must often have been given in such cases by the men of the sword.[7]   In the case of Marseilles we know that the govern-

---

[1] Marquardt, i. 349 ; Schürer, *Hist. of the Jewish People*, i. 401 ; *Staatsr.* i. 159 (Fr. tr.).

[2] Hirschfeld (*Gall. Stud.* i. 293) believes that these *iniqua foedera* did not remain under the Empire.

[3] Cic. *pro Balbo*, 14.   [4] Cic. *pro Balbo*, 8 and 22 ; *pro Archia*, 4.

[5] Cic. *in Verr.* iv. 19.   [6] Ib. ii. 66.

[7] Plut. *Pomp.* 10 : παραιτουμένων γὰρ αὐτοῦ τὸ βῆμα καὶ δικαιοδοσίαν, ὡς νομίμῳ παλαιῷ Ῥωμαίων ἀπειρημένα, Οὐ παύσεσθε, εἶπεν, ἡμῖν ὑπεζωσμένοις ξίφη νόμους ἀναγινώσκοντες ; Cf. id. *Mor.* ii., p. 993 (Didot), *Hermes*, xxxiv. 311 ; *Staatsr.* iii. 687, note 2.

ment was a very pronounced oligarchy[1]: perhaps this is one reason for the elaborate panegyric which Cicero more than once bestows upon the place.[2] Rhodes on the other hand had a peculiar kind of democratic constitution,[3] which doubtless was one reason why the Romans found the place difficult to deal with, and why its privileges were ultimately taken away.

These towns owed their privileged position to services done to Rome in the past, and Rome looked to them to do if necessary similar services in the future. Cicero speaks of Marseilles almost as he speaks of Narbo,[4] and its services were doubtless great. So it was the Remi who took the lead in peaceful measures when part of Gaul revolted under Civilis[5]; and Gades from the time of the Punic wars had given many substantial proofs of loyalty.[6] *Services of these towns to Rome.*

It shows, however, how strong was the tendency to uniformity and how great the attraction exercised by Rome that we find almost all these towns, whose position seems so exceptional and so favourable, gradually renouncing it in order to become colonies or municipia. In Sicily, Tauromenium became a colony, and Messana apparently a municipium.[7] In Spain, Gades becomes a municipium, under *These towns tend to become Roman.*

[1] Cic. *de Republ.* i. 27 ; Strabo, iv. 1, § 5.

[2] Cf. Cic. *pro Flacco*, 26 ; *de Off.* 2, § 28 ; *ad Att.* xiv. 12, 14 ; *Phil.* 8, § 18 ; Vell. Pat. ii. 56.

[3] Cic. *de Republ.* iii. 35 : Omnes erant iidem (Rhodii) tum de plebe, tum senatores, vicissitudinesque habebant, quibus mensibus populari munere fungerentur, quibus senatorio ; utrubique autem conventicium accipiebant ; et in theatro et in curia res capitales et reliquas omnes iudicabant iidem. For Roman dealing with Rhodes, see Vell. Paterc. i. 9, ii. 18, 69; Dio Cass., fr. 66 and 68 ; App. *Bell. Civ.* iv. 67; Cic. *ad Fam.* xii. 14, 15 ; Holm, iv. ch. 22 ; Aul. Gell. vii. 3 ; Dio. Chrys. xxxi.

[4] Cic. *pro Font.* 20 : 'Ea condicione atque eo fato se in iis terris collocatam arbitratur, ne quid nostris hominibus istae gentes nocere possint.'

[5] Tac. *Hist.* iv. 67.

[6] Cf. Cic. *pro Balbo*, 17.

[7] Plin. iii., § 88. He calls Messana 'oppidum civium Romanorum.'

the title of *municipium Augustum Gaditanum*[1]; and so also do Saguntum and Malaca, both of which had previously been federate. The latter case seems to show that an allied town would even accept the minor priviliges of the Latin right in preference to its independent condition. Similarly in Italy, both Heraclea and Neapolis became Roman municipia.[2] Marseilles became a colony. It was doubtless found by these towns that the advantages they enjoyed were not of a very substantial character; and that a more certain protection against tyrannical magistrates as well as a larger opening to ambition were supplied by their being incorporated into the Roman State, instead of remaining outside it in semi-independent isolation.[3]

Free towns.

2. The *civitates sine foedere immunes et liberae*[4] differed for the worse from the federate towns in that their freedom was secured, not by the stipulation of a treaty, but by the voluntary gift of Rome, and could therefore at any time be taken from them. Towns which had sided with Rome in war, for instance Utica and six other towns in Africa, or which, like Troas, enjoyed the special goodwill of the Senate or the emperor, received the gift. A fragment of the Lex Antonia de Termessibus which still exists shows that these towns had the right to use their own laws, to be exempt from soldiers being quartered on them, and to use their own customs duties.[5] They were also, like the federate towns, exempt from taxation; but were also, like them, subject to the supreme disposal of the Senate. The difference then between them and the federate towns lying merely

---

[1] C. I. L. ii. 1313; Orelli, 3690, 3691.

[2] Cic. *pro Archia*, 5, § 10; *ad Fam.* xiii. 30. For Marseilles, see Hirschfeld, *Gall. Stud.* i. 284.

[3] Strictly speaking, the free and allied towns did not belong to the province at all; cf. Mommsen, C. I. L. i. 99.

[4] For *civitates liberae*, see *Staatsrecht*, iii. 655; Henze *de civitatibus liberis* (Berlin, 1892); Mommsen, *Provinces*, i. 262; Kuhn. ii. 23. Some were *immunes*, others not.

[5] C. I. L. i. 204.

in their weaker legal position as against Rome, and not in any practical inferiority of privilege, we may expect to find much the same features visible in them that we have already noted in the cognate class of towns. The same right of exemption from the jurisdiction of the governor appears in these as in the federate cities.[1] Piso had to pay a tribune heavily to bring in a law to authorise him when governor of Macedonia to decide upon cases of debt in the free city of Byzantium.[2] But in the Greek cities at all events, which were always 'free,' it is very certain that taxes were exacted, and that the governor exercised the supreme jurisdiction.[3] It is of the cities in this part of the world that Tacitus is speaking when he describes them with a kind of irony as 'the allied nations and free states *as they were called*'[4]; and we may infer from Strabo that the freedom of 'Corcyra the free' was not a matter of very much consequence.[5] When, as sometimes happened, *e.g.*, in the case of Thessalonica, the governor resided in a free town, there could hardly have been much independence. Perhaps the freedom was sometimes badly used. Suetonius[6] says that Augustus deprived of their independence some of this class of states, 'which by their excessive licence were hastening to their own ruin.' Rome endeavoured to maintain control over them by favouring the aristocratic or rather timocratic

---

[1] Cf. Strabo, iv. 6, § 4 ; Pliny, *Ep.* x. 93 ; Seeck, ' *Selbstverwaltung*,' i., p. 223.

[2] Cic. *de Prov. Cons.* 4.

[3] See Mommsen's note, iii. 271. See the case of Cnidus, to which Augustus sends Asinius to investigate a case of murder referred to him. Dittenberger, *Sylloge Inscr. Graec.*, vol. i., p. 560, Müller's *Handbuch*, iii. 464.

[4] Tac. *Ann.* xv. 45.

[5] Strabo, vii. fragment 7, ὑπὸ πολέμων τινῶν καὶ τυράννων ἐφθάρη· καὶ ὕστερον ὑπὸ Ῥωμαίων ἐλευθερωθεῖσα οὐκ ἐπῃνέθη, ἀλλ' ἐπὶ λοιδορίᾳ παροιμίαν ἔλαβεν.

[6] Suet. *Aug.* 47. Instances are Tyre and Sidon and Cyzicus. Dio Cass. liv. 7. The decree against Cyzicus was afterwards revoked, but Tiberius punished it later in the same way. Suet. *Tib.* 37.

element in their constitutions[1]; we find for instance the Areopagus apparently the chief judicial authority in Athens,[2] —a strange return to the days before Pericles and Ephialtes. But the affairs of these states fell into confusion, and such special missions as that of Pliny to the cities of Bithynia are of frequent occurrence.[3]   A good governor was careful to show one of these towns special respect,[4] but a Verres could disregard their privileges with impunity, and at all events one case occurs of a magistrate of one of these towns being scourged by a Roman governor.[5]   It is no wonder therefore that the same causes which changed the federate cities into municipia should act still more power-fully here, notwithstanding that for a considerable period at all events there was much competition for the privileges of freedom,[6] and that they were purchased with large sums of money.[7]   A free town would naturally enough appeal to Rome for assistance in case of disturbance in its internal affairs.   Thus the free town of Halesa in Sicily requested the Senate to regulate its constitution, which was done by sending C. Claudius Pulcher to the place as extraordinary commissioner.[8]   Similarly Caesar when praetor in Spain regulated the internal affairs of Gades,[9] and a free town of

---

[1] Coulanges, *Cité Antique,* 448-91, 454 ; Marquardt, i. 238, for Syria ; i. 248, for Judaea ; i. 578, for Tarsus and generally.   Cf. Pausanias, vii. 16, 9 ; Livy, xxxiv. 57.   The guard for the defence of Byzantium, Plin. *Ep.* x. 82, which 'protected its privileges,' is not easy to explain. Perhaps it was intended for the support of the aristocratic element against the plebs.   For the insistence on a limited franchise in a Greek town, see Mommsen, *Provinces,* i. 257.

[2] Tac. *Ann.* ii. 55.

[3] Cf. Plin. *Ep.* viii. 24 : ' Messius Maximus missus in provinciam Achaiam ad ordinandum statum liberarum civitatum.'   Henzen, 6483 : ' Legato divi Hadriani Athenis, Thespiis, Plateis, item in Thessalia . . . legato divi Hadriani ad rationes civitatum Syriae putandas.'

[4] Suet. *Cal.* 3 ; Tac. *Ann.* ii. 55, for Germanicus.

[5] Mommsen, iii. 293-4 (Mylasa in Caria).

[6] Cic. *ad Qu. Fr.* ii. 11, for the refusal of freedom to Tenedos.

[7] Cic. *de Off.* iii., § 87 ; Suet. *Jul.* 54.

[8] Cic. *in Verr.* ii. 49.   [9] Cic. *pro Balbo,* 19.

Bithynia, though asserting its right to exemption from all interference of the Roman governor, voluntarily submitted its affairs to Pliny's examination.[1] This was a tendency which once begun would not stop before the assimilation of these towns to the regular municipal type. Thus in Italy Nero made Puteoli, which had been a free town,[2] into a colony[3]; and we find the same change effected in the case of Hadrumetum, Hippo, and Parentum in Africa.[4]

Civitates stipendiariae.

The great mass of provincial towns — civitates stipendiariae — possessed no special privileges. That however their internal affairs were not much interfered with, and that at all events under a good governor, they retained the use of their own laws to a large extent, is proved by all the evidence. Temnos had five praetors, three quaestors, and four mensarii, names which we may no doubt regard as translations of Greek equivalents.[5] Thyatira had a βουλή and an ἄρχων, and its chief magistrates appear to have been στρατηγοί.[6] In Africa we even find Sufetes.[7] So we find a προάγορος at Catina in Sicily,[8] and all the Sicilian cities had apparently their local Senates. Cicero frequently mentions that of Syracuse, and when speaking of it gives it its regular Greek name of βουλευτήριον.[9] The great change made by Rome was in the direction of abolishing the democracies; though we still find the popular assemblies of Asia Minor in some cases apparently the chief source of power, at all events up to quite the end of the Republic.[10]

---

[1] Plin. *Ep.* x. 56.   [2] Cic. *de Leg. Agr.* ii. 31

[3] Zumpt, *Comm. Epig.* i. 458.   [4] Ib.   [5] Cic. *pro Flacco,* 19.

[6] Perrot, pp. 5, 9 of *Inscriptions d'Asie Mineure ;* pp. 8, 16, 23, 27 of *Inscriptions de la Mer Noire.*

[7] For Sufetes, see Orelli, 3056 ; Wilmanns, 89, 2345.

[8] Cic. *in Verr.* iv. 23.

[9] Cic. *in Verr.* ii. 20, 21, iv. 64, 65.

[10] Cic. *pro Flacco,* 6 fin. ; Cic. *in Verr.* ii. 27, for Lampsacus. But such a passage as Cic. *ad Qu. Fr.* i. 1. 8, is significant : ' Provideri abs te ut civitates optimatium consiliis administrentur.' A passage of Caesar, *B. G.* viii. 21, seems to suggest that the populace was always at first unfriendly to Rome, and that Rome made it her business to

Under the Empire timocracies seem to have been everywhere established.[1] Only those possessing a certain income
were permitted the full franchise of the place. So at Tarsus, besides a βουλή, and a δῆμος, there was a 'no small multitude which stood as it were outside the constitution.'[2] In this case the regular franchise could only be purchased at a cost of 500 drachmae. But the greatest change of all was the conversion of these towns into municipia by giving them the Roman or Latin franchise. The Greek towns offered a passive resistance to this change, and though after Caracalla the *decuriones* were introduced everywhere, we still find officers like the ἄρχων at Athens existing up to Constantine.[3] What were the steps by which the different town constitutions changed into the regular decurional arrangements no one can tell.[4]

SECTION III.   *Roman Towns.*

The administration of Italy was a model and anticipation of provincial administration. It will therefore be well in

conciliate the nobles; cf. ib. 49.   See Levy, 'Études sur la vie de l'Asie Mineure sous les Antonins' in *Revue des Études Grecques*, viii. (1895).

[1] *Staatsrecht*, iii. 696.

[2] Πλῆθος οὐκ ὀλίγον ὥσπερ ἔξωθεν τῆς πολιτείας, Dio. Chrys. ii. 43 R ; Marquardt, i. 518; *Staatsr.* iii. 696.

[3] Cnidus had an ἄρχων and βουλή, as had Mylasa. Cyzicus had an hipparch, Dittenberger i. 356, 348; there were archons, boulè, and demos at Ephesus, ib. 404; and Naples, though a colony, still had its demarchus and phratries; Orelli, 3720, 3800, 3801. So there were astynomi at Velia, Orelli, 3804 ; agonothetae and episcopus at Nice, Orelli, 4024 ; and afterwards the decurionate constitution became universal, Kuhn, ii. 3533; Ramsay, *Cities and Bishoprics of Phrygia*, i. 60.

[4] Marquardt, i. 523. Under the later Empire (364) an official called *defensor plebis* or *civitatis* was instituted to protect the plebs against the nobles of the place; Marquardt, i. 522. He must be carefully distinguished from the defensor reipublicae, defensor coloniae, etc., which occur at a much earlier period. See Orelli, 3908, 3909 ; Henzen, 7088, and his note.

this section to consider the case of Italian towns side by side with those in the provinces.

There were three main classes of Roman town—municipia, coloniae, and praefecturae—of which the praefecturae do not require our discussion, as, though frequent in Italy, and perhaps the original type of all municipal towns in that country,[1] they were not carried into the provinces. But it must not be supposed that all Roman towns came under one of these three heads. There were also the smaller units of *fora* and *conciliabula*, which are mentioned along with the three more important classes in the Lex Julia Municipalis.[2] Both of these were in origin the meeting-places of the different pagi of a tribe, and lingered on till late in districts where there was no town. Fora occur in Gaul, and very Fora. frequently in the Transpadane country.[3] They are usually called after some Roman—Forum Appii, Forum Sempronii, etc.—and perhaps were in each case definitely established as markets by some Roman general. In course of time such country towns would be attributed to a neighbouring colony or municipium, or would themselves rise to an independent position. In the provinces the word *vicus* appears to be used Vici. where one of these more definite terms would be used in Italy. It represented the lowest administrative unit, and was applied to a street or a quarter of a town as well as to a a rural group. We know that a vicus regularly had its own aediles,[4] probably elected part of the municipal senate of the

---

[1] Festus maintains this; Marquardt, i. 43; Mommsen, *Staatsr.* iii. 797.

[2] §§ 26 and 27 of this law; see *Hermes*, xxi. 534.

[3] Pliny, *N. H.* iii. 20, gives a list. Jung in *Hist. Zeit.* for 1892, pp. 1-40; Vell. Pat., ii. 39.

[4] Cf. p. 226, on the Canabae, and an inscription of the vicus Furfensis (C. I. L. ix. 3513, Bruns, p. 283), which formed part of the respublica Peltuinum in Sabine territory : 'Venditio locatio aedilis esto, quem quomque veicus Furfensis fecerint.' Cf. Digest L. 1, § 30; Wilmanns, 289, 2071.

republica which it belonged,[1] and could apparently be the
client of its own particular patron.[2] But the history of such
villages, where it can be traced, always shows a development
into the regular municipal system. All these minor towns

Pagi.

met with more or less recognition from Rome ; but the *pagi*
which occur now and then in inscriptions had no such well-
defined legal position. We never, for instance, find them
mentioned in such general municipal laws as that of Rubrius
or Caesar. But we find magistrates calling themselves
' magistri pagi,' an office which Egger compares to that of
the village mayors in France. Thus we find the pagus
Herculaneus decreeing the restoration of a covered walk
with the consent of the *magister pagi*, Cn. Laetorius ; and the
chief official of the Canabae appears to have been given the
same title.[3] Even the aedile of a pagus occurs[4] ; it might
have a deliberative assembly or *ordo ;* and the decrees of a
pagus are more than once mentioned.[5] In Italy these pagi by
the time of the later Republic were a mere relic of antiquity,
perhaps maintained for sentimental and antiquarian reasons;
but in some parts of the provinces (at any rate in Gaul) they
would still be the channel by which the administration reached
the people. Thus we find a prefect of the pagus of the Gallic
Epotes (Upaix).[6]

Colonies.

Apart from all such minor and dependent communities
as the above, there remain two great classes of Roman

[1] Cf. Zumpt, *Comm. Epig.* i. 91, and Marquardt's criticism of Zumpt,
i. 11, note 4.

[2] Cf. an inscription of Yverdon, which was only a *vicus*, in Troyon,
Mon. de l'antiquité dans l'Europe barbare, 1868, p. 523. A case of iiii viri
in a vicus appears to occur in Aosta ; Orelli, 4029. For Swiss *pagi* see
Hermes, xvi. 457.

[3] Wilmanns, No. 2409, and ii. p. 627. For Cn. Laetorius, C. I. L.
xi. 1042.

[4] C. I. L. i. 1279. See Willems, p. 522, who quotes C. I. L. iii.
1405, 1407, 3776-7, v. 1829-30, 4148, etc.

[5] Orelli, 3984.

[6] Orelli-Henzen, 4025 ; Kuhn, *Entstehung der Städte der Alten*, 438 ;
Bullet. Epigr. v. 179 ; Hirschfeld, *Gall. Stud.* i. 304.

towns—the colonies and the municipia. In the course of Roman history we find colonies used for three different purposes,—as fortified outposts in a conquered country, as a means of providing for the poor of Rome, and as settlements for veterans who had served their time. The colonies established in Italy before the latter part of the second century were of the first class, those designed by Gracchus were to be of the second, and those founded by Augustus were of the third. But the first sense of the word never died out; Camulodunum, for instance, was founded exclusively for military purposes. Gracchus' great scheme of transmarine colonisation proved abortive, but it was not long after his death that a Roman colony with full rights was settled at Narbo (118 B.C.). It is not, however, till the latter part of the first century B.C. that the system of transmarine colonisation was extensively employed. Caesar settled 80,000 citizens in different colonies out of Italy, and Augustus in 14 B.C. founded a number in Narbonensian Gaul and Spain ; others in Sicily, Africa, Macedonia, Achaia, Asia, and Syria.[1] In some cases Augustus expelled the existing inhabitants to make room for his colonists, and thus founded entirely new towns; in others merely added his settlers to the existing population, the town then receiving the rank and title of a colony, especially with the object of civilising remote districts like Gallaecia or Lusitania, and protecting new commercial highways.[2] After Augustus the system was much employed, but no doubt rather in the form of ascription of colonists to existing populations, than by making entirely new foundations. In many cases a place was given the rank and privileges of a colony without receiving any new citizens at all. Hadrian largely used this system of honorary colonies. In Sicily

Honorary colonies.

---

[1] For the extra-Italian colonies of Augustus, see Mommsen, *Res gestae*, p. 119 [*Mon. Anc.* 28]. They were all military colonies of veterans, civilian settlements being henceforth exceptional.

[2] Hyginus, *De Lim.*, p. 177 ; Lachm., quoted by Mommsen, *Mon. Anc.*, p. 41.

Lilybaeum and Panormus, in Spain Italica, in Africa Utica, and no less than eight towns in Narbonensis, became colonies during his reign.[1] Probably later emperors carried out the same system; we know from Aulus Gellius that municipia competed for the title of colony[2]; and Commodus is said to have thought of bestowing it upon Rome.

The land of a colony.

The ceremonies usual at the foundation of a colony remained on the whole unchanged in all periods. The land was parcelled out into *centuriae* or squares of 200 acres each; and these again divided into allotments, *sortes*, the size of which differed in different colonies. In military colonies a man received a larger or a smaller share according to his rank.[3] From a comparison of the Mamilian Law with the law of the colony of Urso, which was founded by Caesar, it seems probable that Caesar established a norm of law for all matters connected with the land of a colony, and that from this original model the separate colonies transferred what was needed into their own municipal law.[4]

Relation of the colonists to the natives.

As in most instances these colonists were added to existing towns, there were naturally frequent difficulties between the new settlers and the original inhabitants. Cicero mentions the disputes between the new settlers in Pompeii and the natives of the place, and part of the quarrel seems to have turned upon political questions.[5] In the provinces, where the colonists brought with them a distinct superiority of legal right, the natives must at first have been in a disagreeable position. But they probably very soon, if not at

---

[1] Zumpt, *Comm. Epig.* i. 458. The system of honorary colonies was begun by Julius Caesar in Spain. Dio Cass. xliii. 39. See Jung, *Recht. Lat.* 22 ; *Hermes*, i. 102.

[2] xvi. 13. M. Aurelius made the village where his wife died a colony ; Capitolinus, *M. Aurel.* 26. Diocletian made Nicomedia a colony ; Marquardt, i. 457. Caracalla or Sept. Severus Palmyra ; Marquardt, i. 256.

[3] Marquardt, i. 458 ; cf. Tac. *Ann.* xiv. 27 for the differences of rank.

[4] Bruns, pp. 95 and 120.

' De suffragiis ' ; Cic. *pro Sulla*, 21.

once,[1] obtained equal rights with the colonists. We find the *contributi* forming part of the local militia in the colony of Urso ; and where there were duties there were naturally rights. The new inhabitants and the old intermarried, as in the Colonia Agrippinensis[2]; and these connexions doubtless often extended far beyond the immediate boundaries of the colony.[3] On the other hand, the excessive claims which a colony put forward as the representative of Rome often, no doubt, provoked the jealousy and hostility of neighbouring municipia or other provincial towns. The idea of a colony was that it was another Rome, transferred to the soil of another country. Even in the form and aspect of the place Rome was imitated,[4] and the Roman law, with all its formal usages, was transferred unchanged into the provinces.[5]

The difference between a colony and a full Roman municipium was a difference of history and, to a certain extent, of rank,[6] but not a difference of right or privilege. In regard to their internal arrangements and constitution, what is true of a municipium is true of a colony,[7] and it is therefore possible to discuss the municipal polities as a whole without having to distinguish between the two classes

Municipia.

---

[1] At Carteia this occurred at once, Livy, xliii. 3 [171 B.C.] ; the amalgamation at Cologne was slower, Tac. *Hist.* iv. 65 ; but for the tendency, see Tac. *Ann.* xiv. 33 (Verulamium).

[2] Tac. *Hist.* iv. 65 ; Kuhn, *Entstehung,* 435; *Hermes,* xix. 78.

[3] Tac., ib. iii. 34.

[4] Lentheric makes this remark of Narbo. Jung, *Röm. Land.,* 20.

[5] Cf. the Fragmentum Tudertinum, Bruns, p. 157. Compare § 102 of Lex Ursonitana (about limit of time for speeches) with Cic. *in Verr.* ii. 9 ; Plin. *Ep.* iv. 9 ; see also § 103 of the law. Cf. § 29 of Lex Salpensana, fin. (law of guardianship) ; Lex Malacitana, § 54 fin., § 64 (requirements of candidates for office, and law of sureties).

[6] In an enumeration of the different classes of Roman towns *in Italy* the order is always municipia, coloniae, praefecturae, etc. But *in the provinces* this is reversed, and the colony is always put first. *Hermes,* xxvii. 108.

[7] The few inconsiderable exceptions to this are given by Marquardt, i. 481.

of towns. The word municipium was roughly used for the whole body of towns with Latin or Roman right, and Gellius[1] expressly says that the citizen of a colony would habitually call himself ' municeps ' and his fellow-citizens 'municipes.' We even find cases in which one and the same place (perhaps only by confusion) was called colony and municipium at once,[2] and had both duoviri and quattuorviri. Ordinarily, however, it is possible to say at once whether a place is a colony or a municipium, as the mention of duoviri puts it into the former, while that of quattuorviri puts it into the latter category.[3] A colony was formed by a fixed number of families settled in a definite place by the direction of the competent authority. Its jurisdiction was limited by its charter (*lex coloniae*) ; it therefore did not have *libertas*, but was under the law of Rome. A municipium may be defined as a provincial town—not a colony—which was in possession of the Latin or the full Roman franchise. The phrase so frequent in Pliny[4] to describe a town—quae jure Romanorum civium fruitur—is just as if he had said without periphrasis, 'which is a municipium.' The historical difference between a colony and a municipium is that which is made by Aulus Gellius, namely, that the

[1] xvi. 13.

[2] C. I. L. iii. 183, No. 95 ; Orelli, 81, 3826, 3846 ; cf. 3686 (Apulum) ; Jullian, 31, 32 ; Mommsen, in *Hermes*, xxvii. 108.

[3] There are, however, exceptions. We certainly find duoviri used now and then of the magistrates of a municipium. Rénier particularly notices this in the inscriptions of Numidia (cf. Henzen, 7044, p. 416). In any case the distinction, though important as a key to the student of inscriptions, was one without a difference. In a colony, as well as in a municipium, there were four principal magistrates ; only in a colony they were divided into *duoviri iuri dicundo*, and *duoviri aediles*, whereas in a municipium they were all comprehended under the one name of *quattuorviri*. The powers and duties of each were precisely similar. See Jung, in *Hist. Zeit.* xxi. 8. Mommsen, in *Hermes*, xvi. 40. Quattuorviri are mentioned in regard to Augusta Vindelicorum (a colony). Orelli, 494. There were no municipia in the Greek East, except Stobi in Macedonia.

[4] Pliny, *N. H.* iii. 13, 14, etc.

municipia were taken into the State from without, while the colonies were offshoots from within. A provincial town became a municipium when its inhabitants accepted the Roman or Latin franchise, and when it had received the definite municipal constitution from a Roman governor or special commissioner. This constitution was just as necessary to make a place a municipium as the possession of the Roman franchise[1]; and the occasional dictators, praetors, etc., whom we find in Italian municipia[2] are exceptional in Italy, probably in the great majority of cases came to an end with the introduction of such measures as that of the Lex Julia Municipalis, and do not occur in the provinces.

A municipium meant originally a community which was in possession only of the incomplete franchise. By derivation the word is sometimes referred to the jus hospitii existing between Rome and Italian towns[3]; but its actual usage was for a town possessing the civitas sine suffragio, that is the right of trade and intermarriage, but not the jus suffragii or the jus honorum.[4] Gradually these municipia acquired the full franchise; and as this happened the meaning of the word changed, and municipes came to mean men who were not actually born at Rome, but were full citizens, and included in a tribe. Thus Cicero was ' Civis Romanus, *Origin and various meanings of the term.*

---

[1] Cf. § 53 of the Lex Mamilia: ' Quae colonia hac lege deducta quodve municipium, praefectura, etc., constitutum erit'; § 30 of the Lex Julia Municipalis.

[2] Orelli, 3789, 3786, 3787. Milo was dictator at Lanuvium ; Cic. *bro Mil.* 10 ; cf. Cic. *de Leg. Agr.* ii. 34.

[3] ' The receiving of a gift,' *munus capere*—i.e., Italians from Romans when sojourning in Rome, Romans from Italians when passing through any town connected with them by such a tie. See Marquardt, i. 27. Another explanation is that *munus* meant a ' burden,' and indicated the position of a town, such as Tusculum was the first to occupy—i.e., with the obligation to the levy and to taxation.

[4] Festus, p. 142 M. : ' At Servius filius aiebat municipes initio fuisse, qui ea condicione cives Romani fuissent ut semper rem publicam separatim a populo Romano haberent, Cumanos, etc., qui aeque cives Romani erant . . . sed dignitates non capiebant.' Marquardt, i. 28.

municeps Arpinas.'   At what period the change took place
which established the Italian municipia as independent
communities under the central government of Rome, but
no longer administered by a prefect sent from Rome, it is
impossible to say.   Mommsen ascribes this great change to
Sulla.   There is, however, no direct evidence for his view;
and all that can be said is that after the Social War and the
extension of the franchise to all Italy, some reorganisation
of the Italian towns was necessary; that it had become
obviously impossible to go on treating the towns as if they
were but so many outlying fragments of Rome, and that
Sulla was the only statesman of the period who seems to
have had the head for reorganisation on a great scale.   The
great law of Caesar secured and defined this municipal independence, and was probably applied by Augustus to all

*Transfer-
ence of
the muni-
cipal
arrange-
ments of
Italy to
the pro-
vinces.*
municipia in the provinces.   Roman towns had naturally
grown up in the conquered countries—Italica, to name one
instance,[1] had so grown up in Spain; and now that the
Italian municipia had been regulated, the same process
must have been applied to them.   The arrangements of the
Italian towns had been taken over we may be sure without
much change, and all that had to be done was to regulate
and legalise them.   Augustus was solicitous about the welfare of the municipia,[2] and we shall probably not be wrong
in ascribing to him a considerable share in the carrying out
of the details of the Italian system into the provinces.

SECTION IV.   *Municipal Polity and Law.*

*Composi-
tion of a
muni-
cipium.*
Inscriptions permit us to see clearly what were the constituent elements of a municipal town.   ' The order ' (this
was the regular name for the municipal Senate) 'and the
whole people'[3]; ' the centumviri ' (the Senates consisted of

---

[1] Italica and Carteia were the first of such settlements outside Italy.
Appian, *Iber.* 38; Jung, *Romanische Landschaften* 14, note 1.
[2] See Egger, p. 15.   [3] Orelli, 4045; cf. Henzen, 7171.

100 members) 'and Seviri and Augustales[1] and municipal citizens'[2]; 'the decuriones and the people'[3]; 'the decuriones and Augustales and the commons'[4];—such is the classification which perpetually recurs in inscriptions recorded in the name of the whole municipality. The Senate of 100 members in which sat the magistrates constituted a government of a decidedly oligarchical character, the members being usually kept select by a high property qualification (e.g., at Como 100,000 sesterces)[5]; and it is no wonder that we sometimes find such bitter disputes between the 'order' and the 'commons' as that which Tacitus mentions as occurring at Puteoli.[6] The body of the citizens elected the magistrates of whom the Senate was mainly composed, but had no further control over it. The Senate could also be recruited by co-optation of men who had not been magistrates,[7] and was never filled by direct election in the West. These decuriones formed a town council, with more power and less responsibility than town councils as we know them. And there are indications that it was often unpopular, the members of the municipium sometimes inviting the interference of the Governor against it.

The commonalty was divided into various subordinate bodies, which in the west of the empire formed the voting

[1] These were religious bodies, without political importance—to be discussed later. See Jung, Rom. Recht. 16.

[2] C. I. L. xi. 3808.   [3] Ib. xiv. 2807.   [4] Orelli, 3937, 4009.

[5] The knights whom Augustus made so common in the municipia of Italy at all events must have constituted a sort of ready-made aristocracy, and no doubt were all decuriones; cf. Suet. Aug. 46. The 'hastiferi civitatis Mattiacorum'—Brambach, Inscriptiones Rhenanae, 1336—are perhaps to be similarly explained.

[6] Tac. Ann. xiii. 48, 'Illi vim multitudinis, hi magistratuum et primi cuiusque avaritiam increpantes.'

[7] Hirschfeld, Lat. Recht., p. 234. Pomponius, de verb. signif. 1239, says that the decuriones were so called because on the settlement of a colony a tenth of the settlers were selected to form a council. Eventually these councils became practically composed of ex-magistrates. See Kuhn, Verfassung, i. 242; Marquardt, i. 511.

units, and everywhere formed a kind of corporation with separate officials and meetings, especially of a religious or festal character. In the west the commonest unit was the curia, occasionally the tribe or century; in the east the φυλή or tribe, with occasional local variations, such as *obae* or *phratriae*. Besides the Senate and the citizens there was also a class of settlers or incolae, commonly Roman or Latin citizens who had settled in the municipium, and who for all practical purposes counted as full citizens. We find a special curia set apart for their votes at the municipal elections,[1] and they took their place in the municipal militia.[2] In inscriptions recording the statues or votes of thanks, or other honours offered by a municipium to a benefactor, we frequently find the incolae mentioned along with the regular coloni or municipes of the place,[3] as sharing in the vote, or as bearing their part of the necessary subscriptions; and cases occur of their holding office and becoming members of the Senate.[4] Of the contributi, or native population attached to a colony or municipium, I have already said something. It is only necessary to add that they paid a vectigal to the municipium, and pleaded in the municipal courts.[5]

It used to be commonly supposed before the discovery of the laws of Malaca and Salpensa,[6] that the magistrates

The incolae.

The contributi.

---

[1] Lex Malacitana, § 53. 'Ex curiis sorte ducito unam in qua incolae qui cives R. Latinive cives erunt suffragium ferant.'

[2] Lex Ursonitana, § 103 (classed with coloni and contributi).

[3] C. I. L. ii. 2222-2226, x. 1452.

[4] C. I. L. ii. 2135 ; Orelli, 3709, 3725.

[5] Suet. *Aug.* 46 ; Zumpt, *Decr. Tergest.* p. 15.

[6] The tablets were found together (1861) in a brick-pit near Malaga by two workmen, who sold them to a smith. The peculiarity about the 'find' was that the bronze of Salpensa was discovered along with that of Malaca, though Salpensa was at some distance. As it stands the commencement of the law is wholly lost ; §§ 21-29 are supplied by the bronze of Salpensa; §§ 51-69 by that of Malaca. They are all in Bruns, p. 142 sqq. The law of Osuna, originally of Caesar's time, was found in two parts, the later in order in 1870, the earlier in 1874. Here

were elected by the decuriones, or that at all events all popular elections in the provinces came to an end at the same time as they did at Rome, that is early in the reign of Tiberius. But these laws show this view to be a mistake, and that for the first century of the Empire at all events the elections were of a strictly popular character, and excited a good deal of emulation and a strong political interest. It was only in the next century that popular election was practically superseded by the outgoing magistrate nominating the exact number of magistrates required; their election being then a mere formality, showing of course that these offices were no longer regarded as desirable. It was also confined to the 'order.'

The popular assemblies retained a few other rights, mostly of a formal character, such as decrees in honour of officials; but especially in the Greek parts there are references even in the second century to their continued activity; and they might even address complaints to the emperor about the character of the administration of their city.

The chief magistrates were six in number; two duoviri, two aediles, and two quaestors, and were changed annually. On the day of election the senior duovir, or if he was prevented, his colleague, presided, and was required to see that the curies into which the citizens were divided should give their votes in accordance with the prescribed arrangements.[1] He had to put to the vote first the candidates for the duovirate, then those for the aedileship, and lastly those for the quaestorship, all of them 'from that class of free-born men, concerning which this law has made provision.'[2] No one was to be proposed as duovir who was under twenty-five years of age, or who had held

---

persons who were admissible to decurionate rank could also be accepted as candidates for municipal office (§ 101).

[1] Lex Malacitana, § 52. The part of the law containing these prescribed arrangements is lost.

[2] Ib. § 54.

the office less than five years ago. No one was to be admitted as a candidate for the aedileship or quaestorship who was less than twenty-five, or who had anything against him which, if he were a Roman citizen, would prevent him from being a decurio in a Roman municipium.[1] What these disqualifications were we may infer with some confidence from the great measure of Julius Caesar, where it is provided that no one should be competent to hold office or enter the Senate in any Roman municipium or colony who was engaged in any petty trade, like that of a public crier or an undertaker; no convict; no gladiator; no bankrupt; no exile; no one proved guilty of libel or collusive accusation; no one who had been degraded in the army, or expelled the army; no actor; no pimp; no infamously immoral man; no one who had conspired against the life of a Roman citizen.[2] If no candidates or too few offered themselves, the magistrate holding the elections had to make out a list of sufficient and fit persons. These involuntary candidates were allowed to name the same number of new candidates as they themselves amounted to. Thus five could name five, and ten could name ten; and these latter again could name a similar number. Then the names of the whole number were to be posted, and the elections made from them.[3] The electors gave their votes by curies,—each curia in its own enclosure,—and three citizens were told off to receive the votes of each curia, and were bound by oath to count and

---

[1] Ib. § 54 fin. The last four words which I have supplied may, I think, be inferred from the Latin. Perhaps they were understood to convey a reference to the Lex Julia Municipalis. The age-limit in the Lex Julia is thirty, or alternatively after three years' service in the cavalry or six in the infantry.

[2] See §§ 83-141 of the Lex Julia Municipalis. Caesar did not insist on free-birth in provincial municipalities, but Augustus excluded freedmen from the local senates, an indignity which was to some extent compensated for by the creation of the order of Augustales.

[3] Lex Malacitana, § 51.

report them honestly.[1] Before declaring a successful candidate elected the presiding magistrate made him take an oath of obedience to the municipal law[2]; and each candidate before the voting began had to name securities, who would go bail for him that during his year of office the public money would be safe in his hands. If the securities did not appear to the presiding magistrate to be sufficient, he could refuse to accept any man's candidature.[3]

In this law the provisions as to the nomination of involuntary candidates have a sinister air; but the rest of the evidence would lead us to conclude that this, like other laws, was calculated to meet unusual emergencies as well as everyday circumstances, and that in the first century at all events candidates were by no means slow to offer themselves for the municipal magistracies. Bribery and corruption by means of a good dinner is expressly forbidden in the law of Urso, and the number of guests that a candidate may invite every day is limited to nine.[4] The restrictions of age and other qualifications could hardly have been maintained if there had been much difficulty in obtaining candidates.

The powers of some of these magistrates appear to have been considerable. The aedileship was probably very much of the nature of an honorary post; it was ordinarily the one first held; and was no doubt, as at Rome, an expensive office to the holder. The quaestors (corresponding to _The aediles._ _Quaestors._

---

[1] Ib. § 55.   [2] Ib. § 59.
[3] Ib. § 60.
[4] Lex Ursonitana, § 132. In Italian municipia also there was sometimes such vehement rivalry between candidates that the election was prevented. See Tabula Pisana: Orelli, 643; Wilmanns, 882. The walls of Pompeii still retain election scrawls, showing how the goldsmiths, the fishermen and other trades interested themselves in the elections : 'the fishermen want Popidius Rufus made aedile'— 'the whole body of goldsmiths propose C. Cuspius Pansa to be aedile.'

the less important *tamiai* of the Greek provinces) had the charge of the revenue and expenditure of the municipium, and there were strict regulations as to the rendering of their accounts.[1] The duoviri, corresponding to the earlier Roman consuls, were in the first place magistrates for the administration of justice. All cases which were not of such importance as to come under the jurisdiction of the Roman governor were decided by them, and there is reason to believe that as a rule the governor left the municipia to manage their affairs as they pleased.[2] ' Let no one administer justice in this colony except the duovir, the duovir's prefect, or the aedile,' says the Lex Ursonitana.[3] According to the usual Roman system of administering justice, the duovir appointed the jury to try the case, but it lay with him to secure the presence of the witnesses, to put them on oath, and if need were to expedite the decision of a suit.[4] It was laid down that a duovir should not take his seat before the first, nor keep it after the eleventh hour, except in cases which by the municipal law had to be decided in the course of one day.[5] If a decurio were accused of being unfit for his position, the duovir was called upon to try the matter, and if he gave an adverse decision, that person ipso facto ceased to be decurio.[6] The duovir, prefect, or aedile had the power of imposing fines, subject only to the right of appeal to the municipal Senate.[7] It seems, however, that a too despotic magistrate could be controlled by the interference of his colleague. Duovir

Duoviri.

Judicial functions of the duoviri.

---

[1] Lex Malacitana, § 67, I take to refer to the quaestors. Note that what is here said of aediles and duoviri applies to the quattuorviri of a municipium.

[2] Cf. Strabo, iv. 1, § 12, on Nemausus. ἔχουσα καὶ τὸ καλούμενον Λάτιον, ὥστε τοὺς ἀξιωθέντας ἀγορανομίας καὶ ταμιείας ἐν Νεμαύσῳ Ῥωμαίους ὑπάρχειν· διὰ δὲ τοῦτο οὐδ' ὑπὸ τοῖς προστάγμασι τῶν ἐκ Ῥώμης στρατηγῶν ἐστι τὸ ἔθνος τοῦτο.

[3] § 94.   [4] § 95.   [5] § 102.   [6] § 105.

[7] Lex Malacitana, § 66. For the extent of local jurisdiction at this period cf. Reid *Municipalities*, 483 sq.

could interpose against duovir, quaestor could interpose against quaestor, and aedile against aedile. The duovir could also interpose against the aediles or quaestors, while they on the other hand had no power of interposing against their superiors. The same subordination of these magistrates to the duoviri appears from the fact that though the aedile could impose a fine, he was obliged to acquaint the duoviri with the amount of the fine he had imposed.[1] Nor were the duoviri confined solely to judicial functions. In case of any employment of the local militia, such as is mentioned in the law of Urso, it was the duoviri who received authority from the Senate to command the troops.[2] It was they who were responsible for the appointment of the keepers of the temples, for the performance of the ludi circenses, sacrifices, and pulvinaria[3]; and they seem to have had considerable powers over what we should suppose would be the special business of the quaestors, the municipal finances.[4] If a man wanted to manumit a slave, he could do so by going through the ceremony in the presence of the duovir[5]; and, at all events in Latin municipia, the duovir had the power of appointing a guardian to a ward not already provided with one.[6] In case of need the authority of a duovir would be supported by the special interference of the governor of the province. Thus a letter is extant from Claudius Quartinus, governor of Tarraconensis in the time of Hadrian, to the duoviri of Pompaelo, to the effect that they can carry out the powers of their office against malcontents—'Jus magistratus vestri exsequi adversus contumaces potestis.'[7] But if the power of the duovir was assured as regarded the mass of the citizens, it does not seem to have been equally well defined as against the decuriones, a feature in which the municipia

Relation of the duoviri to the decuriones.

---

[1] Lex Malacitana, § 66.   [2] Lex Urson. § 103 ; cf. Henzen, 5334.
[3] Ib. § 128.   [4] Lex Malac. §§ 60, 63, 64.
[5] Lex Salpens. § 28.   [6] Ib. § 29.
[7] C. I. L. ii. 2959.

sufficiently resembled their great prototype, Rome itself. Apparently any decurio could request the duovir to refer any matter concerning the public money, or fines or punishments, or public sites, lands, and buildings, to the body of the decuriones for investigation or decision; and whatever the decuriones determined was to have the force of law.[1] The duovir seems to have habitually consulted the decuriones in regard to the more important details of the administration[2]; and it is expressly laid down that all duoviri, aediles, prefects, or decuriones of the colony are to obey the decrees of the decuriones, and to carry out whatever they may be ordered by decree of that body.[3] In the absence of all magistrates we find the *universi decuriones colonique* organising themselves into a kind of constituent assembly, and initiating important resolutions, as in the *Tabula Pisana*, already mentioned. But it can easily be imagined that a man of resolution could exercise very extensive powers, and not refer more to the Senate than the Roman consuls had sometimes done. We find a duovir at Vienna ordering the total abolition of the games; and although the matter was brought to Rome on appeal, and it was alleged that he had no powers for such an act, his order was maintained.[4] The men who, as in some cases, were magistrates of several important municipia at once,[5] must have been persons of power and influence, and must to a large extent have escaped the control of the local Senates. It is worth mentioning in this connexion that in the municipia or colonies which were near a frontier or otherwise of any military importance, we frequently find the municipal magistracies held

---

[1] Lex Ursonitana, § 96.

[2] Ib. § 99. On the other hand, for a valid decree the presence of the magistrates was apparently essential; see the Tabula Pisana; Orelli, 643 ; Zumpt, i. 51.

[3] Lex Urson. § 129.   [4] Plin. *Ep.* iv. 22.

[5] Cf. Orelli, 3885, 3985. Perrot, *Mer Noire*, pp. 25, 26, may be referred to, though his remarks relate only to non-Roman towns.

by old soldiers or officers of the army,[1] a fact which looks as if their authority must have been of a very practical kind.

The praefecti who so frequently occur in municipal inscriptions are to be regarded as taking the place of the duoviri. In the municipal laws the commencement of a clause often runs, ' Let the duovir or the prefect ' do this or that. These prefects had the regular authority of the duovir delegated to them, and came into existence in two different ways, either because the duovir was absent, or because at the time there was no duovir. If one of the duoviri absented himself he was represented by his colleague, but if the second duovir also absented himself he had to appoint a prefect to represent them both.[2] More important was the arrangement by which the emperor was elected first magistrate of a municipium, and then appointed a prefect to take his place, ruling apparently without a colleague. ' In case the municipium elected Domitian to be their duovir, and Domitian accepted the honour, and appointed a prefect to represent him, that prefect was to have in every respect the full authority of a duly-elected duovir;'—so runs the twenty-fourth clause of the law of Salpensa. Hadrian used this system largely, and his biographer mentions him as having been dictator, aedile, duovir, demarch, quinquennalis, archon, at all sorts of different towns both in Italy and in the provinces.[3] Juba, the literary king of Numidia, was quinquennalis and patron of Carthagena,[4] as well as his son Ptolemy. But besides prefects of this character, who are important as representing the encroachments of the central government upon the municipia, we also find in cases where the magistracies were

The municipal praefecti.

---

[1] Orelli, 65, 3789, 4025 ; Finazzi, *Antiche Lapide di Bergamo*, p. 83 ; Zumpt, *Comm. Epig.* i. 150. See Patsch, *Dalmatien*, iv. 29.

[2] Cf. Lex Urson. § 93 ; Lex Salp. § 25.

[3] Spartian., *Hadrian*, 19 ; Zumpt, i. 56 ; Marquardt, i. 493, note 3 ; cf. Orelli, 3817.

[4] C. I. L. ii. 465 ; Eckhel, iv. 158 ; Head, *Hist. Num.* ad fin.

vacant a prefect appointed to fill them by the decree of the decuriones. The earlier arrangement had apparently been that in such cases, as at Rome, an interrex [1] should be appointed. But the *Lex Petronia* passed at the end of the Republican period gave the local Senates the power of choosing prefects, and we find prefects of this kind regularly entitled ' praefecti lege Petronia ' or ' praefecti a decurionibus creati.' In some cities of Italy, Spain and Gaul, *Praetores* took the place of duoviri, especially in the earlier period.[2] In the eastern provinces the chief magistrates were usually strategi (occasionally archons), varying in number, and aided by a town-clerk or recorder (γραμματεύς).

The quinquennales.
The quinquennales of a municipium corresponded to the Roman censors. They were charged with the duties connected with the census, looked after the municipal revenues, and contracted for municipal buildings, or for the collection of sums due to the municipality from occupiers or merchants ; local like national revenues being often farmed by Publicani. We find some cases, even under the Empire, for instance Malaga, where the censorial duties were discharged by the ordinary duoviri ; but as these duties became more and more important we find the Romans more and more insisting on something like their own censorship everywhere. In years when there were quinquennales there were no ordinary duoviri; their full title was *duoviri quinquennales;* and they appear to have been chosen instead of the ordinary magistrates. They were called quinquennales not because they held office for five years —their tenure, like that of the other magistrates, was simply annual—but because there was always a five years'

---

[1] Cf. the Lex Urson. § 130. This title looks as if much in the municipal arrangement was borrowed straight from old Rome. It is in any case certain that much was borrowed from old *Italy :* it is only necessary to point to the assembly by curies.

[2] Marquardt, i. 494 ; cf. Orelli, 3679, 3818. At Narbo and Nice the praefectus pro duumviro seems to have been a permanent official ; Orelli, 4023, 4024 ; cf. 4025, 4027.

interval from one census to another.[1]   In the Greek parts
τιμηταί or πολιτόγραφοι performed similar duties.

The *Augustales* so frequent in the inscriptions were The
originally connected with the worship of Augustus, and Augus-
imitated from the sodales Augustales at Rome. The Seviri.
Seviri Augustales are to be distinguished from the regular
Augustales ; they appear to have been for one year priests
of the same college of which the regular Augustales were
life members ; and the latter apparently stood in a relation
of subordination to them. The Augustales were chosen
decreto decurionum, and by the time they were definitely constituted as an Order (second century A.D.), in rank stood next
to the decuriones. While commonest in Italy they occur
also in Spain and Africa, but not in the east, except in a few
colonies inhabited by Romans. When public largesses
took place, decuriones received a triple share, Augustales
a double, members of the commons a single. The officials
such as magistri and quaestor, who had control of the common fund (*arca*) resembled those of other religious colleges.
They were largely freedmen, who had much of the trade of
the west in their hands, and though excluded from public
offices by Augustus, by their membership of a recognized
society were encouraged to place their wealth at the disposal
of the community. Their duties were primarily religious.
Before very long the office, like that of decurio, came to be
a burden, and became hereditary. An instance occurs of a
man's bequeathing money to Barcino (Barcelona) on
condition that his freedmen and their freedmen, if elected
seviri, should be ' excused all the burdens of the sevirate.'[2]

The municipal Senate was composed of a definite number The de-
of life members, generally 100—we sometimes find the term curiones.

---

[1] Marquardt, i. 487 ; Henzen, p. 423. A few of the inscriptions
referring to quinquennales are : Orelli, 3821, 3822, 3823 ; C. I. L. ix.
2855, xi. 4087. If the emperor was elected quinquennalis, there was a
praefectus quinquennalitatis ; Orelli, 3876. See Neumann, ' *De Quin-
quennalibus Coloniarum et Municipiorum* ' (1892).

[2] C. I. L. ii. 4514.

centumviri used instead of decuriones, though in provinces where such a body had previously existed the original number was often retained. It would have been an impertinence for these municipal assemblies to call themselves 'Senate,' and if we do occasionally find the terms 'patres' or 'senatores' used of the decuriones, the case was at all events a very exceptional one.[1] We do not know how these municipal Senates were first set going; perhaps the members were chosen by the founder of the colony, or the man who constituted the municipium; but once started, the arrangement was that every five years the quinquennales should hold a lectio senatus, and make up the list of decuriones.[2] In this were put down first the old senators, then the magistrates whose office gave them a claim to a seat, then those citizens who without having held office were qualified by their property to be decuriones. In fact, a municipal Senate copied that of Rome in being made up of ex-officials. It was not any more than the Roman Senate a popular or representative body, but consisted like it mainly of ex-officials. It should however be observed that most detailed information relates to western towns closely modelled on Rome. In the East βουλαί, elective and holding office for a year, often lasted on, and included far larger numbers than western Curiae. Eventually life-membership became the rule here as in the West.

Taking an actual album, of Canusium, still existing (A.D. 223), we find the following list: thirty-one patrons of senatorial rank; eight patrons of equestrian rank; seven quinquennalicii (men who had been quinquennales); four allecti inter quinquennales; twenty-nine duoviralicii; nineteen aedilicii; nine quaestoricii; thirty-two pedani; twenty-

---

[1] E.g., C. I. L. v. 4392, x. 8038 and 5807. *Ordo* (sc. senatorius) was the commonest title in the early empire, afterwards *curia*. Members were often called conscripti, and in the Greek-speaking parts Bouleutae, Synedroi, or Timouchoi.

[2] Marquardt, i. 50, note.

five praetextati. These patrons were influential Romans (elected by the decuriones), from whom a certain protection and assistance at Rome was expected, and who were put first by way of compliment. Two-thirds of the decuriones had to vote for a patronus for the vote to have validity; and if any one offered the patrocinium to any Roman except in accordance with such a vote, he was to be fined 10,000 sesterces, and the offer was to be null and void.[1] That they were not really acting members of the Senate is proved by the fact that if we cut them and the praetextati off the list, we have the normal number of 100 left.[2] But if they were not acting members of the municipium they were often considerable benefactors of it, and an immense number of inscriptions record the gratitude of the citizens to some rich and powerful patron.[3] By the *allecti inter quinquennales* must be understood men elected in an extraordinary manner, and not possessing the usual qualifications.[4] They were generally men who had done special services, and who, with the emperor's leave, were made decuriones by decision of the Senate. *Pedani* is explained by Aulus Gellius (iii. 18) to mean those who had the right to a place in the Senate, but who were not yet called senators because they had come in after the last lectio Senatus, and so had not yet been formally chosen by the quinquennales.[5] By

---

[1] Lex Malac. § 61 ; cf. Lex Urson. § 97. For the *Album Canusinum*, Orelli, 3721.

[2] Marquardt, i. 508 ; Cic. *de Leg. Agr.* ii. 35 for 100 as the normal number. See Nissen in *Rhein. Mus.* xlv. 108.

[3] Orelli, 3771. It is curious to find several instances of women as patrons of municipia ; cf. a remarkable inscription, Orelli, 4036, and see Orelli, 5773, 3774. Perhaps such women were friends of the empress, or in other ways possessed exceptional influence.

[4] For the way the verb *adlego* is used cf. Suet. *Claud.* 24, ' Appium Caecum censorem . . . libertinorum filios in senatum adlegisse docuit;' Marquardt, i. 508 ; cf. Orelli, 3725, 3745, 3816.

[5] Zumpt, *Stud. Rom.*, p. 297, discusses the *Pedani.* Their position seems to be analogous with that of the pedarii in the Roman Senate. See Willems, *Le Sénat*, pp. 192 and 506.

praetextati are meant sons of decuriones, included in the album as having the right to be present at the meetings, but not capable of voting.[1]   All decuriones, to whichever of these classes they might belong, had to possess a certain amount of property to be eligible,[2] and had to pay into the municipal treasury a certain sum of money as honorarium.[3] As the system decayed the possession of wealth was the one thing sought for, and even boys came to be enrolled.

Authority of the de-curiones.
The decuriones were in theory, like the Senate at Rome, the standing executive body, from which the magistrates received their orders, and with whom they consulted on all important matters.   They were required to live in or close to their town.   Appeal could be made to them from a fine imposed by a duovir; and all magistrates who had the handling of public moneys were obliged to send in their accounts either to the decuriones or to some inspector appointed by the decuriones.[4]   It was to the decuriones that rescripts of the emperor touching the affairs of the municipium were directed,[5] and on all public occasions they represented the municipium; for instance, they had the first seats at the games.[6]   No valid decree could be passed without a quorum, which was often made a large one, being

---

[1] Marquardt, i. 509 ; cf. Orelli, 3745 : 'Hunc decuriones, cum esset annorum sexs, ob liberalitatem ordini suo gratis adlegerunt.'   Apparently the father wanted the boy made a decurio at the age of six, one cannot tell why, and so restored a temple in the boy's name ; cf. 3747.

[2] If, however, a decurio lost his fortune he might remain a member. Willems, p. 506 ; Dig. L. 4, 6 ; 2, 8.

[3] Cf. Plin. *Ep.* x. 48, 113.   Thus the Decretum Tergestinum (supr. p. 164) refers to the gain to the municipal chest from the addition of fresh members to the local curia.   For a use of this pecunia honoraria see Kandler, *Inscrizioni dei tempi Romani rinvenute nell' Istria* (1853), 43.

[4] Lex Malac. § 67.

[5] So the curious letter of Vespasian to Sabora in Spain is addressed to the quattuorviri et decuriones, C. I. L. ii., p. 195 ; as also another letter of Vespasian ' to the magistrates and senators of the Vanacini ' (N. Corsica), C. I. L. x. 8038 ; Bruns, p. 225.

[6] Lex Urson. § 125.

present.[1] A number of such decrees have been preserved to us in the form of inscriptions. Most often they refer to statues or some such honour, which is offered in return for some benefaction received. A curious one is the decree of *biselliatus*, or of the right of sitting by yourself in a seat large enough for two,—an honour that appears to have been highly coveted.[2] The most important among such decrees is that of Tergeste, but hardly any of them are without antiquarian or historical interest of some kind.

There was little local taxation; water was sold to con- sumers by the municipality, and rent was in some cases exacted for the use of shops or other buildings belonging to the town. Most of the revenue was, however, derived from the public lands, which might be extensive, and at some distance from the town. Further, private generosity, and the custom of giving gratuitous personal service to the community in many capacities, relieved ancient municipalities of many of the expenses now met by local rates. Woods, fisheries, mines and harbour-dues, or dues on goods brought by land also contributed something, as well as fines, and payments of new officials or senators.

With a constitution, in which, though not perfect, there was apparently a fair balance of power, the municipal towns seem to have flourished at all events during the first century of the Empire. But about the reign of Trajan we see signs of a decay in the vigour and resources of the municipia, one clear evidence of which is the establishment of the new officials known as curators.[3]

---

[1] Orelli, 4034, 'In Decurionibus fuerunt xxvi.;' Lex. Urson. § 130. Two-thirds necessary to elect a patron; cf. §§ 96 and 97 of the same law.

[2] Cf. Millin, *Pompeii*, p. 78, referred to by Orelli on 4044; cf. Orelli, 4046: 'Liceatque ei omnibus spectaculis municipio nostro bisellio proprio inter Augustales considere.' Cf. 4047, 4048.

[3] See Zumpt, *Comm. Epig.* i. 148-158; Rénier, *Mélanges d'Epigraphie*, p. 46 *et seq.;* Marquardt, i. 488 *et seq.*, to whom I refer for more details. Also Reid *Municipalities of the Roman Empire*, 473-4. For the time of the first creation of *curatores* see C. I. L. iii. 291.

The curators.

The curators in the long run superseded the quinquennales, but their functions do not seem to have been identical. The principal function of the quinquennalis was the lectio senatus, whereas with that the curator had nothing whatever to do. The business of the curator was purely financial : he had the charge of the municipal moneys. This is indicated by the Greek name for the office—λογιστής,—by the Latin term ratiocinatio civitatis,[1] which is applied to it, and by several passages from the Digest.[2] It was probable that it was an annual magistracy, as otherwise it is difficult to account for its being held by such important personages. If we wish to discover how the curators were elected, it is necessary first to distinguish the two different kinds of curators.

Two classes of curators.

1. Curators for special purposes.   2. Curatores rei publicae (in Greek λογισταί). The first class of curators are frequently mentioned in the municipia, and were generally chosen by the assembly.[3] Occasionally we find even these curators appointed by the emperor.[4] Perhaps, as Zumpt conjectures, these towns themselves petitioned the emperor to appoint such officials for them, or else when he had spent money on their buildings he appointed a curator to see that the work was properly performed. Quite different from these special curators were the curatores rei publicae, of whom the first example occurs under Nerva or Trajan. If the emperor wanted the accounts of any town to be reoganised he appointed an extraordinary curator, generally a municipal citizen. Thus we have a duovir quinquennalis of Brixia acting as ' curator rei publicae Bergomatium

Curators for special purposes.

Curatores rei publicae.

---

[1] Dig. xxvii. 1, 15, 7.

[2] Dig. l. 4, 18, 9 : ' Sed et curatores qui ad colligendos civitatum publicos reditus eligi solent.'   Cf. Ulpian, *in Dig.* l. 8, 3, 1 ; Paulus, *in Dig.* xxxix. 3, 46 ; Zumpt, *Comm. Epig.*   In an inscription given by Zumpt, i. 158, we find the same man quinquennalis and curator *of the same place.*

[3] Orelli, 3882 : ' In comitiis facto curatori.'

[4] Orelli, 4006, 4007, 4011 ; cf. Suet. *Tit.* 8.

datus ab imperatore Trajano, curator rei publicae Comensis datus ab imperatore Hadriano.'[1] We never find these curators mentioned as appointed in any other way than this. So we gather the origin of these curators. They were always appointed by the emperor. But as long as there is added to their title the phrase ' given by such and such an emperor,' they are extraordinary magistrates. Now after Septimius Severus this phrase does not occur, although it is known that there were curators in every municipium. Zumpt's conclusion is that they then ceased to be extraordinary and became ordinary magistrates. The reasons for making this magistracy a permanent one are obvious. Being directly appointed by the emperor the curators had naturally greater powers than the ordinary municipal magistrates; and as the local finances all over the Empire became more and more embarrassed, the old magistrates were less and less able to deal with them. Either Sept. Severus or Alex. Severus made the curator a regular magistrate. We learn from Ulpian[2] that the curator presided in the municipal senate; and he discusses the office in other respects, in a way which shows that it was a regular one in his time, though novel. Originally then *curatores* were appointed by the emperor to meet some special need or distress of a municipality; and then little by little became regular and permanent magistrates, appointed by the local senate as a kind of burgomaster.

Besides finance, all matters relating to public buildings, etc., within a municipium were regulated by the curator. Thus we find an inscription of Caere which records that a certain Vesbinus wanted to build a phretrium for the municipium at his own expense. It was determined by the decuriones to write to the curator to ask permission for the

Matters regulated by the curator.

---

[1] Orelli, 3898, 3899, 3902. The necessity for such an officer often arose from municipal extravagance or mismanagement of finance, See *Philol. Woch.* xxi. 178 (1901); Liebenam's *Curator reipublicae* in Philologus for 1897, pp. 290 ; Ramsay, *Cities and Bishoprics of Phrygia.* i., pp. 370, 464.   [2] Dig. l. 9, 4.

work.   The curator, who was at Ameria, writes back to give his consent, with a number of complimentary expressions.[1] We find a man curator of several municipia at once,[2] or curator of one municipium and decurio of another; and in some cases the duties are discharged by an official of very high rank,[3] no doubt in one of the intervals of leisure in Italy which intervened between important provincial commands.

Decay of the municipia.   This system of substituting imperial for municipal officials was probably begun with the best intentions, but it marked a change for the worse.[4]   The brightest feature in the whole Roman system fades before us, as we see this government official taking the duties and the responsibilities out of the hands of the municipal magistrates. With the decrease in their power came an increase in the burdens laid upon the magistrates and decuriones.   Already in the decree of Tergeste under Antoninus Pius we find the inhabitants eager for the incorporation of new citizens, that they might share the duties of the decurionate, 'which are burdensome to a few.'   The local magistrates were now appointed from the Senate, and the Senate was compulsorily filled up from landholders possessing the needful amount of property.   Even before this change came about, and while the elections were still in the hands of the assemblies, we find in an inscription of Aquileia the record of a vote of thanks on a statue being offered to a man because he had of his own accord given in his name to the quattuorvir for municipal office.[5]   The tendency in the inscriptions is either to substitute the word *onus* or *munus* for *honor* when the municipal offices are mentioned, or at all events to put the two words side by side.[6]   The office of

---

[1] Orelli, 3787; Wilmanns, 2083.   [2] Ib. 3898.   [3] Ib. 3851.

[4] For the decay of the municipia see Liebenam. *Stadteverwaltung* (1900); Vanlaer, *La fin d'un peuple*, *Philol. Woch.*, xxi. 181. Hegel, *Gesch. der Städteverfassung in Italien*, i. 66-98.   [5] Orelli, 4041.

[6] Ib. 3940: 'Omnibus oneribus honoribusque functo; cf. Cod. Theod. xii. 1, 40, ut nec muniis militaribus obsequantur, nec oneribus oppidaneis prosint.

decurio became hereditary, and in the fourth century it was a regular punishment to make a man decurio.[1] A man could not avoid his responsibilities to the State even by enlisting in the army. The reason of this was that the decuriones were held responsible for the quota of taxation which the town was called upon to furnish. Concentration of wealth in a few hands, dislocation of commerce and industry caused by the barbarian inroads, and increasing demands of the central administration for the payment of its countless officials and the maintenance of its troops all made themselves felt. Thus the weight of the taxation both upon the middle and lower classes, and upon the decuriones who had to make good a deficit, became more than human nature could endure.[2]

With the burdensome taxation, enforced by an immense host of unproductive officials, went a steady diminution in the population, due to the falling birthrate, the growth of a monastic system, and the flight of oppressed artisans and coloni to the barbarian tribes across the frontier. Free workers disappear from towns, rural labourers sink more and more to mere serfs, and the invasions of the German peoples are looked on at last with indifference if not actual relief. These evils were less marked in the more conservative East, and there the Empire held its own for many centuries longer.

How far did this great mass of the Roman Empire form a unity? Along with the many causes which tended to bring about a certain uniformity between all its parts, Elements of union and disunion.

---

[1] Marquardt, i. 512. He illustrates, by Cod. Theod. xii. 1, 66, Ordinibus curiarum, quorum nobis splendor vel maxime cordi est, non aggregentur nisi nominati nisi electi, quos ipsi ordines coetibus suis duxerint aggregandos; *nec quis ob culpam, ob quam eximi deberet ex ordine, mittatur in curiam.* From the same book of the Cod. Theod. may be gathered evidence that the offices of decurio and duovir in the fourth century were regarded as a burden to be escaped by every means. See especially §§ 3, 11, 13, 16, 22, 40, 48, etc.

[2] For the municipia in the Constantine period, see Finlay, i. 110.

there were at least two centrifugal causes at work. The essential difference between East and West was never surmounted, and the rise of a new religion divided for some time the Roman world into the two great classes of Pagans and Christians. It is only with Constantine that Christianity ceases to divide and becomes rather a bond of union. It was as introducing disunion and division that it was so fiercely attacked; and persecutors would have justified themselves by similar reasons to those which have been urged in modern times.[1] But the universal peace, the active trade, the community of feeling caused by the possession of like privileges and like interests, the diffusion of the Romans over the provinces, and the way the different races of the Empire penetrated into the parts most removed from their own homes,[2] the one language, and the one administration,—all these tended to make of Europe a single brilliant whole. Nor were the frontiers a strict and impassable line, and we should err if we looked upon the Roman world as a space of light and civilisation surrounded by a black night of barbarism. On every side the light radiated out beyond the frontier, and it was only by slow degrees that it faded into the dim Northern world. The races just beyond the frontier were in many cases in a condition of more or less real subjection. They were visited by Roman traders, and now and then had even the pleasure of listening to a company of Greek or

[1] Ramsay, *The Church in the Roman Empire*, p. 356. The Christians looked to a non-Roman unity; they decided on a common action independent of Rome; they looked on themselves as Christians first and Roman subjects afterwards; and when required to accept this secondary allegiance they ceased to feel themselves Roman subjects at all. When this was the case, it seems idle to look about for reasons why Rome should proscribe the Christians. If it was true to itself it must compel obedience; and to do so meant death to all firm Christians.

[2] Partly in the course of trade, partly through service in the army, but perhaps more still owing to slavery, which largely Orientalised the population of Italy, and prepared the way for an Oriental despotism.

Roman players. If the barbarians had been wholly barbarians they would hardly have shattered the power of Rome. Mere savages never have held their own against civilised troops and never will. Even the typically German hero Arminius had served in the Roman legions and could apparently talk Latin, while his brother Flavus remained faithful to the service which he forsook. Tacfarinas had served as an auxiliary in the Roman camp in Africa, and Boiocalus, chief of the Ampsivarii, had served under Tiberius and Germanicus. When Classicus rebelled he assumed the insignia of a Roman general and Civilis had himself saluted Caesar. Among the Parthians there were the Roman prisoners who had survived Carrhae, and the Germans also had often spared and taken back their captives with them across the Rhine.[1] As the burden of the taxes and the conscription grew heavier, it became a common practice for Roman subjects to settle beyond the frontier, and so secure themselves from the recruiting officer and the tax-gatherer. In this way the barbarians themselves were half Romanised, often adopting for their own government the *leges Romanae;* and it was not till the brutal Huns, lying far outside the radius of Roman influence, had fought their way southwards, that the Southern world felt the full bitterness of conquest. The rapidity with which the invaders of the fourth century adapted themselves to their new position, adopting in a great measure both Roman law and the Latin language; and the almost timid conservatism which their leaders in some points showed, attest the impression made both on their intellects and their imaginations by the colossal and majestic system which Rome had reared.

[1] Even those of the army of Varus, Tac. *Ann.* xii. 27, cf. Dio Cass. lxxi. 16 for the 100,000 Roman prisoners sold by the Quadi and Marcomanni (A.D. 174). For the early Romanisation of the Pannonici see Vel. Pat. ii. 110, ' In omnibus autem Pannonicis non disciplinæ tantummodo, sed linguae quoque notitia Romanae.' For the survivors of Carrhae, Ib. ii. 82 ; Dio Cass., liv. 8 ; Hor. *Od.* iii. 5, 5.

APPENDICES

APPENDIX I

TABLE OF PROVINCES, ACCORDING TO ORDER OF ACQUISITION

SICILY.—Passed to Rome in 241 B.C. at the close of the first Punic war, except Syracuse and six dependent towns in the east, which were added after the fall of the city in 212. It was governed by a praetor from 227, by a propraetor from 122. Syracuse was the seat of government, but one of the two quaestors who assisted the governor was stationed at Lilybaeum, for financial business in the west. In 27 B.C. it became a senatorial province. Large slave-worked estates prevailed, and many of the slaves, who caused serious revolts 135-2, 103-100 B.C., were Orientals. During the war with Sextus Pompeius Sicily was practically severed from the Empire. Taxation was on the tithe system, but this was probably abandoned under Caesar or Augustus, when Sicily ceased to be one of the chief corn-producing provinces. Caesar largely extended Latin rights, and Augustus founded seven military colonies. Several judicial *conventus* existed.

Under Diocletian it was governed by a Corrector, subject to the Vicar of Southern Italy. It belonged successively to the Vandals, Ostrogoths, the Eastern Empire, and the Arabs.

SARDINIA AND CORSICA.—A military occupation of part of Corsica took place before the end of the first Punic war ; the Carthaginians were forced to resign Sardinia in 238 ; Manlius Torquatus subdued the inhabitants of the coast districts in 235 ; by 227 both islands were sufficiently conquered to be placed under a regular praetor. From 122 there was a propraetor. In the first division by Augustus they became senatorial under a praetorian proconsul, in A.D. 6 imperial under a procurator, in A.D. 67 were restored by Nero to the senate in exchange for the liberation of Achaia. After being again made imperial under Vespasian, they were probably given to the Senate by M. Aurelius in exchange for Baetica, which needed protection against the Moors. The natives were restless, many of them brigands, and they were often enslaved. Tithes of corn were paid in the earlier period, and the towns were mostly under prefects nominated by the governor. Carales, a municipium in the early Empire, was the seat of government. Corsica had two military colonies, Mariana and Aleria. The islands followed the fortunes of Africa, being conquered successively by the Vandals, the Eastern Empire, and the Arabs.

SPAIN.—The east and south of Spain came into the Romans' possession in the second Punic war (206), and were organised as the Hither and Further Provinces, with the capitals at Carthago Nova and Corduba, in 197 B.C. A *stipendium* was exacted, in some parts taking the form of one-twentieth of the corn-crop. The rest of the peninsula was slowly conquered, a process completed under Augustus, who planted several military colonies and reorganised the provincial divisions, the capital of the Hither Province being henceforth Tarraco, those of the subdivided Further Province Corduba for Baetica, Emerita Augusta (Merida) for Lusitania. Further subdivisions took place in the third century, when part of Mauritania was also attached to Spain. Under the republic an immense export trade was carried on in metals, especially silver, corn, wine, and oil. Later iron, copper, and lead were much worked, and linen and wool-stuffs, esparto grass, steel blades and dried fish, were exported to Italy.

German settlements began in Spain early in the fifth century, and by A.D. 476 the Visigothic kingdom was firmly established.

ILLYRICUM.—The coast district between Dalmatia and Epirus was annexed by Rome in 167 B.C., after the deposition of King Gentius, who had supported Perseus in the third Macedonian war. It was then subjected to tribute, except for a few towns which had sided wtth Rome, but no regular governor appears for another century. In the first division (27 B.C.) Illyricum became proconsular, but owing to barbarian attacks an imperial legate was sent from 11 B.C. ; and the province was shortly after extended to the Danube on the north. In A.D. 10 it was subdivided by the formation of the province of Pannonia out of the northern section. The older portion came to be known as Dalmatia, and was governed by a consular legate residing at Salonae, having three judicial *conventus*, made up of groups of tribes, as well as some Roman colonies and municipia, such as Scardona, Epidaurus, and Narona. Gold, silver, and iron were all worked here ; and the province corresponded to the modern Albania, Montenegro, and most of Bosnia.

MACEDONIA.—The division of the old kingdom into four separate republics having proved a failure, a regular provincial organisation was undertaken in 146 B.C., probably including, for certain purposes at least, not only Macedonia, but Thessaly, Epirus,and all Greece, except a few favoured districts. In 27 B.C. it was separated from Epirus and Greece, and became senatorial;

but between A.D. 15 and 44 was governed by imperial legates, and was only restored to the senate by Claudius. Thessalonica was the governor's headquarters, but Roman colonies existed at Pella, Philippi, and several other places. Thessaly seems to have been again annexed to Macedonia under Vespasian. The country was rich in metals, exporting silver, copper, iron, besides wine, timber, and textile fabrics.

AFRICA.—Only a small district, the remains of the greatly attenuated Carthaginian dominion, was annexed by the Romans at the close of the third Punic war (146 B.C.). It was surrounded, except towards the Mediterranean, by the extensive kingdom of Numidia, which reached from Mauritania on the west to Cyrenaica on the east. After the Jugurthine war (106) the eastern portion of this was incorporated in the province of Africa, including the three Tripolitan towns, which had a mixed Greek and Phoenician population. In the Civil war Juba, king of Numidia, supported the Pompeians, and in 46 B.C. Caesar formed his kingdom into a new province, *Africa Nova*. This was for a time restored to Juba's son by Augustus, but on the transference of the former to Mauritania, Numidia was definitely incorporated in the Empire (25 B.C.). It was placed under the rule of the African proconsul, whose headquarters were removed by Augustus from Utica to Carthage, which had lately been resettled. Though a senatorial governor, he commanded a legion, and governed different parts of his province by legates. In A.D. 37 Caligula created a separate legate for the African legion, and as the headquarters of this were in Numidia (first at Theveste, later at Lambaesis), though Africa and Numidia seem not to have been officially separated before the time of Severus, Numidia differed little from an ordinary imperial province. The commercial and judicial centre was Cirta (Constantine), formerly the capital of the Numidian kings, and a Roman colony of Caesar's age.

There was a wide export trade from both districts, especially in corn, oil, and marble, and important caravan routes led from the interior to the coast of these provinces, by which slaves, wild beasts for Roman shows, gold-dust, ivory, and ebony were conveyed to Europe. The greatest prosperity was under the Antonines, when Africa enjoyed a primacy in the west, both in Christian and heathen letters, and Carthage was regarded as the second city in the Empire. Africa and Numidia were conquered by the Vandals about 430, recovered by the Eastern Empire a century later, and occupied by the Arabs before 700.

ASIA represented the ancient kingdom of Pergamum, the last king of which died in 133 B.C., and which was organised by Aquillius in 129. It included most of Mysia, Lydia, and Caria, except for the Rhodian possessions, but not Rhodes, until the time of Vespasian, nor the inland territories of Phrygia and

Pisidia, until the middle of the first century B.C. The proconsul, who was supported by three legates, had his headquarters at Ephesus, but Apamea on the Maeander was also a rich and important town. After the changes of C. Gracchus the taxation, which until Caesar's time took the form of tithes farmed by Roman equestrian companies, was most oppressive, and may explain the readiness with which the cause of Mithridates was embraced in the Pontic war. Through the whole period of the civil wars this rich province suffered severely from the exactions of successive Roman armies and leaders. There were several free towns and a few colonies, such as Parium and Alexandria Troas. The proconsulate under the Empire was the most honourable post that the Senate could confer ; and the trade of Asia remained considerable, especially in wine, fruit, woollen, and textile fabrics, and marble from Synnada in Phrygia. The country was never conquered by the Arabs, and remained in possession of the Empire till the coming of the Turks. The defeat of the emperor, Romanus, at the battle of Manzikert in 1071 by the Seljuk leader, Alp Arslan, ended the long Roman dominion.

NARBONENSIS.—This province originated from successful wars against the Ligurians and Allobroges, ending in 121 B.C. The district was needed to secure land communications with Spain, the Via Domitia being carried from the Rhone to the Pyrenees ; to provide settlements for poorer citizens ; and to enable Roman merchants to compete with Massilia in the trade of the West. The citizen colony of Narbo was established by Licinius Crassus in 118, and Caesar's campaigns added the whole of the rest of Gaul, which was kept under the same administration till 44, when a separate governor was provided for Narbonensis. Much of the territory of Massilia was confiscated in 49, and the province, the inhabitants of which were Iberian rather than Celtic in origin, was rapidly Romanised. It was bounded on the east by the Alps, on the south by the sea and Pyrenees, on the west by the Garumna (Garonne) and the Mons Cebenna (Cevennes), on the north by the Rhone between Vienna and Lacus Lemanus. Many colonies, such as Arelate (Arles), Forum Julii (Fréjus), Arausio (Orange), were founded by Caesar and Augustus, and others received Latin rights. Between 27-22 B.C. it was under senatorial governors, later under imperial.

CILICIA.—After the piratical war of 103 B.C. a district called the province of Cilicia was occupied, and the names of a series of governors are recorded, but it seems to have only consisted of eastern Cilicia (*Campestris*), with parts of Phrygia and Pisidia which had once belonged to the Pergamene Kingdom, but had not been included in the province of Asia. In the course of the next generation Isauria, Lycaonia, and Cilicia Aspera were added, but some native princes were left as tributaries. There were a number of judicial *conventus*, as appears from the letters of Cicero, who was governor here ; and Tarsus, one of the principal seats of learning in the East, was the chief town.   Caesar lessened the area by adding the Phrygian districts to Asia ; Antony and Augustus both granted wide domains to native kings, and in the latter's reign the province only included Cilicia Campestris under a pro-curator, who was soon subordinated to the legate of Syria.

Vespasian's suppression of various local dynasties, including the last remnant of the Seleucid kingdom, Commagene, produced a wider area, which was henceforth governed by an imperial legate ; and Isauria and Lycaonia were again added by Severus.   There were six free towns and, by the third century, three with colonial rights.   Lead and copper were among the chief products.

BITHYNIA.—The kingdom on the south coast of the Euxine be-queathed by Nicomedes in 74 B.C. was greatly enlarged nine years later by Pompey, who added the greater part of Paphlagonia, as far as the Halys.   The governor was at first a propraetor, after 27 B.C. a senatorial proconsul.   The administration proved un-satisfactory ; some rearrangement was made by Augustus, and Pliny was sent thither by Trajan as a special envoy, chiefly for financial organisation.   Hadrian placed the province under an imperial legate, whose headquarters were at Nicomedia.   There were several Greek towns on the coast, some of which were free states or received colonial rights ; and a few colonies were founded under the Empire, but the municipal system was not well developed. The eastern portion, Paphlagonia or Pontus, had a separate provincial assembly, meeting at Amastris.

CYRENE AND CRETE.—Cyrenaica had been held by a member of the Ptolemaic family, Apion, who bequeathed it to Rome in 96 B.C.   The kingdom consisted mainly of the Doric colony of Cyrene with four offshoots, forming together a pentapolis with a common assembly.   The Senate took possession of the royal domains, and the country was subjected to a toll payable in kind by means of the valuable plant Silphium, but the pentapolis re-tained its internal administration till 74 B.C. when a quaestor pro praetore was sent out as governor.   Late in the republic it again became for a time an independent kingdom, but was definitely made into a province by Augustus, and conjoined with Crete, which had been conquered from the pirates by Q. Caec. Metellus in 68-7 B.C. The governor was a senatorial proconsul of praetorian rank.   In 20 B.C. Cyrenaica was enlarged by the conquest of Marmarica, a strip of African coast towards Egypt.   Crete had suffered much from the pirates and the Roman conquest, and was not prosperous. Gnossus was the principal town, and wide estates were held by the Campanians of Capua, in virtue of a grant of Augustus.

SYRIA.—The Seleucid dynasty which had ruled Syria for 250 years was deprived by Pompey in 64 B.C., at a time when the kingdom was encroached on in every direction by native peoples, Arabs, Parthians, and Jews ; so that its annexation by Rome was probably the only means by which western civilization could then be preserved. Several client principalities were allowed to subsist on the outskirts for some generations, such as Commagene on the north, with the capital Samosata ; Chalcis, occupied by the Romans in the Flavian age ; Abilene, Emesa, and Damascus. Judaea underwent several variations, being at one time (63-40 B.C.) part of Syria, but under a separate procurator, at others under one or more native rulers. After the capture of Jerusalem by Titus in A.D. 70 Judaea became a separate imperial province under a legate, with a legion, stationed at Caesarea.

Several Syrian towns of Greek origin were left their freedom, but placed under aristocracies. The governor, whose headquarters were at Antioch, was a propraetor or proconsul, under the Empire a consular legate, provided with a great military force, owing to the position of Syria as a barrier against the Parthians. It amounted to three or four legions in the Early Empire, to five in the second century. Roads were laid out and trade encouraged, especially in flax, Tyrian purple, and glass. There were several through routes from the Persian Gulf, the Red Sea, even from China, whence silk was imported. Petra and Palmyra were important entrepôts for goods brought by eastern caravans. Syrian merchants established themselves in most large Mediterranean ports, carrying with them the orgiastic cult of their moon-goddess, Astarte. Berytus, an Augustan veteran colony, became a famous school of Roman law in the Later Empire, and other colonies were due to Claudius and Vespasian. The province was divided by Sept. Severus into Coele Syria, and Phoenice, and remained attached to the Eastern Empire till the Arab conquests of the seventh century.

CYPRUS.—This island, which had been an appanage of the Ptolemaic family, was occupied by M. Cato in 58 B.C. and attached to the province of Cilicia, thus being subject to Cicero during his governorship. It was later restored by Caesar and by Antonius to members of the Alexandrine royal house, but after the battle of Actium reverted to Rome. At first treated as an imperial province, and perhaps again attached to Cilicia, in 22 B.C. it was placed under a senatorial proconsul, usually residing at Paphos, which was dignified with the title of Sebaste or Augusta. Great quantities of copper were dug in the island, which has given its name to that metal in late Latin and most modern European languages. Cyprus was conquered in the seventh century by the Arabs, was recovered by the Eastern Empire, and passed to the dynasty of the Lusignans in compensation for the loss of Jerusalem.

GAUL.—The conquest of Gaul outside the Narbonensian province was effected by Caesar in a series of campaigns ending in 51 B.C., but the country was in too disturbed a state for a provincial system to be introduced at once. In 44 he parted the new conquests from Narbonensis by the appointment of separate governors for Belgica, and for the central and western parts. Augustus completed the organisation, and formed three provinces, all under imperial government, out of the recent acquisitions. These were *Aquitania*, the south-west portion (between the Pyrenees and the Loire, the Bay of Biscay and the Cevennes), from which the southern portion, inhabited chiefly by Iberians, was later cut off by Trajan under the title of Novempopuli ; *Lugdunensis*, or central and western Gaul, between the Loire, the Seine and the Saône, with the Roman colony of Lugdunum (43 B.C.) as its capital ; and *Belgica*, or north-east and east Gaul, reaching to the Rhine, and including the modern Belgium with part of Germany and Switzerland. The capital of this last of the *Tres Galliae* was Durocortorum Remorum (Rheims), but Augusta Trevirorum (Trêves) was a place of importance. Under Augustus all three had a common legate, with three subordinates to represent him. The country had few towns, and though some Roman colonies were planted the prevalent cantonal system was recognised by the administration, sixty-four districts being grouped round some centre, called after the name of the people or tribe. Tiberius in A.D. 17 separated the three provinces, but some community of action remained in the general meeting of the provincial parliament at Lugdunum in connection with the imperial worships. Druidism was severely repressed, and Roman manners readily adopted, such towns as Augustodunum (Autun) and Burdigala (Bordeaux) developing a high civilisation, with famous schools of rhetoric and literature. Minerals were not plentiful, but much trade was done in manufactured goods, pottery, glass, woollen and woven fabrics, and wine ; and there were important trade routes from the Mediterranean to the Bay of Biscay and to the Channel.

EGYPT was annexed by Augustus in 30 B.C. after the battle of Actium, and organised as a private imperial domain, governed by a procurator with the title of prefect, having under him a staff of freedmen, and a military force (three legions under Augustus, two under Tiberius, one in the second century), officered by equestrian prefects. It extended southwards to the first cataract of the Nile. Internal administration remained almost as it had been under the Ptolemies. Great centralisation prevailed, with an elaborate bureaucracy, graded downwards from the heads of the three great divisions or epistrategiae, through Nomes, down to the village units. The epistrategi were Roman officials with both military and civil power, but the subordinate magistrates might be Greeks or Egyptians. The native religion was left undisturbed, and exercised a powerful influence over nearly the whole Empire in the first and second centuries. A municipal system, except for a few Greek towns, was almost absent, and difficulties were put in the way of the enfranchisement of Egyptians. Alexandria was ruled directly by imperial officials, the chief a *juridicus* and a *procurator*, but the Greeks and Jews had their own magistrates. There was a great export trade to Rome, both of Egyptian produce, such as corn, papyrus, and linen, and in goods brought from Asia or the interior of Africa, as cotton, ivory, and dried fruits. Egypt remained part of the Empire till the Arab conquest in the seventh century.

ACHAIA.—It is still doubtful whether Greece was formally reduced to the rank of a province after the suppression of the Achaean revolt in 146 B.C. Probably it was subjected for some purposes only to the governor of Macedonia, the various states being treated favourably or unfavourably according to their past attitude. Athens and Sparta became federate states; others were made free from toll; Corinth, Thebes, and Chalcis were destroyed; leagues were broken up, fortifications done away with, and the Greeks generally were disarmed. Small communities were attached to the larger centres, which retained their local magistrates and judicature, but were placed under aristocratic governments by the enforcement of a high census. In 27 B.C. Achaia, with Thessaly, Epirus, and Acarnania, became a senatorial province; between A.D. 15 and 44 it was subject to the same imperial government as Macedonia; then restored to the proconsul (Gallio in A.D. 53, at the time of St. Paul's visit to Corinth); and for a few years after 67 enjoyed nominal freedom. It was placed for a third time under a senatorial governor, supported by a legate and quaestor, in the time of Vespasian (74), when Thessaly seems to have been attached to Macedonia, and Epirus placed under an imperial pro-curator. Corinth, restored by Caesar's orders, was the seat of government; Patrae, Actium and Buthrotum had colonial rights. Little trade was done; both population and wealth declined, and the ruin of Greece was completed by the Gothic and Slav invasions.

GALATIA, including a heterogeneous collection of peoples in the interior of Asia Minor, was annexed after the death of Amyntas the king, in 25 B.C. It comprised, besides Galatia proper, with the capital Ancyra, eastern Phrygia, Pisidia and Lycaonia. A great part of Pontus was added a few years later, but subsequently transferred to Cappadocia. The governor was a praetorian legate, after Vespasian a consular; and a few towns, such as Iconium and Antioch in Pisidia, had colonial rights. Three of the old Gallic tribes, Tectosages, Tolistobogii and Trocmi, still inhabited Galatia proper, each with its national assembly; and the district was the centre of the worship of the Asiatic earth-goddess Cybele, which extended widely over the Empire.

PAMPHYLIA was at first included in the adjoining province of Cilicia (103 B.C.), but was established as a separate unit in 25 B.C., being probably administered by a representative of the legate of Syria. The Lycian league was suppressed as a political body by Claudius, and Lycia joined to Pamphylia to form a separate province (A.D. 43). Further changes took place under Nero or Galba; Pamphylia was attached to Galatia, and Lycia temporarily freed. From about 74 the two countries again became imperial, but were transferred by Hadrian to the senate in exchange for Bithynia. Each had a national assembly, the principal towns of Pamphylia being Side, Perge, and Aspendus; of Lycia, Myra, Xanthus, and Patara.

NORICUM.—This province was an independent kingdom till 15 B.C., and its king had supported Caesar in the civil war. In consequence of an invasion of Histria in 16 B.C. by the Noricans and Pannonians, who were repelled by P. Silius, governor of Illyricum, it became a province, still known for a time as *Regnum Noricum*; at first under a procurator without troops, but in the second century with a legate and legion, stationed at Lauriacum (Lorch). A few Roman colonies existed, as Virunum and Ovilava, and important iron mines were worked. It corresponded to the east of modern Bavaria, with Upper and part of Lower Austria, and was bounded on the north by the Danube.

RHAETIA was conquered by Drusus and Tiberius in 15 B.C., and placed under an imperial procurator or vice-legate, who commanded only local levies, both horse and foot. In the second century there was a legion under a legatus. The chief town was Augusta Vindelicorum (Augsburg), founded by Augustus, at first only a *forum*, later raised to municipal rights. Rhaetia, including Vindelicia on the north, corresponded to southern Bavaria, part of the Tyrol, and the country round Lake Constance, thus containing portions of modern Germany, Austria and Switzerland.

ALPINE PROVINCES.—The oldest was *Alpes Maritimae*, reduced to a province by Augustus in 14 B.C., and placed under a procurator, occasionally replaced by a prefect. It included the French department Alpes Maritimes and part of Basses Alpes, with the important town of Nicaea, a Greek colony from Massilia. Latin rights were conferred on the provincials by Nero. *Alpes Cottiae* lay immediately to the north, partly in the department of Hautes Alpes, partly in Piedmont; Segusio was the chief town. It was a client kingdom till the time of Nero, and then placed under a procurator, the inhabitants receiving Latin rights. *Alpes Poeninae* (French Savoy and western Switzerland) was perhaps at first attached to Rhaetia, but received a procurator by the second century; important towns were Civitas Sedunorum (Sion) and Octodurus (Martigny).

MOESIA, a large province south of the Danube, corresponded to Servia, Bulgaria, and the coast districts of Roumania. The first definite reference to a governor is in A.D. 6, and it does not seem to have been permanently annexed before the later years of Augustus. It was under an imperial legate, usually of consular rank, who in the years 15-44 was also charged with the supervision of Macedonia and Greece. Domitian subdivided Moesia into eastern and western halves—Inferior and Superior—separated by the river Ciabrus, each under a consular legate. There was a small group of Greek cities, such as Tomi and Odessus, on the Euxine coast, and several Roman colonies were founded in the interior, especially about the age of Trajan. There was a considerable trade and even some political connection between the shores of Moesia and the Greek colonies and native principalities along the north shores of the Euxine, a district never technically forming a part of the Empire.

PANNONIA, corresponding to the south of Austria, and Hungary west of the Danube, was first occupied by the Romans in 34 B.C., when as a result of native risings Siscia (Siszek) was garrisoned. Twenty-five years later further disturbances induced Augustus to have the territory incorporated in Illyricum ; but before the end of the reign, about A.D. 9, it was made an independent province, under a legate who, in view of the fact that its safe-keeping was vital for the safety of the most accessible portion of the Italian frontier, was supported by the large force of three legions. In Trajan's time it was subdivided into eastern and western halves— Superior and Inferior—both under legates, and in the next reign some Roman colonies were planted. In the western province some settlements, as Siscia and Claudia Savaria, dated from the Early Empire ; in the eastern the chief town was Aquincum, on the Danube.

GERMANY.—The two provinces of Germania—Superior and Inferior—though perhaps originally intended to reach to the Elbe, in the redistribution of Gallic commands in A.D. 17, covered comparatively small areas west of the Rhine, which had been conquered under Caesar and Augustus, and settled in part with Germans. For financial purposes they remained attached to Belgica, but were each governed by a consular legate, at the head of a powerful military force. Lower Germany corresponded to Belgium and Rhenish Prussia, with Colonia Agrippinensis (Cologne) as the capital; Upper, which was extended considerably to the east, and protected by a wall under Hadrian, to Hesse, the Palatinate, Alsace and Baden, with Mogontiacum (Mayence) as the chief town.

CAPPADOCIA.—An imperial procurator existed in this state while it was still a native kingdom, and after the death of King Archelaus in A.D. 17, Tiberius made it an imperial province, bounded by Pontus and Armenia Minor, the Euphrates, Mount Taurus and Galatia. There were few materials for an ordinary provincial organisation, and local government did not develop till late in the Empire. As in Egypt, the administration, taken over from the native kings, was a centralised bureaucracy, the country being distributed into ten *strategiae*. The procurator had no troops, but could be supported by the Syrian legions if necessary. Vespasian, realising the importance of the district as an outpost against the Parthians, placed it under a consular legate with a strong force. Galatia was added for a time, and when this was given a separate government, about the age of Trajan, the Pontic districts, reaching to the Euxine, as well as Armenia Minor and Lycaonia, were subjected to the Cappadocian legate. Much of the land was imperial property, and there were few towns. Some colonies were founded by the Romans, and certain *Vici* raised to municipal rank.

MAURITANIA became an imperial province on the deposition of Ptolemy, son of Juba, in A.D. 40. It consisted of two portions, Caesariensis or eastern, with the capital Caesarea ; and, separated from this by the river Mulucha and extending to the Atlantic, Mauritania Tingitana, with the capital Tingi, which in the third century was attached for administrative purposes to Spain. Each was under an equestrian *procurator pro legato*, who commanded some auxiliary forces, chiefly cavalry. Several colonies were founded, and some native towns raised to municipal rights ; but the Moors resisted Romanisation, and after the Vandal conquest of Africa and Numidia the Romans never regained more than a few outposts in Mauritania. The country was not very fertile, but there was some trade in fish, purple dye, marble, and in wild beasts for the Roman amphitheatre.

BRITAIN.—Caesar's expeditions of 55-4 B.C. had familiarised the Romans with the south of the island ; tribute was paid for a time, and some trade was carried on in the Early Empire. In A.D. 43 a large part of England was permanently occupied, with an army under an imperial legate, and a colony was founded at Camulodunum in 50. Agricola (recalled in 84) extended the province to the line of forts which he built between the Forth and Clyde. A revolt led to the abandonment of the more northerly portion, and the construction of an earth wall and trench from the Solway to the Tyne by Hadrian (120). The Forth-Clyde frontier was restored under Antoninus Pius, but the southern wall was the recognised Limes by the time of Sept. Severus, who greatly strengthened it, and subdivided the province into Upper and Lower portions. Britain was in revolt for many years in the third and fourth centuries, and under Honorius (410) all Roman troops were withdrawn. Lead, copper, and tin were worked, and there was some export trade in hides, woollen goods, baskets, hunting dogs, and in corn for the troops in Germany.

THRACE.—Part of the Thracian coast had already in the later days of the Republic been placed under the control of the governor of Macedonia, but the tribes of the interior were left to the rule of native princes until the time of Claudius (A.D. 46), when Thrace became a province under an imperial procurator, apparently different from the procurator who managed the Thracian Chersonese as a private domain of the emperor. The general supervision of the province was left to the legate of Moesia until the time of Trajan, who created a special praetorian legate. Several Greek colonies on the coast retained at least a nominal freedom, and a few Roman towns were planted by the emperors, one of the most famous being Hadrianopolis. Thrace was bounded on the north by Mount Haemus, on the west by the River Nestus, and on the other sides by the Euxine, Propontis, and Aegean. There was a considerable coasting-trade, and wine, timber, and textile fabrics were exported.

ARABIA.—This province was formed in A.D. 105 with a view to protecting caravans arriving in Syria from the further east, by Cornelius Palma, on behalf of Trajan. It included the regions extending southwards from Syria and Palestine to the Red Sea, but only a strip of the peninsula of Arabia. A praetorian legate in command of a legion governed Arabia, the chief towns of which were Bostra, a century later raised to colonial rank, and further south Petra. In the third century Arabia was divided into two, with these towns as the respective capitals ; and towards the end of that century the northern half was enlarged by the transference from Syria of the regions of Auranitis, Trachonitis, and Batanea.

DACIA corresponded to eastern Hungary, Transylvania, and most of Roumania, being bounded on the south by the Danube. It was annexed by Trajan as a result of the successful wars ending in 106. The inhabitants were mostly driven out into Sarmatia, and their place taken by settlers from other parts of the Empire, including many Asiatics. Several of these small settlements were ultimately raised to colonial rank. Among the chief towns were Sarmizegethusa, or Ulpia Trajana, called a 'metropolis,' with provincial assembly and imperial worships, Apulum, the legionary headquarters, and Napoca ; and there were some important gold mines. It was subsequently divided into two, later into three, provinces.

Dacia was lost to the Goths under Gallienus and Aurelian ; and the provincials were moved to two new provinces taken out of Moesia, *Dacia Ripensis* (capital, Ratiaria), south of the Danube, and Dacia Mediterranea beyond this (capital, Sardica). Thence they appear at a later date to have recrossed the Danube into the present Roumania, where a corrupt Romance dialect is still spoken.

ARMENIA MAJOR.—This kingdom, with the capital Artaxata, reached from the upper course of the Euphrates north-eastwards to the Caspian Sea. The Romans long contented themselves with retaining it in their interests by supporting their own nominees on the throne.   In the course of Trajan's eastern campaign he temporarily annexed it, placing it under a legate and procurator (114), but it was surrendered by Hadrian three years later.

MESOPOTAMIA, with the west district of Osrhoene, which had long been ruled by the royal house of Edessa, was annexed by Trajan in the course of the Parthian wars, abandoned by Hadrian, but reconquered by L. Verus, and not finally resigned till the reign of Jovian (363).   No tribute was raised, the district being looked on as a military outpost, and guarded by several colonies, such as Ninus, Carrhae, Singara, and probably Edessa.

ASSYRIA.—A district east of the Tigris, according to some authorities made a province for a short time by Trajan, but not retained even to the end of his reign.   Its boundaries are doubtful.

ITALY.—Cisalpine Gaul was established as a separate military command, probably by Sulla in 81 B.C., when the Rubicon seems to have been fixed as the boundary of Italy.   Its provincial status was ended on the proposal of Octavian, according to Caesar's known desire, in 42 B.C.

The process of reducing Italy to the rank of a province was almost coeval with the principate.   The division into eleven *regions* by Augustus, in order to facilitate the new system of taxation, marks the first step.   Hadrian's four *consulares*, and the *juridici* of a somewhat later date foreshadow the *correctores* of the third century.   These seem to have been at first temporary officials appointed by the emperor in particular districts for special purposes, sometimes commanding troops, and also exercising judicial functions.   In the age of Diocletian a regular provincial system was set up.   Italy lost its immunity from tribute, and was placed under two Vicars, one of whom resided at Milan, and was charged with the supervision of the *correctores* of the northern provinces of Italy ; while the *Vicarius in urbe* similarly supervised southern Italy with Sicily, Sardinia, and Corsica.   Rome and its neighbourhood (*urbicaria regio*) for some years longer remained exempt from tribute, and was governed by the urban prefect, who had both civil and military authority, and presided over the senate.

TABLE OF PROVINCES TOWARDS THE END OF
AUGUSTUS' REIGN.

Senatorial :
  1. Under consular proconsul : Asia, Africa.
  2. Under praetorian proconsul : Sicily, Baetica, Gallia Narbonensis, Macedonia, Achaia, Bithynia, Pontus, Cyprus, Crete with Cyrene.

Imperial:
1. Under consular legati: Hispania Tarraconensis, Pannonia, Dalmatia, Moesia, Syria.
2. Under praetorian legati: Lusitania, Aquitania, Gallia Lugdunensis, Gallia Belgica, Galatia.
3. Under procurator: Rhaetia, Alpes Maritimae, Noricum, Sardinia, Judaea, Cilicia.
4. Under prefect: Egypt.

TABLE OF DIOCESES UNDER VICARS AT THE END OF THE THIRD CENTURY A.D.

1. *Orient diocese* (sixteen provinces): Covering Cyrenaica, Egypt, Arabia, Syria, Mesopotamia, the south-east of Asia Minor, and Cyprus.
2. *Pontic diocese* (seven provinces): The centre and north of Asia Minor.
3. *Asian diocese* (nine provinces): The west of Asia Minor and the Aegean islands.
4. *Thracian diocese* (six provinces): Thrace and part of Moesia.
5. *Moesian diocese* (ten provinces): The districts south of the Danube, Macedonia, Epirus, Thessaly, Achaia, and Crete.
6. *Pannonian diocese* (seven provinces): Pannonia, Noricum, and Dalmatia.
7. *Italic diocese* (fifteen provinces): Italy with Venetia, Histria, Sicily, Sardinia and Corsica, and Alpes Cottiae.
8. *Spanish diocese* (six provinces): Spain and western Mauritania.
9. *African diocese* (six provinces): The rest of Mauritania, Numidia, and proconsular Africa.
10. *Britannic diocese* (four provinces): Britain south of walls of Hadrian.
11. *Gallic diocese* (eight provinces): North and central Gaul, and Roman Germany.
12. *Viennensian diocese* (five provinces): South and south-east Gaul with Aquitania and Narbonensis.

Of these, under the tetrarchy system set up by Diocletian, and corresponding generally to the quadruple praetorian prefecture of Constantine, dioceses 1-3 fell to Diocletian himself, 4-6 to Galerius, 7-9 to Maximian, 10-12 to Constantius.

APPENDIX II
CHRONOLOGICAL TABLE
B.C.

241. Annexation of most of Sicily.
238-1. Reduction of Sardinia and Corsica.
227. Two additional praetors for new provinces.
206. Carthaginians abandon Spain.
197. Spain divided into Hither and Further Provinces.
    Two additional praetors govern them.
171. First Latin colony outside Italy—Carteia.
167. End of Macedonian kingdom; probable annexation of Illyricum.
149. First law against provincial extortion (Lex Calpurnia).
146. Macedonia (perhaps including Achaia) and Africa become provinces.
131. Sicily settled by Lex Rupilia.
129. Organisation of province of Asia (bequeathed 133).
123. Provincial measures of C. Gracchus. Balearic islands attached to Hither Spain.
121-18. Establishment of Narbonensian province; Narbo founded 118.
103. War with pirates and annexation of Cilicia.
96. Cyrenaica bequeathed to Rome.
88. Asiatic possessions occupied by Mithridates.
81. Sulla separates home and provincial commands. Cisalpine Gaul a province.
74. Bithynia bequeathed to Rome; government of Cyrenaica organised.
67. Conquest of Crete by Metellus, ultimately attached to Cyrenaica.
65. Pontus annexed.
64. Syria made a province by Pompey.
58. Occupation of Cyprus.
51. Cicero in Cilicia; conquest of Gaul completed.
46. Africa Nova (Numidia) formed by Caesar.
43. Gallic colony of Lugdunum founded.
30. Annexation of Egypt.
29. Province of Moesia.
27. Division of provinces between emperor and Senate.
25. Annexation of Galatia. Numidian kingdom attached to Africa.
22. Cyprus made a senatorial province.
19. Final reduction of Spain by Agrippa. Further Spain divided into Lusitania and Baetica about this time.

B.C.
15. Formation of provinces of Rhaetia and Noricum.
14. Province of Alpes Maritimae.
11. Illyria made an imperial province.

A.D.
6. Sardinia and Moesia transferred to the emperor ; Judaea with Samaria made a procuratorial province.
9. Pannonia established as a separate province.
15. Macedonia placed under imperial legate (till 44).
17. Cappadocia and Commagene annexed. Organisation of the Gallic and German commands by Tiberius.
37. A military legate appointed for Africa.
40. Organisation of the two Mauritaniae as procuratorial provinces.
43. Conquest of southern and eastern Britain.
46. Thrace made an imperial province.
50. Foundation of Camulodunum.
61. Rising in Britain suppressed by Paulinus.
63. Province of Alpes Maritimae receives Latin rights.
67. Provincial changes of Nero.
70. End of the Jewish war, Judaea an imperial province.
73-4. Vespasian's reforms ; several client kingdoms and free states annexed ; Pamphylia, with Lycia, an imperial province ; wide grant of Latinity in Spain. Sardinia again imperial.
84. Agricola extends Roman dominions into Caledonia, but is recalled.
105. Province of Arabia formed.
106. Trajan's conquest of Dacia leads to a new province.
114. Provinces of Armenia Major, Assyria, and Mesopotamia ; the first two soon abandoned.
122. Construction of Hadrian's Wall in Britain.
125. *Juridici* appointed in Italy.
131-5. Last Jewish War.
143. Antonine wall in Britain.
197. Britain divided into Superior and Inferior.
259. Western empire of Postumus.
293. Quadruple division of the Empire by Diocletian.
297. Subdivision of the provinces, Italy included ; and separation of military and civil power.
324. Constantine the Great sole emperor.

APPENDIX III

ON ROMAN SWITZERLAND

A GREAT subject is often best seen by a close examination of some small portion of it. It may be of interest, therefore, if I subjoin what can be made out of a little country which formed part of several different provinces, and the account of which should throw light on points of interest. I refer to Switzerland.[1]

There is no such thing, strictly speaking, as a Roman Switzerland. Different parts of it belonged to different border countries. Geneva was in the district of Vienna, and so belonged to Provence. West Switzerland, including Nyon, the lake shore, and Rhone valley, belonged to Lugdunensis. East Switzerland was part of Rhaetia ; Tessin belonged to Italy. A special administrative district was made out of the Rhone valley and part of Savoy, under a governor called *Procurator Alpium Attractianarum et Poeninarum*.[2] For some purposes of administration the whole of Gaul, including West Switzerland, formed a unit, e.g., there is a uniform mile-stone system over the whole area, from which we may argue to a uniform road and postal system, and a central administration of them. Also all Gaul had one system of tax and customs, and as part of this there was an important custom-house at Zurich, another at St. Maurice, and at Conflans in the valley of the Isère. The Zurich *statio* was connected with the Julier Septimer and Splugen routes from Milan ; that of St. Maurice with the Great, that of Conflans with the Little St. Bernard. There was thus a ring of posts at the edge of the Gallic frontier, directly behind which edge is Western Switzerland. Also there were probably Swiss representatives at the great religious festival of Lyons.

By the later arrangements of Constantine, West Switzerland comes under the vicar of Gaul, Spain, and Britain ; while East Switzerland went with Italy, Illyricum, and Africa.

The military importance of Switzerland rested on its being part of the frontier. The chief military station was at Vindonissa, a very strong position on the tongue of land between the Reuss and the Aar, commanding the roads from Como by the Splugen, etc., and that from Avenches coming over the Great St. Bernard. Augusta Rauracorum (Augst) and Augusta Vindelicorum (Augs-

---

[1] My account is obtained from Orelli, *Inscriptiones Helvetiae;* Mommsen, *Schweiz in römischer Zeit;* Troyon, *Monuments de l'Antiquité dans l'Europe barbare.* The inscriptions have also been collected by Mommsen. See also Hunziker's *Schweiz* (1898), Jung's *Alpinae Civitates*, Buckhardt-Biedermann, *Helvetien unter den Römern* (Basle, 1886) ; Mommsen, in *Hermes*, xvi. 445.

[2] Mommsen, *Schweiz*, 6.

burg) provided an easy connection with the Rhine and the Danube. The passage of the Rhine at Zurzach was secured by a bridge, and thence the road went to Coblenz. Vindonissa also communicated with the head-quarters at Mogontiacum (Mayence), and this road crossed the Rhine at Breisach, which was guarded by a detachment of the troops quartered at Vindonissa. Later on we find Vindonissa connected with the Danube through Zurzach, Rottenburg on the Neckar, and Ratisbon. Switzerland flourished for about 250 years, but towards A.D. 260 the Alemanni invaded it and burnt Aventicum. A few years afterwards Augusta Rauraca was burnt. The frontier line now became the Rhine, which was guarded more carefully than ever. There was a Roman fleet on Lake Constance. But no coins of Augusta are found later than the end of the fourth century, and in that time we must put the the victory of the barbarian deluge. The same thing applies to coins found all over Switzerland, and the last inscription is of the year 377. By 395 all connexion between Italy and Gaul was at an end. In Switzerland the Valais remained Roman longest, and was not overrun till Italy was. Latin was the official and common language. But West Switzerland was much more Romanised than East. The Rhone valley was Romanised fully and completely, owing to the great trade route over the Great St. Bernard ; so was Geneva, as part of Provence. There are very few inscriptions in East Switzerland, and when we find names of Helvetii or Rauraci occurring, they are very barbarous and un-Roman. The same thing occurs on the North French coast, where inscriptions are very rare. The present divisions of Switzerland explain themselves by these facts. For the Burgundians in West Switzerland found an old civilisation already, and became Romanised, while the Alemanni in the East started on quite new ground.

Gaul fell naturally into *pagi*. There were eight of these in Switzerland, of which the Nantuates were the most important.

The first considerable town was Colonia Equestris (Nyon),[1] belonging to no *pagus*, but wedged in between the Sequani, Helvetii, and Allobroges. Other towns are Aquae (Baden near Zurich), Vindonissa (Windisch), Turicum (Zurich), Salodunum (Soleure), Lousanna.[2] But by constitution these were never regular municipia. No duoviri or quattuorviri occur in any of them. Under the Empire, however, we get important towns, e.g., Martigny, Sion, and St. Maurice, with Latin right. Augusta Rauraca and Aventicum were Roman colonies, and the surrounding *pagi* were subject to their jurisdiction. Citizens of Aventicum were scattered about the

---

[1] The *Colonia Equestris* of Noviodunum was a very considerable place, much larger than the present Nyon. See Troyon, p. 481.

[2] At Lausanne have been found a bronze Diana, bust of Cato, medals of Victorina, Trajan, Zenobia ; Troyon, p. 485. The remains of Roman columns were employed in building Lausanne Cathedral ; ib. 487.

country, and their interests were well looked after. As to the natives, they probably got the *civitas* of the place in time, and therefore Roman *civitas* also—as was the ordinary procedure with natives. Apparently these citizens of Roman colonies were exempt from military service. But troops were obtained from the rest of the country,—an *ala* was raised in Valais, and the Helvetii must have contributed at least two cohorts of infantry.

Commerce was very unimportant in early times. But the foundation of Aosta and consequent extension of the Great St. Bernard as a trade route changed this. From Martigny the road went down the Rhone valley to Nyon, or diverged from Vevey to Solothurn and Augst.[1] After this we find articles of commerce passing through Switzerland from Germany and Flanders, and Switzerland exporting its own cheese, timber, etc., and importing oil, wine, etc.

[1] Between Vevey and Solothurn discoveries of Roman remains have been pretty frequent, e.g., at Moudon ; Troyon, 492. Extensive discoveries have been made at Avenches—frescoes, ib. 495 ; aqueducts, temples, statues, ib. 497. It had a patron, ib. 498 ; an amphitheatre, ib. 502 ; fragments of statues, Hercules and Faun, Apollo, ib. 503. Remains also at Yverdon, ib. 505 ; Orbe, ib. 506. See Hirschfeld in *Westdeutsche Zeitschrift*, viii. 122. Meisterhans, *Aelteste Geschichte des Kantons Solothurns, Philol. Woch.* xii. 89.

INDEX